Out of Joint

OUT OF JOINT

POWER, CRISIS, AND
THE RHETORIC OF TIME

NOMI CLAIRE LAZAR

Yale
UNIVERSITY PRESS
New Haven and London

Published with assistance from the Mary Cady Tew Memorial Fund.

Copyright © 2019 by Nomi Claire Lazar.
All rights reserved.
This book may not be reproduced, in whole or in part, including illustrations, in any form (beyond that copying permitted by Sections 107 and 108 of the U.S. Copyright Law and except by reviewers for the public press), without written permission from the publishers.

Yale University Press books may be purchased in quantity for educational, business, or promotional use. For information, please e-mail sales.press@yale.edu (U.S. office) or sales@yaleup.co.uk (U.K. office).

Set in Gotham and Adobe Garamond types by IDS Infotech Ltd., Chandigarh, India.
Printed in the United States of America.

Library of Congress Control Number: 2018957334
ISBN 978-0-300-16633-0 (paperback : alk. paper)

A catalogue record for this book is available from the British Library.
This paper meets the requirements of ANSI/NISO Z39.48-1992 (Permanence of Paper).

For Talia Tsephora

Contents

Acknowledgments ix

Introduction: Framing Time 1
1 The Political Construction of Time 16
2 Calendars and the Politics of Order Alignment 60
3 Khubilai Khan's Calendar and the Politics of Performance 101
4 The Primitivist's Lament 130
5 A Dead End? 166
Conclusion: Transcending Time 209

Notes 219
Index 253

Acknowledgments

The idea for this book came about in three stages over fifteen years. It was in the course of a freshman conversation about postmodernism and campus politics with the linguistic anthropologist Monica Heller that the idea first occurred to me that the way people talk about time impacts forms of political action. In graduate school, while studying Machiavelli with John McCormick, I began to think about how ideas about time structure the questions political thinkers formulate. Reading a history of calendars made the problem finally coalesce. So I gratefully acknowledge, in the first instance, Monica Heller for patient engagement with her adolescent neighbor, John McCormick for thinking with me about Machiavelli, and the late Evelyn Greene for the fateful gift of the calendar history.

In the long course of writing this book, a number of scholars and specialists have offered various kinds of assistance, including area experts such as Eckart Frahm, Lawrence Kelly, and Nora Forgacs, among many others. Their guidance was invaluable given the breadth of the cases considered in this work, and their assistance is gratefully noted throughout the text. I am grateful also to those whose thought-provoking questions and comments lit up discussions with audiences at the universities of Cambridge, Carleton, Michigan, Nanjing, St. Andrews, Singapore, and Yale, the Florida International University, Hebrew University of Jerusalem, the Vrije Universiteit

ACKNOWLEDGMENTS

Amsterdam, UCLA, Eötvös Loránd University in Budapest, the Oñati Institute for the Sociology of Law, the London School of Economics, and the China Research Centre in Sydney, Australia. I note with special thanks helpful feedback from anonymous reviewers and from Ed Andrew, Elton Chan, Ci Jiwei, Joshua Foa Dienstag, Lisa Disch, Rick French, Alex Himelfarb, Bart van Klink, Terry Nardin, David Runciman, Ian Shapiro, Sharon Sutherland, Michael Williams, and all the kind participants at manuscript workshops organized by Steven Smith at Yale and by Lyana Francot and Tanja Alberts at the Time and Law Research Centre in Amsterdam.

For financial support, I am grateful to Yale University for funds to visit Copan, and to Yale-NUS College and Singapore's Ministry of Education for supporting a sabbatical visit to Amsterdam and the manuscript workshops. I also thank the Social Sciences and Humanities Research Council of Canada for funds to do everything else. For excellent research assistance, I'm grateful to Margaret Rae Heard Julian (aka "Agent Meg"), Lee Jin Hee, Nisa Malli, and Anushua Nag.

It is a sincere pleasure to thank my superb editor, Bill Frucht. His insightfulness, humor, and unwavering support have been invaluable.

In many ways, this has been a challenging book to write, and not only because of the range of subject matter. Gratitude for forbearance of a scholar's absence from other roles in the later stages of writing is a trope in academic acknowledgments. But absence is a luxury not universally available. I persevered in some particularly challenging role juggling through the encouragement of my husband, Emanuel Mayer, my family and friends, especially Naomi K. Lewis and the late and warmly missed Mayling Birney. It was my daughter who provided the final impetus. She was born with this book, and the two grew together. Early on, I typed with one finger while she nursed and read standing up as I rocked her while she slept on my back. As the project neared its end, Talia was reading and writing notes beside me. She wrote: "I hope I can read your book someday." Well, my child, here it is. This book, which has always been with you, is now as much yours as it is mine.

Out of Joint

INTRODUCTION

Framing Time

In the midst of innovation or upheaval, leaders frame lofty claims in the rhetoric of time. Lincoln, at Gettysburg, framed a moment of luminous power by stretching a hand toward the past, a hand toward the future.[1] Robespierre, at the dawn of the Terror, invoked overarching destiny to subdue the transitory qualms of his political present.[2] More recently, the populist speeches of Viktor Orbán not only call out events in Hungary's past but also address the shape of that past, promising, through extrapolation, a shape for the future.[3] Constitutions, too, are framed in time talk. Russia, China, and Korea, Hungary, South Africa, and Kyrgyzstan, among many others, have constitutional preambles that go beyond the mention of historical events to situate the occasion of a nation's constitutional renewal in an arc of time. Other time frames cost more than words. The shape of time is constructed not only rhetorically but by means of clocks and calendars. And historically, political innovators have spent huge sums on calendar reform at fraught political moments, changing the shape of time to frame their political present.

Consider the Julian reform. In the year 49 BCE, Julius Caesar crossed the river Rubicon with his legions, thwarting a taboo against bringing arms into Rome. Transforming the office of the dictatorship to formalize his extensive informal power, Caesar executed a range of political reforms to quell Rome's civil conflict and cement his

INTRODUCTION

position. These included reforms to the police, land tenure, and population policy, all of which serve clear political purposes. But in that resource-intensive environment, he also devoted funds and political capital to the reform of the calendar. For the casual observer who might see in this an isolated case, it may be tempting to attribute the calendar reform to some personal eccentricity on Caesar's part, or perhaps to Rome's then current vogue for Egyptian science. But then consider the example of Khubilai Khan. Until his father's generation, the language of Khubilai's nomadic people had had no written form and voiced no scientific tradition. Yet in the mid-thirteenth century CE, having effectively conquered and unified China and founded the Yuan dynasty, Khubilai diverted vast sums and expertise to the development and production of new precision astronomical instruments and to the reform of the Chinese calendar. In doing so, Khubilai followed in the footsteps of every previous dynasty-founding Chinese emperor, each of whom reformed the calendar, though none as extensively as Khubilai.

Then there is the famous French revolutionary calendar and clock. In the wake of the execution of Louis XVI in 1793, and in the midst of social and political chaos, the Jacobin Council devoted resources to the propagation of a new calendar and clock, based on the decimal system. The Julio-Gregorian calendar was reinstated only after the restoration of the monarchy in 1806. There is Lenin, who led Russia to adopt the Gregorian calendar in 1918, and Atatürk, who did the same for Turkey in 1925, abolishing the Rumi calendar amid wide-ranging reforms. Stalin, and more recently Turkmenbashi, amended the Julio-Gregorian calendar too. Pol Pot, among myriad others, declared a new base year, Year Zero.

Why, in the profound, spare speech of Lincoln, would time figure prominently among his few and precious words? Why would countries spend the rationed words of a constitutional preamble this way? Why would so many conquerors, reformers, and revolutionaries devote resources, at a most resource-needy time, to what may look like an eccentric, technical exercise? It is a commonplace that political actors invoke historical *events* to justify their political endeavors, but here they invoke not just events but the *place of these events in shaped time,* their sequence and synchrony, and their meaning not only for the present but for the future. Structuring or restructuring time tracks several forms of political innovation. The correlation, though imperfect, is common enough to cry out for explanation. If we assume that political leaders faced with the myriad problems of a new or expectant regime will spend human, fiscal, and political-rhetorical capital with care, it would follow that leaders expect some political return. What work does time talk do at moments of political change?

The conjunction of time talk with periods of innovation or upheaval is suggestive, and it would be reasonable to posit that the phenomenon responds to a challenge common to these political circumstances. The challenge every regime or leader shares, regardless of place, era, or culture, and that figures most prominently at moments of innovation or upheaval, is the challenge of establishing legitimacy. The process of establishing and maintaining legitimacy is *legitimation.* In the toolbox of legitimation strategies and tactics, a leader will find a variety of means to shape and reshape time. Time talk and temporal framing, I shall argue, serve the project of legitimation.

How? The politics of legitimation is partly conducted by means of storytelling. Narrative gives meaning to action and event generally. But narrative, in turn, draws its meaning from a combination of the substance of events and the structures that fit those events together. When a narrative extends beyond the level of anecdote or localized explanation, which is to say, when it is intended to have meaning and

INTRODUCTION

resonance beyond itself, beyond its value as entertainment or information, it is normally situated in an additional structure that conveys the relevance of that story to the present or the future. One such structure is causal: how one event not only precedes but precipitates another. But there are others. Do we expect the form of the story to repeat? For instance, not that *this* empire would rise and fall repeatedly, but that a temporal structure of cyclicality would characterize empires? Do we understand the story as an episode, a mark along an ever-upward (or downward) route? Is it evidence of an anyway-assured progress or decline? Is it the fulfillment of a promised station on the road to an imminent end and subsequent rebirth? Is it simply a reiteration, a continual repetition with the power to stall or stop time, the means to an eternal present? That is, what a narrative means for us depends not only on the substantive content of the events it relates but on the meaning of the temporal pattern that the choice of that event sequence draws out. I will call such temporal patterns conceptions of the flow of time. Conceptions of the flow of time illuminate not what happened in the past but in what way the past is meaningful for the present and the future.

As I will argue in chapter 1, because time can be experienced only through marks and measures, reshaping these reshapes the experience of time too. Some marks and measures are "found," like the rising and setting of the sun, moon, and stars, the tides, cycles of dry and wet, hot and cold. Some are constructed, like hourglasses and sundials, water clocks and atomic clocks, lunar or solar calendars. Everyone, both across and within cultures, uses a range of time measures for a range of purposes, moving with ease from one technology to another as needed: from an academic calendar to a religious one, from a sense of one's child's progress at school to the knowledge of one's ultimate end, from an egg timer to timely arrival at a meeting, aided by a watch. Familiarity with diverse conceptions and measures of time makes rhetorical transitions from one to another relatively easy. Reshaping our experience of time by changing marks and measures is thus a ready political-rhetorical technique. It is a useful technique because the choice of a time frame impacts the received meaning of events. Meaning depends on narrative structure, and narrative structure depends on a conception of the flow of time.

This technique of temporal-rhetorical framing is particularly useful in the politics of legitimation because it enables political leaders to draw from two wells of legitimacy. One contains already accepted forms of order, like nature, reason, or cosmic harmony, with which innovations can be aligned. Because time *feels* natural—though experience of time is always constructed—what is associated with its flow may borrow its "natural" self-evidence. The other contains cues about political capacity and means of performing that capacity. In chapter 2, I argue that calendars can be used to create frame alignment with an order already understood to be legitimate. These rhetorical tactics are illustrated by means of three examples: the conquest of Mayan Copan by K'inich Yax K'uk' Mo', the Julio-Augustan calendar reform, and the 2012 Hungarian Basic Law. In chapter 3, I argue that calendars serve the aims of performance legitimacy and performing legitimacy. My examples here are the calendar reform of Khubilai Khan and the calendrical practices of the long-enduring Assyrian-Babylonian Empire.

Chapter 2 shows how calendars are effective tools of frame alignment because they are Janus-headed, made to invoke the familiar but with a novel intent. Like the technique of recension in biblical studies, calendar reform provides a means of "rereading" the past in light of a future-serving interpretation of the present. This is important because whether an innovation (reform, conquest, or revolution) is understood to be legitimate depends partly on whether it can be cast

INTRODUCTION

at the same time as a restoration, and calendars provide a number of means of calling out alignment with what is already accepted.

Further, calendars' linearity, counting forward in blocks of Gregorian centuries or Mayan baktuns, facilitates the framing of actions in the context of grand historical cycles. By aligning a political event or innovation with a juncture along a cyclically structured narrative, a political leader can imply the inevitability of imminent glory. However, a grand cyclic frame implies an ultimate and inevitable decline, conceding in advance serious limitations on human agency. This poses a challenge to anyone who would use this rhetorical tactic. But calendars provide a means of addressing this problem also. If what politics can achieve is colored by the assumption of decay, the question is how decay might be delayed, the regime helped to linger longer at its peak. Machiavelli argued that a successful regime must, in the face of inevitable decline, regularly bring the people back to core principles and loyalties, a practice he called "resuming the government." To engineer this requires that the cyclic flow of time be regularly punctuated, and because one cannot rely on external factors to unite the people and bring them back to their first principles, ideally, a political agent ought to punctuate cycles herself. But because one cannot rely on future agents either, a political innovator can harness calendars to serve as automated tools of punctuation, and this can be achieved through the inscription into the calendar of festivals and holidays. All polities automate the rehearsal of civic religion through national holidays, and this policy is explicitly advised by political thinkers such as Rousseau.[4] In these ways, both the linear and cyclic features of calendars can be put to use in conjuring already accepted forms of order, framing claims of legitimacy.

Chapter 3 shows how calendars frame claims of performance capacity, particularly in the fraught legitimation environments faced by colonizers and imperial powers. Even conquering regimes have a strong interest in legitimating their power to minimize the costs associated with the use of force. Weber argued that the perception of legitimacy rests on charisma, legality, or tradition, but in addition to these, legitimate power relies on competence (for which charisma is sometimes a proxy). So a conquering power must focus not only on constructing its formal legitimacy, perhaps through the adoption of legal-traditional structures accepted domestically as legitimate, but also on effective provision of public goods and an effective infrastructure of risk mitigation. Particularly in imperial states, the substantive and symbolic performance of competence has, historically, generated impressive risk-mitigation infrastructures, complete with sizeable and prestigious bureaucracies staffed with highly trained and sometimes esoterically knowledgeable elites and equipped with sophisticated technology and resources. This may sound like a description of our own contemporary risk-focused bureaucracies, but through an alternative epistemological frame, it equally describes those of lasting empires like Assyria and imperial China. In these latter cases, the production of calendars and almanacs, the purpose of which is to anticipate and mitigate sources of risk with respect to the appropriate timing of political and religious-political activity, is an important element in the broader risk-management infrastructure. Their production and maintenance are resource intensive, and so in such regimes a number of legitimating threads come together. A regime that successfully anticipates and mitigates risk, effectively manages contingency. When contingency is effectively managed, this creates the appearance of harmony with cosmic forces, whether that is understood as special luck or, in Confucian regimes, the Mandate of Heaven. Furthermore, to maintain the extensive infrastructure necessary for risk management is itself a means of displaying capacity through wealth and power. And finally, in some imperial regimes, the provision of a calendar and almanac is—purely formally—a symbolic act that signals legitimate power. If a form of action is associated with a role, then the person who does that action implies that she inhabits that role. We assume the person checking our vital signs is the nurse, because this is what we expect nurses to do. Each dynasty-founding emperor of China reforms the calendar, so the person who reforms it communicates that he is a dynasty founder. Through all these means of managing contingency, some substantive, some suggestive, reshaping calendar time is one means through which leaders can draw from the well of competence, framing claims of performance legitimacy.

Temporal framing serves the politics of legitimation, but leaders of radical political movements, rebellions, revolutions, or insurgencies must undermine order and supersede capacity to provide their followers with the moral narratives necessary to justify violence. Chapters 4 and 5 show how, to serve this project of *de*legitimation, temporal-rhetorical techniques can be inverted.

Alignment with order may serve legitimation, but where order is the villain, primitivism can be used to expose it. Primitivism—a cluster of views that link increased civilization to declines in wisdom or morality—frequently frames radical rhetoric of this kind and forms the subject of chapter 4. When primitivism is used as a temporal-rhetorical frame, its ultimate function is to associate order with constraint, domination, and alienation, and hence to associate order not with security and gradual improvement in the conditions of life but instead with loss. Primitivist rhetoric achieves this by implying that our original, natural condition, a condition of peace and freedom, is also a generic condition, free of particularities. Any determination that brings us out of this condition entails loss and alienation. All determination, as Spinoza taught, is negation.[5] To become one determinate thing restricts or negates alternatives, and this is true of every form of specificity, whether metaphysical, communal, or literally concrete (as when a building divides space in a way that negates any other possible division, constraining movement). Because order is necessarily a condition of determination, negating, by its very existence, every alternative order, primitivism stands opposed to any nonnatural or nonspontaneous order. In parallel, the primitive is also fundamentally opposed to politics: what is generic has no capacity for agency or action because action is choice, and choice both relies upon particularity and, in turn, creates determinations. Without action and agency, there can be no politics. Since any order in the primitive condition is natural and self-enforcing, domination is unknown. Without action, without politics, the primitive remains not just free of domination but stalled or undulating in slow, peaceful time—that is, a time opposed to events, indeed to any chronotic or regular, sequential experience of time. Hence, for the radical politician who deploys primitivism, the enemy of the primitive is the intrusion from outside of some mechanism of imposed order or else the intervention of chronotic time, of events, into that stalled time. It is through an external, violent intervention that alienation takes hold as people are forced into a shaped, highly constraining temporal-physical environment in which they must contort themselves into particular creatures whose active contestation over power is the only means of persistence. In this way, order generates domination, institutes alienation. Only in a condition of abstraction is there freedom from domination, which means freedom from politics too.

Illustrations here include some campaigns of the environmental movement and E. P. Thompson's critique of clock time.[6] Thompson's work on clocks has been a pillar of leftist social thought, and it is its primitivist frame that preserves the work's continuing rhetorical power

INTRODUCTION

in the face of trenchant normative, empirical, and conceptual critiques. Primitivism is a temporal frame of particular resonance and power for radical critiques of order, and understanding its conceptual underpinnings—uprooting our faith in those forms of order on which legitimate power stakes its claim—illuminates, in turn, how radical politics comes apart from justice, which is always entwined with order, and from progressive politics in particular. In disputes between leftist factions, it is normally the frame (often temporal) that drives the substance and hence constructs the disagreement. The primitivist frame precludes just order and thus any institutional means of restoring freedom. It negates the legitimacy of *any* enforced—and hence nonspontaneous—order. Thus, all that primitivism itself allows is lament. This drives radical political rhetoric toward eschatology, the subject of chapter 5.

As primitivism becomes lament, eschatology is the paramount rhetorical technique for managing violence in contexts of injustice: time becomes a proxy for order, with its inherent violence, domination, and constraint. The promise of the eschaton, time's end, creates the illusion of a substantive alternative to enforced order, an inverted world ruled by love, not law. Eschatology directly undermines performative legitimacy by rendering concrete progress, amelioration of conditions in the here and now, an act of treachery. The existing political world holds back the eschaton, and its performance distracts from this encompassing final aim.

When the leaders of eschatological political movements are effective in gaining adherents and managing political action, they work through a strategic configuration of a triad of forces. Together, divine sanction, identification of historical patterns, and individual motive power create the illusion of inevitable success: a luminous, lasting, perfect freedom and harmony await, bypassing the need for legitimation entirely. Performative capacity is rendered irrelevant, even treasonous. But if this motive structure breaks down, as it arguably has in the work of key contemporary radical-left thinkers, undermining both order and performance as traditional sources of legitimacy leaves a rhetorical vacuum, with potentially volatile political results.

Ultimately, temporal framing is effective in political speech because time drives both the demand for and the possibility of experiencing meaning, for the paramount and universal fact about time, experienced by every person as objective and inexorable, is the inevitability of death. Whatever one imagines comes after, death is, for each of us, an imminent fact. It is this limitation of time, this sense that we will one day run out of time, that creates the demand for meaning, the necessity of finding or creating it, to rescue transience from insignificance. The drive for meaning in human life stems from this desire to transcend death, this one objective fact about time. But if it is our limited time that drives the need for meaning, it is also limitations that constitute and construct our experience of time—that shape time—that provide a range of sources of meaning. For shaped time is constrained time, and meaning is always reliant on constraint. Constraint and determination are what give anything its content, its shape and qualities. The way that shaped time constrains understanding of events presents an opportunity for constructing the meaning of events or event sequences, whether political or individual, and hence for mapping one's own life onto something beyond itself. Time presents both the need for meaning and the opportunity to construct it. A human life, inherently limited, placed in the context of shaped time, gains purpose, binds individuals to projects beyond themselves—to the achievement of a military victory, the attainment of grace, the realization of the cultural renewal, advancement, or fruition of a family, people, or polity. Beyond the limited and objective scope of each life, the narrative structures enabled by shaped time provide a means of transcendence.

This ready fact provides limitless opportunities for political entrepreneurs who can tap into this need for meaning and map, by means of shaped time, each individual's sense of herself onto political time—which, if not eternal, is at least longer. It is no new insight that political leaders call citizens or subjects to feel subservient to a purpose beyond themselves, beyond the constraints of birth and death. But attention to temporal rhetoric shows a common and important mechanism through which this is communicated and achieved. The meaning of any event emerges only within a sequential arc. A political leader can construct that arc in a range of ways, as it best suits his rhetorical aims, by carefully picking out an event series from the great expanse that is the set of all occurrences.

Before proceeding, it is worth addressing an easy and erroneous conflation. The argument concerns events in time as a means of tracing out arced shapes of time. As history and conceptions of the flow of time may thus seem to overlap, it is worth clarifying the relation and distinction between history or a theory of history, and time and the present theory of time. The range of historical examples, speeches, and texts with historical content used as illustrations in the pages that follow may further this confusion. But these cases serve not to establish claims about what happened in the past, the character of the past, or how historians interpret the past, but instead to develop a theory that illuminates aspects of common *political practice* that look toward the future. My interest here is in politics and political rhetoric, not history and its construction.[7]

That history has its uses in politics is a commonplace. But to say that temporal framing, and not just history, is important in politics is to underscore that it is not merely the character of the events them-

INTRODUCTION

selves and their causal relationship—as, for example, when a leader reminds her people of a historical injustice—but the perceived shape of event series that alters our perception of an event's significance. It is the shape of time and its directionality, perceived by means of a chosen series of events, at issue here. History, by contrast, is the *content* of these events and their substantive or causal relations to each other, substance beyond sequence. The confusion is abetted because temporal framing is as often at work in the historian's craft as it is in the politician's, as Braudel and the Annalistes school, and more recently Corfield and White, have noted.[8] This is to be expected. Just as temporal framing shapes political narratives, it shapes historical narrative too: where meaning can be modulated by sequence and synchrony, there a practice of temporal framing makes rhetorical sense. Wherever narrative is purposively constructed for an end beyond itself, there we should expect to find temporal framing. Narrative that purports to have meaning beyond itself will usually rely on a tacit or explicit account of how time flows, because this impacts our understanding of the relationship between any given token and the various types through which it is understood and interpreted. But time, in historical narrative, frames rather than constitutes history, just as it can frame and give meaning to political events. While conceptions of the flow of time and theories and practices of history are often found together, they are not the same.[9]

Here is an example to clarify the distinction between the deployment of history (an account of the substance of events) and the deployment of structured time. Each February 1 at 9:33 a.m., the minute in 1979 that the Ayatollah Ruhollah Khomeini returned from exile, Iranians launch the "ten days of dawn." These represent the ten days between the ayatollah's return and the success of the Iranian revolution. As Ayatollah Ali Khamenei explained: "Since the victory of the Islamic Revolution up to the present time . . . people have always attended the feast of the Revolution. . . . Most of those who have taken part . . . in recent years had not experienced the days of the Revolution . . . due to their [young] age, but this never-ending chain [of demonstrations] proves the [nation's] power to recreate the Revolution. . . . The truth about the Revolution must always remain alive in the minds of people, because the Islamic Revolution is just halfway through and it needs its main goals to be kept alive in order to strengthen its pillars and achieve its lofty goals."[10]

The purpose of the festival is first to recall the specific events of the revolution and celebrate the achievement as a matter of national pride. This is the use of history for politics. But both the name, "ten days of dawn," and the ayatollah's talk of re-creation and rejuvenation show that structures of time are at work here as well. The event is framed in a conception of the flow of time: at work here is not just the recollection of the revolution as a historical fact but the cyclical renewal of revolutionary feeling and fervor through a framed re-creation, and thereby a regeneration of the experience of the event. This rhetoric situates the substantive historical event of the revolution in a constructed flow of time: progressive but propelled forward through annual, cyclical renewal. A conception of the flow of time frames the event of the revolution not just as a moment of national pride—a deployment of history for politics—but as a means of understanding one's present relative place in time and what is possible in the future. This is not just remembering events but reliving them, and not for nostalgia but for reinvigoration and recommitment, looking not just backward but forward. It is not just past events but the character of the present moment in relation to them; it is not just causal relations but the shape of a people's future path to which such rhetorical efforts gesture. History is in the past. Conceptions of the flow of time—here, a cyclically reinvigorated progress—help show the relevance of that past for the present and future. This distinction between history and conceptions of the flow of time should become increasingly clear through the myriad examples in the pages that follow.

Attention to temporal-rhetorical framing quickly reveals its ubiquity in periods of political change across cultures, traditions, regime types, and eras. When order fractures, when "the time is out of joint," as Hamlet put it, then political leaders can use temporal-rhetorical framing to create the perception that order will be restored.[11] It is because time is malleable that techniques of reframing are possible. Time can be shaped and reshaped around the same event series, changing the meaning of that event series or a specific event within it. This is not to say that political innovation is always accompanied by time talk. There are, after all, many other tools in the toolbox of legitimation. Nor do I claim that all fiddling with structures of time is driven by the need for political legitimation. Sometimes, for instance, practical coordination is the fundamental driver. My claim, rather, is that in the toolbox of legitimation (and delegitimation) are an array of techniques from which any leader may draw, and among them is this form of rhetoric, the temporal-rhetorical frame.

The use of temporal-rhetorical framing provides a range of more and less sophisticated techniques to help legitimize or delegitimize political innovations. There are few political problems as enduringly pressing as that of legitimation, and it is my aim to illuminate this common element by examining the rhetorical practices through which it is negotiated.

1

The Political Construction of Time

> From the point of view of prophecy, events are merely symbols of that which is already known.
> —*Reinhart Koselleck*

How is it that time, commonly understood as an objective measure naturally inherent in the rational structure through which we perceive the world, or else as an organic element of culture, could be made a tool of politics? This chapter shows how time technologies can serve as framing devices that further the aim of political legitimation. Even were time something pure and essential, a thing in itself, we could not experience it as such, since we perceive time only through marks and measures. This means that we only ever experience mediated, shaped time. It is we who shape time, picking out or constructing a set of marks and measures useful for a given task. Because time is useful for diverse tasks, we use diverse sets of marks and measures. Time is thus both malleable—because we shape it through the marks and measures we draw out—and multiple. Because there is no, or at least no experience of, time-itself, time is always available for reshaping. Nonetheless, the marks and measures through which we experience time often have the appearance of objective manifestations of order, in part because many marks and measures are found in nature.

POLITICAL CONSTRUCTION OF TIME

Time thus functions as an ordering mechanism that is open to reshaping while maintaining an illusory organicism. Marks and measures overlap substantially between cultures and across time due to universal human needs and experiences. A range of times, which are constructed, not organic, and primarily aim-relative, rather than culture-relative, animate every society and structure the life of every person.

Time, whether mechanically shaped by means of a clock or conceptually shaped by means of, say, the idea of progress, can act as a rhetorical frame. What an event means depends in part on its place in a sequence and the shape that sequence picks out. By framing a claim, event, or innovation in a construction of time, political leaders can shape what that event is understood to mean. If we recall that temporal constructions often come to seem natural or objective, then by a process of frame alignment, innovations can be made to seem natural or objective also. Temporal framing can make innovations seem old and constructions of time seem like the children of nature or reason.

With this established, it becomes clear how temporal framing suits the politics of legitimation. Claims about legitimacy ultimately draw from two wells. First, leaders may try to associate a political order with some underlying idea of order that is already accepted as legitimate. Here, because a temporal construction invokes nature or reason, time framing is among the useful available tools. Second, leaders may stake their legitimacy on a claim (and performance) of capacity to maintain just order and security. Through the apt organization of time in the service of managing risk, and the display of a capacity to do so, using time as a frame helps leaders draw from this other well of legitimacy too.

To illustrate the argument, I conclude with an example of a straightforward temporal framing technique in the service of legitimation—the shift in temporal frame between China's last Maoist (1978) and first

Deng-era (1982) constitutional preambles—before proceeding to more complex temporal framing techniques in subsequent chapters.

Time Technologies

Time technologies mark out a measure to track, order, and synchronize events. Anything that marks a sequence may serve as a time technology, whether found or constructed, mechanical or cognitive/conceptual. Constructed time technologies, like clocks, crank out their measure with task-suitable predictability: a well-built water clock will empty regularly; atoms and pendulums and pieces of quartz, in the right mechanism, oscillate reliably. But tools for marking time are not limited to clocks. The sun rises, constellations appear to move about the sky, tides and monsoon rains come and go, solstices and equinoxes occur regularly. All of these can be used to mark time. The first light-rail train of the morning or a waste-collection truck coming by every Tuesday may roar as reliably as a rooster crows. Quadrennial Olympiads mark and measure, and so do cycles of market days and cycles of the moon. These other technologies, whether in nature or the built environment, are "found technologies," but they are functionally parallel to those we construct. Because temporal measures are simply recurring marks, each mark itself an event, any reasonably regular event series can be used to measure time. Each oscillation, each time a mark on the water clock cistern is reached, the start of each sequentially numbered year is itself an event like the arrival of a train or the rising of the sun, and through the measure any series provides, we can order other, less regular events.[1]

Some found technologies have been regularized into concepts, such as our notions of "day" or "month" or "year," and because these concepts become divorced from original markers, *conceptual* time technologies—of which there are several kinds—form another class. The concept "year" is not identical with a full rotation of the earth around the sun: the stretch of time that requires varies by geographical point. Nor, of course, is the concept precisely equivalent to 365 days, or even 365 1/4 days, or fifty-two weeks, or twelve months. These are all context-dependent overlapping approximations of the concept of a year. Similarly, a day is not identical with the passing of twenty-four hours on an atomic clock, nor is it obvious that a new day starts at midnight rather than at sunset or dawn. Cave experiments challenge even our intuition that a day is a consistent cycle of sleeping and waking: bodily cycles vary dramatically when neither clocks nor found markers like sunrise and sunset are available.[2] The time concept "day" captures an independent measure related to each but identical with none. And while conceptual time technologies like "day" and "year" have different cultural resonance, they are, at least in family resemblance, robust cross-culturally.

Conceptual time technologies include recurring units of time like days and years. But they also include what we might call conceptions of the flow of time, such as progress, grand historical cycles, eschatology, and primitivism. These constructions provide schemata for sequentially organizing events in ways that make sense of their substantive relationship. They frame what kinds of narrative structure are possible in what contexts. Most simply, progress suggests a means of organizing and understanding the relationship between events in time by asserting from the outset that there is an overall pattern of improvement (whether moral, technological, or otherwise). This pattern then keys perception of any given event's meaning within that series. Or, eschatology is a conception of time's flow that implies an event's meaning is given by its relationship to a future anticipated rupture or redemption. And primitivism frames understanding of contemporary events by means of their temporal relationship to originary events, representing a past peak of perfection.

What does it mean to say that a technology is conceptual? A technology is an organization or application of knowledge for the simplification of tasks. So concepts may be understood as a kind of technology, as they are tools for simplifying and accomplishing cognitive tasks. Concepts are a form of *cognitive* technology. This notion was developed in work on numeracy by Frank et al. These scholars performed a series of experiments with speakers of English and of the indigenous Amazon language Pirahã—a language containing no numeral words—to illustrate how cognitive technologies function. Speakers of Pirahã or of English can both easily match objects by quantity. However, when memory-based tasks related to sequential numbers are introduced, Pirahã speakers perform worse, unless English speakers' memory function is artificially distracted or disrupted. Numbers, it would seem, are a technology for holding information about quantity. They are a technology for efficiently performing quantitative cognitive tasks.[3] Hence Frank et al. defined a cognitive technology as "a method for quickly and efficiently storing information via abstraction."[4] Rapid thought requires not only abstraction of concrete tokens into cognitive technologies like numbers but heuristic maps of the relationship of such abstractions to one another. Concepts are the cognitive technologies that perform this function: they are tools for organizing and symbolizing information in ways that increase speed and agility in relating ideas to one another. This aptly describes the function of conceptions of the flow of time. At a primary level, we use these to organize and symbolize information about expected sequences of events. In rhetorical practice, conceptions of the flow of time are cognitive technologies for shaping and reshaping an understanding of specific events within the sequential context of other events. Whether time technologies are found, like the rising and setting of the sun, constructed mechanically, like clocks, or constructed cognitively, like the concept of a day or the concept of progress, all these technologies are tools for relating events to one another with respect to sequence and synchrony. And it is *only* through technologies that we can experience time.

All experienced time is shaped time. In delineating different kinds of keeping time, it is tempting to sort by categories of more and less precise, more and less objective or archaic, sophisticated or advanced. This implies a single objective measure, accurately instantiating time-as-such. While many philosophers have argued, following McTaggart, that there really is no such thing as time, time feels both profoundly real and profoundly natural; it seems as though the day really is some*thing,* as sure as the sun rises and sets.[5] A precise time technology, then, would accurately reflect actual time-in-nature: it captures, in its count of a year, an orbit about the sun. Or alternatively, it may be tempting to claim that real, natural time is abstract, regular time, and it is this that the best, most precise time technology will capture. This perspective is manifest in claims like this one: "Atomic clocks," a popular science website tells us, "keep time better than any other clock. They even keep time better than the rotation of the Earth and the movement of the stars."[6] If time is in nature, then there might be, at least in theory, an objective single measure of better and worse time technologies, their accuracy and precision, which would mean time cannot be reshaped, only warped.

But what would guarantee the objectivity of this measure? If time has a single objective measure, it would have to stand somewhere between time-itself (time as it "really is") and our everyday technologies of time. Time-itself—if there is such a thing, and I am entirely agnostic on this point—never presents itself in a manner that can be measured except by means of the imposition of marks and a measure upon it. This is evident theoretically: can time be imagined unmediated by marks and measures? And it is evident empirically too. When all marks and measures are removed, the experience of sleeping, waking, and eating become measures of time. The body itself becomes a clock, albeit a highly irregular one. We know this from the peculiar cave experiments of the speleologist Michel Siffre. On several occasions between 1972 and 2000, Siffre secluded himself in caves and glaciers for stretches of two to six months with nothing to indicate clock or "natural" time. Whenever he woke, ate, or lay down to sleep, he would use a radio to call his colleagues above ground so that they could keep a clock-time record. Siffre himself recorded his subjective experiences in a diary. During the six months he spent in a Texas cave in 1972, his sleep rhythms expanded. His "days" varied randomly from eighteen to fifty-two clock-hours, but he reported no subjective awareness that his days varied in clock-time length, nor could he later find in the diaries he kept any indication of having had such awareness. Siffre's sense of time was now shaped by new marks: sleeping and waking itself.[7] Variations of the experiment have since been conducted hundreds of times, yielding similar results: after an initial period of relative stability, days often get longer and longer. If relative stability is again achieved, it may be punctuated with further periods of disruption.[8] With no external supporting technologies, the researchers' *experience* of time was radically dependent on the sleep/wake cycle, which itself became the only available (cognitive) technology through which a day could be experienced. The day had been redefined.

Even if it were possible to experience time without marks and measures, it would not be possible to express or share this experience. There may be something that is unmediated time-itself, but the moment we mark or measure it, once it takes on form, it ceases to be time-itself. Hence, any stipulated mediating, uniform, and objective measure against which our technologies might be compared would necessarily fail to reflect time-as-such, and would, instead, shape time in a specific way that in turn had no objective measure. The atomic clock may standardize time, but it is a Wittgensteinian standard, like the meter bar near Paris, not a reflection of some objectively understood time-itself. Whatever time is, if it is any*thing*, it has no objective measure beyond what we might stipulate.

But while there is no objective measure of time that would show any given technology is accurate with respect to time-itself, it is not quite right to say there is no such thing as temporal accuracy. Rather, accuracy is context-dependent, where context is dictated by our aims. An atomic clock does not mark morning more accurately than the dawn because it may be the light, and not the hour, that matters in a specific context. No natural phenomenon can accurately denote, of itself, when Easter is, and no mechanical clock alone can accurately denote the time for Sabbath candle lighting or Ramadan fast breaking. Accuracy, in each case, is context-dependent. It may make perfect sense to require children to be home "by dark," but no sense whatsoever to land a plane at a busy airport "by dark." It makes perfect sense to measure out a share of a night watch by the fall of sand. But anyone who wants to track the movements of stars and planets might want gears and casings.[9] It makes good sense to use a church clock to observe the hours for Benedictine monks or to regulate business hours, but a captain wants a marine chronometer to find time, and hence longitude, at sea.[10] "What time is it *actually?*" makes sense only with reference to a specific contextual aim and its suitable technology, not with reference to time in itself. Whatever time is in itself—if indeed it is anything—it can be understood and experienced only in terms of the sequential and synchronic relations of events superimposed by time technologies: mechanical, cognitive, or conceptual. Time does not come ready-marked. There is no means of accessing naked time, and there is no time-tracking mechanism that tracks time-as-such. For each task its time, and for each task-in-context its technology.

This claim shares features with those of the "temporal relationists." For example, in the *Physics,* Aristotle defines time as "number of motion in respect to *before* and *after*."[11] For Aristotle, "We describe the time as much or little measuring it by the movement, just as we know the number by what is numbered, e.g., the number of horses by one horse as the unit. . . . So it is with the time and the movement, for we measure the movement by the time and vice versa."[12] Time, here, is a means of determining relations and it is one measure of change: it measures the sequence of movement. But it also uses change *as* the measure, one change compared to another that is known-to-be-regular. The achievements of marks provided by the technology are events in time rather than time-itself.

Nonetheless, by constant conjunction, it may become remarkably difficult to shake the sense that time really is (objectively, organically) made up of seconds, minutes, and hours, that the rising and setting of the sun really does *manifest,* rather than merely *constitute,* the passing of time. It is perhaps for this reason that Augustine, famously, had so much trouble saying what time was, despite his certainty that he knew.[13] It is difficult to separate such measures from time-itself, and the ease of conflating marks and measures with some objective temporal order contributes to the political usefulness of time technologies. The appearance of objectivity makes temporal frames that much less visible.

I have thus far argued that time technologies cannot be judged according to the accuracy with which they capture "actual" time; rather, the accuracy of a technology is relative to its purpose. Each technology gives time a different shape, and that shape is accurate or not, better or worse, insofar as it achieves a specific aim.[14] Because there are multiple and overlapping temporal aims, there are multiple, overlapping—even conflicting—time technologies. The same student may, in the space of a single day, make use of an academic calendar to determine a course schedule, a religious calendar to determine ritual observance, and the Gregorian calendar to mark and celebrate a friend's birthday. He may use the turning of leaves as a mark that fall has come, the sunrise as a mark of morning, and the concept of day to plot out a study schedule. In the course of that day that person might also rely on an atomic clock–powered GPS system to reach his destination and an egg timer to make supper. He may meditate on regime cycles in a history class, on his own mortality at the doctor's office, and on the Second Coming of Christ and the end of time in the small hours of the night. Each of us lives in the throes of a profound temporal relativism: intraculturally, and intraindividually, we are steeped in a variety of times.[15]

This relativism is importantly different from the cultural time relativism that has sometimes dominated twentieth- and twenty-first-century scholarship. Such views tend to emphasize intracultural homogeneity and some level of intercultural incommensurability. It is important to consider this contrast because the tension between the multiple availability of time shapes and our sense that time really *is* something—something captured and represented, not shaped—drive the political use of time technologies. If time were culturally determined, if it were culturally organic, then it would be much more difficult to shape time in the manner I want to suggest is common. It is therefore important to entertain the objection inherent in scholarship on time: that notions of time or experiences of time are fundamentally culturally determined.

A strong line of temporal cultural relativism winds its way through the last century's scholarship on time. Most radical is the set of views associated with Benjamin Whorf and his colleagues and students. Whorf claimed that members of the Hopi nation of the southwestern United States have no conception of time whatsoever, at least in the way that Europeans understand time.[16] Evans-Pritchard claimed that the Nuer have no notion of "abstract" time.[17] More recently, sociologists give accounts of the plight of the homeless and jobless, who must somehow navigate the foreign time of social services provision.[18] Other accounts describe the slow tempo of rural life and its massive disjuncture from urban time.[19] Hans Schwartz has gone so far as to make the peculiar claim that Jews and Christians invented linear time, and that this is why everyone else, particularly Buddhists and Hindus, have not been inclined to plan for the future.[20] In Hanson's *Time and Revolution,* he tidily provides a summary account of this kind of relativism, claiming that for the "other,"

> time is conceived of as concrete, tied to the actual flow of events; in modern societies, by contrast, time appears as abstract, a kind of universal grid against which the duration of all particular events can be measured. The clearest manifestation of this distinction is the shift in the predominant mode of time measurement, from observing the movements of heavenly bodies to the keeping of mechanical clocks. The traditional world was one governed by the sun's position in the sky, the phases of the moon, and the seasons of the year; the modern world relies on recent social inventions such as abstract "seconds" and "minutes."
>
> Related to this distinction between concrete and abstract time is a secondary distinction between cyclical and linear conceptions of time. Since the time measurement of traditional cultures is most intimately connected with the cyclical

movements of the heavenly bodies, these cosmic patterns tend to provide a framework for understanding time itself in terms of repeating cycles, and it is the cyclical metaphor for time that is predominant in traditional religion and philosophy. Conversely, once time is seen as an abstract grid outside all concrete events, only the addition of directionality—from the past toward the future—is required to make time appear to be an infinite line.[21]

Hanson contrasts a "modern" abstract, linear time, divorced not only from the undulations of nature but from concrete events, with an "other" or premodern time that is natural, cyclic, task-oriented, and opposed to invented or artificial time. Though such claims echo widely in scholarship, and though they may accurately describe an aim-driven shift in emphases, they also reflect a range of fallacies and errors.

First, it is fallacious to distinguish between the time marking of a mechanical clock and the time marking of found technologies, like stars, claiming that while a mechanical clock abstracts, the stars are an unmediated, nonabstracted manifestation of time-as-such. There are several errors here. First, both star movements and clock-hand movements are, fundamentally, series of events—not identical with time but rather mediations of time. Stars are distant balls of gas, after all, no more "time-in-nature" than mechanical clocks. In other words, while stars may be a found technology and clocks are constructed, both are tools of abstraction, abstract mechanisms for tracking the passage of time. Moderns are as likely as anyone to conflate a measure of time with time-itself. Both atomic clocks and stars serve precisely the same basic function: they provide a regular, abstracted series of events against which other events may be sequenced and situated.

There is no fundamental conceptual difference here. The difference is with respect to shifting aims and available technological materials.

Furthermore, it is simply false to suggest that the seasons and sun now lack relevance compared with seconds and minutes, or that events no longer play a role in marking the passage of the day. Again, this depends on context and aims. An individual's sense of the day's flow may grow as much from tasks routinely completed as from the passing of minutes or seconds. A retail worker knows it's lunchtime as much because of the rush of arriving office workers as from a glance at the clock. A nursing mother's day may be marked by the baby's sleeping, waking, and feeding, regardless of the clock. Nanoseconds aren't much use to a doctor or a bus driver. In fact, how often do most of us, unless taking a pulse or timing a race (aim-specific time measurements), make use of the second in daily life? Outside a laboratory or sporting context, minutes, or any unit less than quarter-hours, matter rarely: perhaps to catch a train or time customer service in a retail setting. Where these units are important, that importance is clearly aim-dependent.

Conversely, minutes and seconds are no modern inventions, as Hanson falsely asserts. It was, in fact, the Greek astronomer Claudius Ptolemy who, in his *Almagest* of the second century CE, first described the second as one-sixtieth of a minute. And a *fen* 分, an artificial unit similar to a minute, was evident in Chinese time keeping from very early on. Ancient societies evidently sought technologies of greater regularity and precision whenever they had the need. Again, time measurement is aim-relative. Water clocks and hourglasses were widely in use in the ancient world, as Danielle Allen notes, for timing political speeches and night watches.[22] And any ancient society that took astronomy seriously was at work on the problem of mechanical precision in time marking, not so much to *follow* the heavens as to have an instrument that, because abstracted from those heavenly movements, had the capacity to *predict* them. With respect to abstraction, neither the division of a day into hours nor the premodern delineation of a market cycle into work and rest (that is, a week) is related to any concrete natural phenomenon. Even societies without a strong astronomical tradition had these. These are abstractions as surely as the atomic second.

Perhaps the association of abstract linear time-in-nature with Western modernity stems partly from its important role in Newton's *Principia Mathematica,* where he says, "Absolute, true, and mathematical time, of itself, and from its own nature flows equably without regard to anything external, and by another name is called duration."[23] Contrasting absolute time with vulgar time, "a *measure* of duration . . . such as an hour, a day, a month, a year," he goes on that

A fifth-century BCE Greek clepsydra, or water clock, used to time political and legal speeches. (De Agostini Picture Library/G. Nimatallah/ Bridgeman Images)

"the natural days are truly unequal, though they are commonly considered as equal, and used for a measure of time; astronomers correct this inequality for their more accurate deducing of the celestial motions. It may be, that there is no such thing as an equable motion, whereby time may be accurately measured."[24] For Newton, no motion could be found regular enough to accurately track what he understood to be time-itself.[25]

But this is no modern innovation. Plato thought of time in parallel terms of regularity and abstraction. In the *Timaeus,* he describes time as the movement of the heavens, constant and unending. But Plato thinks that this is not a series of events, as a concrete task-connected or organic conception of time might suggest, but rather it is what makes an event sequence possible: absolutely an abstraction. The image he employs to communicate this involves a creator who made an image of the eternal world, a *kosmos* that moved "according to number."[26] Time is what enables the kosmos to imitate the Forms dynamically. In other words, time, as movement, is a means of making the kosmos perceivable. For Plato, planetary movement was understood to be regular and eternal, potentially providing a stable definition for what time was in itself: as abstract and regular as Newton might have wished.

Conversely, there have always been those who lamented any separation of time from the undulating and irregular rhythms of nature. This is certainly not an exclusive feature of pre- or postmodernity, of "women's time" or of non-Western time. Indeed, one might hypothesize that regular time and undulating time, as the key notions of natural time, are partly dependent on each other for articulation. For example, in a comic fragment, the third century BCE Roman playwright Plautus has a parasite say:

> The gods confound the man who first found out
> How to distinguish hours! Confound him too,
> Who in this place set up a sundial
> To cut and hack my days so wretchedly
> Into small portions—When I was a boy,
> My belly was my sundial: one more sure,
> Truer, and more exact than any of them.
> This dial told me when 'twas proper time
> To go to dinner, when I had aught to eat—
> But now-a-days, why, even when I have,
> I can't fall to, unless the sun give leave.
> The town's so full of these confounded dials,
> The greatest part of its inhabitants
> Shrunk up with hunger, creep along the streets.[27]

Near-identical sentiments, less comically expressed, echo among contemporary critics of modernity. Time, divorced from these natural rhythms, is corrupted time on this view.[28] Only the time of found technologies in nature is true time. What one might call naturalism about time is no more a feature specific to premodern thought than the scientific essentialism embodied in the notion of abstract duration is a feature of specifically modern thought.

How many would accept that there is no context in which the sun and the moon are involved in defining the day? How many are aware atomic clocks even exist? To claim atomic time has displaced these other measures is a vast overstatement. For most, the notion that time is an abstract continuum and the notion that it is somehow bound to nature are *both* compelling, each in context-dependent ways. Consider the puzzles in the following examples:

1. Atomic clocks use leap seconds to keep in line with the cycle of night and day. So this suggests that we must hold nature as the ultimate arbiter. But nobody would set a watch by the dawn, which suggests it is not.
2. The Gregorian and Julian calendars require leap years to remain consistent with the seasons: again, is nature the ultimate arbiter? But a solar year is not consistent because orbits change over time.

The clock seems to distort nature, and nature seems to distort the clock. Yet, in context-dependent ways, both perspectives seem right.

The same challenge may be pressed against the claim that we now use linear time while ancient or "other" people used cyclical time.[29] The fascist scholar Mircea Eliade, in an influential work, argued that what he called primitive people do not experience time as linear because only acts of the gods, in mythical time, have meaning and value for them. Primitive people used the cyclical recurrence of rites and rituals to reinstantiate mythical time, which is thereby actually made present for them. "In *imitating* the exemplary acts of a god or of a mythical hero, or simply by recounting their adventures, the man of an archaic society detaches himself from profane time and magically re-enters the Great Time, the sacred time."[30] Ritual cycles displace linear event tokens as the source of meaning. Whether or not it makes sense to claim that some people find no meaning in the linear aspects of their everyday lives, echoes of this view are common. Tsvetan Todorov, for instance, makes use of this assumption in his discussions of the Spanish conquest of Mexico, arguing that differing conceptions of the flow of time made the conquest easier.[31] And the sociologist Gurvich, who held Durkheim's chair at the University of Paris in the 1960s, claimed that French peasants move through a wholly different time field than their urban cousins. The French peasant has "an inclination to move in retarded time turned in on itself" because of his adherence to "traditional patterns and symbols" that require this form of time.[32] Parallel claims about the differential shape of time are common, and have been systematically debunked in the work of Alfred Gell.[33]

But the Romans were quite at home with the linear time recorded in the *fasti,* which listed officeholders and events chronologically, and with dates *ab urbe condita,* counting forward from Rome's founding. And every French peasant, no matter how backward Gurvich may have taken her to be, knows her life is linear and that one day she will die. Indeed, as Gershuny and Sullivan pointed out, "The linear segmentation of time into 'clock time' . . . [is] a feature of any complex, large-scale technological society."[34] This is not simply because these societies have the *capacity* to build mechanical clocks but because the need for such clocks arises in that context. Wherever the need has arisen, so have mechanical clocks.

And, while of course Hesiod and Chaucer wrote of seasons and cycles, even the Victorian age's fixation with progress could not diminish John Stuart Mill's equal fascination with pendular cyclicality.[35] Mill is the totemic philosopher of progress. For him, politics is fundamentally structured by the possibility of moving forward toward truth and happiness. His political concerns with liberty, democracy, and representative government all arise specifically in the context of the centrality of progress: our capacity to find the truth and the good life. But for Mill, no progress is made without cyclical oscillation, nor is progress indefinite. Any forward lurch results from an alternation between periods of stasis and periods of conflict. Events move through time not in a straight-arrow motion, an endless accumulation of knowledge, technology, and moral fortitude, but dialectically. In organic periods, those that are static, "mankind accepts with firm conviction some positive creed, claiming jurisdiction over all their actions, and containing more or less of truth and adaptation to the needs of humanity."[36] It is during the critical periods that progress is made, but this does not mean that the direction is always a forward one. Mill expresses some nervousness about critical periods in which everything is called into question at once. There must be, he says, at least *something* settled or else society will come apart at the seams.[37] After each cycle, humanity grows some little bit closer to truth and the safe exercise of liberty, and this movement exhibits "an ever increasing tendency . . . to settle finally in [the center]."[38] Progress, then, comes to an end. Because ideal conditions are rarely met, Mill acknowledges that knowledge is not just gained but lost. Books are written but they are also burned. New York flourishes but Carthage was destroyed. Cyclicality describes the movement between organic and critical periods, these cycles move forward, but they are cycles nonetheless, and they move toward an end point, a telos or an eschaton. Mill, the quintessential progressive modern, makes ample use of cyclical and rupture-oriented conceptions of time in developing his conception of progress, particularly in his *Autobiography* and his essay *On Coleridge*.[39] This tension between progressive and alternative time shapes is evident in Mill's sometimes fraught correspondence with Auguste Comte, where Comte, comparing the relative intelligence of various thinkers, addresses the time sense of Giambattista Vico. Vico had argued for a grand cyclic arc of time through which civilizations passed: "People first sense what is necessary, then consider what is useful, next attend to comfort, later delight in pleasures, soon grow dissolute in luxury, and finally go mad squandering their estates."[40] Comte, who held a tripartite (theological-metaphysical-scientific) conception of movement in time, says, "His strange theory of the cycles of society [is] . . . absurd" because it ignores "the general superiority of the modern condition over that of ancient days."[41] Yet even Comte was not immune to the draw of other time shapes.[42] The work of many other nineteenth-century thinkers engages a similar ambivalence.[43] These include, notably, Hegel and Marx. And the twentieth century has its Oswald Spengler, Thomas Kuhn, and Stephen Skowronek.[44] Modern time is not straightforwardly linear.[45] For every bubble, there is a crash.

Quintessentially cyclic ancient thinkers, like Polybius, are, on closer inspection, just as complex in the incorporation of linear and disruptive aspects. Polybius clearly held that regime types went in circles, but the ambivalence in his discussions of the meaning of Roman political innovation shows the real presence of temporal directionality in his thought too.[46] Similarly, the appropriately cyclic time of Hesiod's *Works and Days,* concerned with the turn of seasons, may be paired with his *Theogony,* which is clearly linear in orientation. People are fond of pointing to the cyclicality of the Mayan calendar, but Mayan pictographic rhetoric is ripe with evidence of calendrical linearity too. Mayan time stelae record sequences of events characterizing a reign or a lifetime in a decidedly linear fashion, and relate these to the functionally linear Mayan long count. In the case of China, while the annals have a set form that seems to emphasize the repetition of patterns, "the Chinese never claimed that real history (even dynastic history) 'repeated' itself, even though they often cited 'past examples' to illustrate moral or political lessons to be learned from history."[47] Our modern Gregorian calendars, too, go in circles and lines all at once. It may be January once more, but it is, each time, a new January, succeeding the last and preceding the next. The view that time among ancients or primitives is cyclic while time for moderns is linear and progressive is simply not supported empirically.

Types and tokens are fundamental to every human conceptual system and, most simply, linear time is always necessary to the sequencing

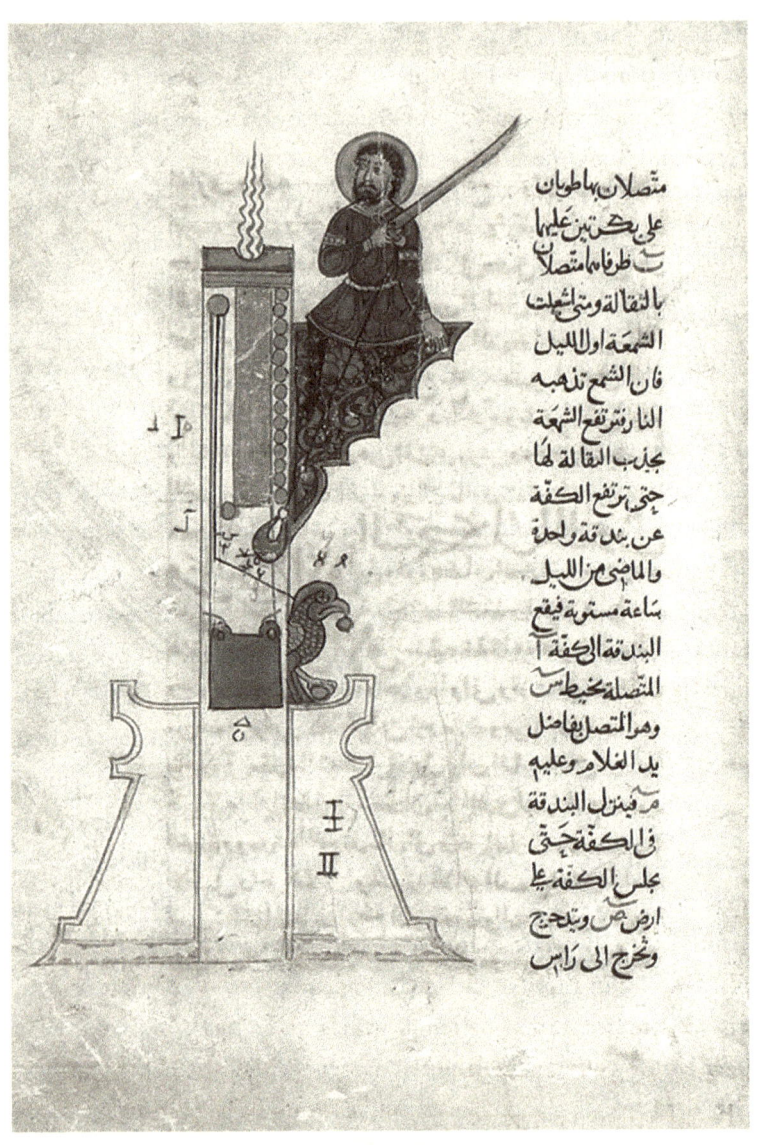

This Syrian candle clock measures a conception of time that is both linear and abstract. (From Al-Jazari's *Book of Knowledge of Ingenious Mechanical Devices* (1315 CE). Pictures from History/Bridgeman Images)

of tokens, while cyclical time suits the sequencing of types. The very pattern of human life suggests linear, cyclic, and rupture/eschatological-oriented time conceptions: a burst into life, a series of milestones—personal to the person living them but cyclical to those who observe the course of the community as a whole—the shrivel of death, and the timeless hereafter. These various time conceptions overlap and intersperse for each person individually, for the community collectively, and across communities and times.

While I certainly do not suggest that there is no difference in ancient and modern or intercultural ways of marking and measuring time, or at least their relative prominence, the strength of the contrast is often overdrawn.[48] As Maurice Bloch once chastised his colleagues, it "is a recurrent professional malpractice of anthropologists to exaggerate the exotic character of other cultures."[49] Where they are different, the differences are in aims and materials. Everyone, Western or Eastern, ancient or modern, rural or urban, unemployed or working, uses a variety of regular events, found or constructed, to meet a variety of time-tracking needs.[50] While culture may drive a florescent variety of manifestations of time keeping—specific devices and emphases—it is not culture itself that determines temporal perspective. Rather, different conceptions of the flow of time, different notions of its shape, and different kinds of clocks are developed and deployed for different purposes. Both across and within cultures, a range of characterizations of time and a range of marks and measures of time are always available simultaneously because we do so many things with time.[51] The technologies that relate events to each other are aim-relative but are also culture-relative precisely to the extent that aims and available materials are culture-relative.

If time is a measure of change relating one set of events to another, then all these time technologies—found, constructed, or abstracted—organize events sequentially in a variety of purpose-dependent ways, with accuracy relative to the requirements of each aim. So experience of time may be—perhaps necessarily is—shaped for specific purposes and ends. These include a variety of first-order aims of sequencing and synchronizing: providing equal time, measuring who is first, coordinating location. But constructed time serves a range of second-order purposes too, and it is in the service of these second-order purposes that time's radical malleability comes to the fore. Beyond sequencing and synchronizing in myriad ways, shaped time can also be put to work as a rhetorical frame, in the service of the politics of legitimation, as I now turn to demonstrate.

Framing

My claim is that rhetorical framing is one means of shaping our experiences in time. Rhetors can deploy a conception of the flow of time to impact how an event, claim, or innovation is understood. This is possible because all experienced time is shaped time and because we are open to multiple time shapes, as I have just shown. Now, what do I mean by a rhetorical frame?

Goffman pioneered the study of frames as technologies of meaning transmission in his book *Frame Analysis*. A frame, for Goffman, consists of "schemata of interpretation" used "to locate, perceive, identify, and label" events or objects in ways that give them significance, enabling the cognitive organization of experience looking back and intention going forward.[52] Frames are cognitive structures that provide heuristic means for making sense of experience. The social meaning of a person, circumstance, object, or claim is given partly by its frame, and when a frame shifts, the meaning shifts also.

People normally remain unaware of these background conditions, moving between them with ease, interpreting and reinterpreting the meaning of actions and events as the frame shifts. What does a doctor's lab coat communicate? At a Halloween party, it is a costume; in an emergency room, it suggests the wearer is a doctor. On a stage, the wearer may be an actor playing a doctor. On a mannequin in a shop, it is goods for sale. It would be false to claim that the coat has no meaning on its own. As Goffman notes, "Whatever goes on within an interpreted and organized stream of activity draws on material that comes from the world and in some traceable continuation of substance must go back into the world."[53] But meaning is modulated in critical ways by contextual factors without which objects and actions would be capable of only incomplete signification. This draws on the related epistemological work of philosophers like Wittgenstein and Quine: nothing has its own complete, independent, discrete meaning; everything must always draw part of its significance from the web of meaningful events, words, objects, and beliefs in which it is embedded.

The most basic frame, Goffman claims, concerns whether an event came about because of someone's intention or whether it is simply the result of chemical or physical forces.[54] To be hit by a fist is a fact, but how we understand the action and what comes next depend radically on whether that fist was intentionally flung or whether, say, a person slipped and the fist found its mark, as a matter of physics, on the way down. This and a range of other frames manage the unconscious flow of experience, guiding interpretation and reaction. With such examples, Goffman was concerned primarily with what he termed micro-interactions on the interpersonal scale. But all meaning is modulated by frames, including the frame of intentionality. Frames together make up the context of every form of communication, interpersonal or mass, direct or symbolic. Frames draw on related facts and relevant aspects of the web of cosmological and epistemological assumptions that hold our every belief in place. So we should expect anyone concerned with the meaning of action, speech, and event to have some interest in framing practices, both as they are constructed intentionally and as they are conducted semi- or subconsciously as standard elements of verbal and nonverbal communication.[55]

Sometimes framing is done consciously for purposes of persuasion. As Todd Gitlin notes, frames can be "principles of selection, emphasis and presentation composed of little tacit theories about what exists, what happens, and what matters."[56] Kuypers has called this practice "*rhetorical* framing," that is, "a process whereby communicators, consciously or unconsciously, act to construct a point of view that encourages the facts of a given situation to be interpreted by others in a particular manner."[57] And Lakoff and others have argued that rhetorical framing works because framing is such a key element of communication more generally, embedded in the very structure of human thought.[58] A rhetor can use a frame to pick out and subtly invoke those background elements that best support a desired interpretation, relying on our empirically established propensity to take cognitive shortcuts where possible.

Framing's role in persuasion drives an explosion of interest among social scientists. Persuasion comes into play in situations of contention, where two or more perspectives are defensible and compete for support. Because meaning relies on framing, persuasion is always frame-modulated and so the study of persuasion must involve the study of frames. So-called purposive framing works to create resonance in a target audience. "When we persuade," Garsten notes, "we want to change our listeners' minds by linking our position to their existing opinions and emotions."[59] An effective frame is resonant with broader beliefs and prior knowledge, invoking existing cosmologies, epistemological assumptions, narratives, myths, and understandings to orient an audience's response to a new claim. Benford and Snow call this task "frame alignment."[60] They show how strategists of social movements use this technique to generate resonance among the social movement's target demographics, people who may not initially recognize a cause as *their* cause. To achieve this, rhetors can draw on related frames, joining the frame of their cause to other "ideologically congruent but structurally unconnected frames regarding a particular issue or problem."[61] Or they can "amplify" their frame through "clarification and invigoration" to animate a particular understanding of events or concerns.[62] In response to a target audience, a rhetor can extend the frame, embracing perspectives offered by the audience or, if a frame is failing, can transform it.[63] Hence rhetorical framing, like the practice Goffman describes at the interpersonal level, is dynamic, not static, and interactive, not unidirectional. As Garsten notes, the study of persuasion ought to be embraced—even by normative scholars—because it "consists partly in ruling and partly in following [and hence] shares more generally in the character of democratic citizenship."[64] Of course, persuasion is not limited to democratic contexts but is important wherever power must be negotiated and maintained. And Garsten's claim that rhetoric is never unidirectional is important in a range of contexts beyond the democratic. Persuasion is a negotiation that engages whole human persons; it is never simply a spectacle that is passively consumed. Framing helps explain how this dynamic feature of persuasion works.

Shaped time is a powerful frame for political talk. I have argued above that time is available to be shaped because of its malleability and the diversity of subjective experiences of time, both within and across cultures. And I have argued that there is a permanent gap between experienced time and anything that might count as time-itself. This means the right measure of time or the right conception of time is permanently underdetermined. This in turn entails the permanent possibility of temporal reshaping, revision, and manipulation. Because people are always open to other time shapes, at home with a wide range of aim-dependent time technologies and conceptions of the flow of time, a rhetor can structure and restructure the meaning of actions or events by situating or resituating them in temporal frames. The meaning of actions and events is always also partly a function of their position within a narrative structure. That is, the synchrony and sequence of events affect their meaning; it is not just the substance of the event itself on its own. Section 1 of the Fourteenth Amendment of the U.S. Constitution looks uncontroversial, its purport assumed. But it looks decidedly different when understood in a linear sequence with the Three-fifths Compromise and Dred Scott. To call out this aspect of meaning is the work of what I will call a *temporal*-rhetorical frame, which dictates the shape of narrative structure. Certain kinds of narratives are enabled, and certain kinds precluded, once situated in a progressive, primitivist, or eschatological frame. If how events are sequenced or synchronized impacts meaning, then the temporal structure in which the event or action is implicitly understood to be situated acts as one among those rhetorical frames that shape its meaning.

It is worth noting, too, that time is not just an available, because malleable, frame, and it is not just an effective, because meaning-modulating, frame—it is also obligingly subtle. Shaped time fades from view precisely because of the habit of conflating the measure of time with time-itself. The notion that time is natural is hard to resist, even where our measures—as with hours, weeks, even the delineated number of seasons—are arbitrary, or at least not objectively compulsory. Most people never question why the year starts in January or the day at midnight. Time frames do their work with particular stealth both because we are inclined not to attend to them and because they have the appearance of neutrality: we do not normally think of clocks and calendars as political tools. Because we generally understand time technologies as neutral, as part of, or at least mirrors of, nature or the objective order of reason and science, they often—though by no means always—recede starkly into the realm of noncontestation. Steven Lukes famously observed that the more invisible the power, the more effective it is.[65] Frames do their work quietly—temporal frames, often, particularly so.

Legitimation

What kind of work do temporal frames do? Time framing effectively serves the politics of legitimation in particular. Legitimation is a special case of persuasion. It is a process that aims not at bringing people around to a judgment with respect to a specific policy, claim, or law but rather at persuading people to accept as morally defensible a general authority to make and enforce policies and law over time. Legitimation is a concern of every power because without legitimacy, control becomes unsustainably expensive. It is a commonplace that if power is not accepted as legitimate, a consistent deployment of force is necessary to secure obedience. This generates substantial costs that spiral outward, as use of force may further erode legitimacy. So any successful leader must engage in a practice of legitimation both for herself individually and for the institutions through which she exercises power.

Legitimation is not a task with a clear end point. A moment of mass consent or a third-party determination that a regime meets with some abstract normative criteria of legitimacy is never the end of the matter because exogenous shocks, poor performance, or the presence of effective antilegitimating rhetoric can threaten legitimacy. Furthermore, it may be difficult to determine at what point legitimacy begins to lag because people obey for a range of reasons—self-interest or lack of interest, habit or fear—that they themselves may be hard pressed to distinguish. And perceptions of legitimacy are uneven across populations too, which makes trust in the solidity of legitimacy even more precarious.[66] Because legitimacy is in flux, the practice of legitimation must be, if not continual, then at least periodic. This challenges the characterization of a legitimate state as one whose denizens *believe* in its legitimacy. Certainly, some people, perhaps a mass of people in some states, normally hold the legitimacy of the power to which they submit as an unquestioned belief. But there are times when legitimacy is threatened because beliefs are unsettled or not yet established; then legitimacy is not a matter of passive belief but of active judgment. At such moments belief in legitimacy may be foregrounded and called into question as people may want to see what a new regime has to offer or hear what a new leader has to say before passing judgment. These cases constitute what I will call a legitimation challenge. If a legitimation crisis, in Habermas's sense, is a situation in which people have lost faith en masse in the capacity of political institutions to fulfill their intended role, a legitimation challenge is a moment—aligned with the classical, medical sense of a crisis—when things could go either way, a cusp of public judgment. While legitimation is a continual dialogic process, this process is at its most acute and visible at such moments.

This is a moment of active engagement between rulers and ruled, and it makes the practice of legitimation normatively scintillating. On one hand, it recalls the fundamental dependence of every regime, no matter how authoritarian, on performance and recognition. On the other, the descriptive study of the practice of legitimation illuminates on what grounds people in fact make judgments about a regime or political agent, which is to say *why* they consent to (however weakly, however grudgingly), tolerate, or reject power.

Hence, consent itself, despite its centrality in normative political philosophy, is of only secondary interest here. At least from Grotius onward, consent has played a key role in theories of legitimacy. As Grotius put it, "The right which the Sovereign has over his subjects [is not] to be measured by this or that form, of which divers men have different opinions, but by the extent of the will of those who conferred it upon him."[67] That is, on this widely accepted view, when the people consent, then power is legitimate. Consent switches on legitimacy. Because it seems to some scholars that people might consent to a morally illegitimate government when they ought not to, a normative rule is sometimes appended to this, as when Allen Buchanan argues that legitimacy must depend on "some threshold approximation to full or perfect justice."[68] But can't people, as autonomous agents, choose their own threshold approximation of what "full or perfect justice" is reasonable in their circumstances? And isn't this collective decision on what will count as good enough at that moment in effect consent? On the other hand, a reliance on consent raises the question of why people in fact give, withhold, or withdraw their consent. Aren't the various possible characteristics of that "threshold approximation to full or perfect justice" important to articulate, or at least contemplate, for the purposes of a judgment of legitimacy? It seems reasonable to suppose that what people in fact expect from government should matter to normative philosophers, and it also seems reasonable to suppose that some of those expectations are defined by a diverse range of criteria understood to be normative. To the extent that consent is interesting, it is interesting because it *marks* a judgment of legitimacy, bridging normative and empirical study.

Furthermore, a focus on consent has the perhaps uncomfortable effect of implying that a vast majority of people have historically lived under illegitimate government, since few, including in our liberal democracies, have had the opportunity to consent to both regime type and officeholders. Then there are the refugees and the stateless who dwell where they have no right or opportunity to freely consent but who may nonetheless acknowledge the legitimate power of the state in which they dwell. And then there are all those historical forms of government that did not provide opportunities for consent but that nonetheless have sometimes seemed to hold legitimacy in the eyes of subjects. Even now, some authoritarian and authoritative countries with limited opportunities for robust and direct consent have very strong markers of legitimacy.[69]

Finally, consent is too static to capture the ebb and flow of legitimacy politics. At what point can we say that consent has been withdrawn? It may be tempting to pinpoint elections in democratic regimes, but even here a leader with weak support is sometimes said to lack a mandate for major policy change, even if he has the official marks of consent or his power was engendered through the appropriate procedure. Consent may be a *mark* but not the constitutive substance of legitimacy: consent is given, when there is an opportunity to do so, to a regime (or individual) that (whom) members of the population already judge or consider to have a legitimate claim to structure or exercise power. And it is the procedure of election—at least in a democracy—not the consent itself that turns that potential into actual power. This makes sense of the fact that in many democratic regimes, someone may legitimately hold power without having even got the majority of votes, in accordance with a procedure nobody voted for and few may support or even understand.

It is because consent is, at best, one marker of legitimacy, not its fundamental constituent element, that no one's legitimation practice involves simply asking for peoples' approval and then announcing that one has received it. Those engaged in the practice of legitimation give reasons, however indirect, however rhetorically dressed, for why they deserve popular support or approval. Because consent sometimes marks but does not substantively and exclusively constitute a judgment of legitimacy, it plays a minor role in this study of legitimation practices.

What is, then, involved in a dynamic practice of legitimation? The empirical study of legitimacy has generated a variety of taxonomies of sources of legitimacy. There is Weber's famous account of the three ideal types: traditional, legal-rational, and charismatic legitimacy. More recently, scholars of legitimacy in China work with a performance/procedural dichotomy, while scholars of legitimacy in Europe have largely adopted Fritz Scharpf's related input/output classification.[70] In Beetham's justly famous analysis, legitimacy rests on three pillars, all of which must be present. He says: "Power can be said to be legitimate where it does not breach established rules; where acquisition and exercise are normatively validated in terms of socially accepted beliefs about rightful authorization and due performance; and where it is confirmed through appropriate acts of recognition and acknowledgement. Together these give those in power moral as well as de facto authority, and those subject to them sufficient grounds for obedience and cooperation."[71]

All of these taxonomies have merit, though each has its peculiarities. For example, charisma is more a proxy for performative capacity than a justification for authority one could proffer in the way one could explicitly offer tradition or legality as justification. No one says, "I am your leader because of my powerful charisma," while, by contrast, claims to tradition and legality could explicitly be proffered as justifications for legitimate authority. Hobbes, in his analysis of power, recognized this explicitly, noting how the constituent elements of charisma serve as a proxy for capacity. He defines power as a "present means to obtain some future apparent good," and then notes a range of features associated with charisma as power's ingredients: eloquence, nobility, affability, a track record of success, wealth combined with generosity, reputation, good looks, prudence.[72] As for the performance/procedural dichotomy, it largely ignores the range of other normative reasons people might give for their obedience. And Beetham's analysis separates rule-based from other forms of normative validation in a way that is perhaps unwarranted. In a crisis, for instance, breaching established rules might not only be tolerated but expected, particularly from a leader who already enjoys a legitimacy surplus on the basis of past performance. Nonetheless, these demonstrably valid sources of legitimacy, when reordered, together constitute a useful overall framework for a study of practices of legitimation.

Within this proposed framework, all sources of legitimation (distinct from but related to criteria of legitimacy) are found in one of two wells, and it is from these wells that legitimation rhetoric always draws. One well contains what I will call underlying self-justifying orders. Examples include tradition, legal and procedural rules, and normative arguments, but also the order of nature, cosmic harmony or divine order, and the order of fate or destiny. Like any claim to justification, whether epistemological, normative, or otherwise, a claim of legitimacy must anchor itself in an already existing cosmological/ontological and epistemological scheme. That is to say, people come to accept something as true partly on the basis of its correspondence with other things whose truth or validity they already accept. This preserves cognitive harmony. For the most part, people prefer order to its alternatives—whatever order means for them—and take measures to maintain it and to expel discordant elements unless they are held in place by a simultaneous rival frame. Justice is restoring a balance of right. Rationality rejects fantastic or incongruent claims. Expiation of sin restores moral wholeness. People employ a range of conceptions of right order, and nearly all forms of justification—rational, normative, and even empirical—draw on one or more of them. Justification involves a normally implicit premise that an action or claim *ought* to be in harmony, in line with right order, and if it is not, some adjustment is necessary.

It is often framing that carries this implicit premise. The frame invokes the relevant order and implies a good fit. All legitimation claims, like justification in general, invoke both some order and this implicit normative claim about the necessity of maintaining it. This is likely a political universal, but it still allows for a diverse range of intra- and intercultural epistemologies and cosmologies, an array of orders, that could be invoked. Notably, while these orders may clash with or even contradict one another, for the most part they are taken as self-justifying and recede into the background. So from the first well, the person engaged in a practice of legitimation can draw on one or more available orders and use an appropriate frame to imply that a certain innovation, action, or claim to power is concordant.

The other well provides arguments from performance or capacity. No regime and no political agent, no matter how procedurally solid its coming to power, no matter how traditional, can maintain legitimacy indefinitely without solid performance. What passes for solid performance may, in terms of specifics, vary substantially from place to place, time to time. It may mean economic growth and progress toward equality in one context, and staving off marauders or securing food supply in another. But the maintenance of order perceived as relatively just, whatever this means locally, is likely a universal requirement of solid performance. More locally, offices defined by a specific task set distinct criteria for the officeholder's performance: it is pretty clear when a tax collector, say, or a director of emergency management has performed well. Elsewhere, legitimation in the realm of performance is normally partly performative. That is, a regime or its leaders must not only do well—or at least not badly—but communicate this effectiveness too. Such practices may take the form of an actual performance of capacity: military parades, celebrations of victory or rehearsals of civic religion on national days, even the architecture of legislatures may form part of this performance of performance. Capacity is communicated not just by statistics themselves—showing, for example, economic growth or a decline in infant mortality—but by the ability to produce those statistics in the first place. This is the second well from which legitimation rhetoric can be drawn: performance and the performance of performance.

Beetham notes that the job of a social scientist is not, in the Weberian tradition, to "report on people's 'belief in legitimacy'" because "[a] given power relationship is not legitimate because people believe in its legitimacy, but because it can be justified in terms of their beliefs."[73] Drawing on the two-well framework I have described leads to the following claims: people have comparatively stable beliefs about what a good government ought to do and be. A government engaged in legitimation attempts to persuade people, largely by invoking suitably resonant frames, that what it has to offer is in accordance with that set of beliefs, and from there, people make a judgment (which they may later revisit) about whether and to what extent a claim to power is indeed legitimate. Drawing from these two sources of legitimation, power makes its pitch.

Time talk helps to frame that pitch. Because of the ease of shaping and reshaping time, because of the ways time frames suggest the significance of events for the present and the future, because modes of ordering time create frame alignment with underlying, already accepted forms of order, and because of the way temporal order communicates capacity, temporal framing serves the politics of legitimation. Conversely, time talk can likewise frame the pitch of political agents who seek to undermine order and power.

Judgments of legitimacy may settle for a time. Or legitimacy may be negotiated and renegotiated repeatedly through a variety of forms of performance and communication, symbolic and direct. It is my contention that the ubiquity of time talk where legitimacy faces a challenge can be explained by the particular capacity of temporal framing to draw from both these wells of legitimation: performance and underlying, self-justifying claims of order. And an atrophied temporal frame in the form of, for instance, a calendar, can reinforce those claims over time at very low cost to a regime.

China's Preambles: An Example

So what does a temporal frame engaged for the work of legitimation look like? Before moving on to analyses of specific techniques in the coming chapters, I want to close this chapter with a straightforward example of temporal framing in the politics of legitimation. A comparison between the preambles of China's two most recent constitutions shows how time talk can be used to create frame alignment, making an innovation appear to be a restoration.

Constitutional preambles have historically been nonjusticiable, but over recent decades they have taken on substantial importance in influencing the interpretation of constitutions. Their length and complexity have increased accordingly. Flagrant nationalist rhetoric is to be expected in preambles, which often name a range of symbolic and historical touchpoints. But recent preambles are commonly also framed specifically by conceptions of the flow of time. Among them, China's constitutional preambles are of particular interest for two reasons. First, as Elazar has argued, Communist constitutions serve, if not primarily then at least substantially, as manifestos.[74] In the Chinese context, the superior importance of mandates, above and beyond ideology and institutions, may explain China's particularly long and programmatic preambles.[75] Because they are so extensive, their temporal framing is especially clear. While temporal framing is pervasive in recent Western constitutional preambles also, for example, in Hungary's millennial 2012 preamble, the clarity of the Chinese case makes it apt as an illustration. The second reason China's preambles are particularly useful here is that the constitutions of 1978 and 1982, so close in chronological time, are worlds apart in political time, providing a stark example of how competing frames serve as rhetorical proxies for fiercely divergent political aims at crucial junctures. Beginning with some brief historical background, this section illustrates how changing the conception of the flow of time in each of these preambles framed efforts to communicate and legitimate opposing political aims.

In 1975, with Zhou Enlai dying of cancer and Mao struggling with Lou Gehrig's disease, China's leadership succession remained unclear. Initially, the radical-left Gang of Four, led by Mao's wife Jiang Qing, held sway. She, Zhang Chunqiao, Yao Wenyuan, and Wang Hongwen had cheered on the Cultural Revolution's excesses. But Mao had not trusted Jiang's political and ideological leadership. Deng Xiaoping, the obvious leadership choice, was in political limbo, purged in the Cultural Revolution and deeply distrusted by the Gang of Four. Brought back into the fold briefly in 1974, Deng was again repudiated after the death of Zhou in 1976. So Mao instead appointed as his successor the relatively unknown Hua Guofeng.

The heart of contention at this political moment was the Gang of Four's plan to continue along a radical-left path, while Deng and a growing number of Chinese saw the need for reform and modernization if China was to survive. The recent assassination of party leader

Lin Bao and his family meant that everyone involved must have known what was at stake in this dispute: not just China's future but their own personal safety.

Between Mao's death in 1976 and 1980, the power struggle was intense. Immediately after assuming the premiership in late 1976, Hua engineered the arrest of the Gang of Four and a number of their associates, and Deng was again brought back from the fringe. However, Hua's personal loyalty to Mao and his leadership of the Cultural Revolutionary forces in Hunan made reform difficult. The more experienced, increasingly powerful, and politically astute Deng began pushing his strategy of market reform against Hua's Soviet-style industrial planning. It was in this highly uncertain and tumultuous environment that the 1978 constitution was drafted and then passed at the first meeting of the Fifth National People's Congress.

The body of Hua's 1978 constitution returns to moderate institutional elements drawn from the 1954 constitution. But the preamble looks vividly ahead to reinvigorated class struggle and continuing revolution. Notably, the story it tells stretches back a mere 150 years. This frame implies that China in its relevant form *begins* with the struggle to throw off feudalism. Then, with Mao's victory in 1949, "the founding of the People's Republic of China marked the beginning of the historical period of socialism in our country."[76] And although China has "won great victories" and the "dictatorship of the proletariat in [China] has been consolidated and strengthened," China must still "struggle in unity and carry the proletarian revolution through to the end."[77] The Cultural Revolution marked a shift to a new era but the people must "persevere in continuing the revolution" and "persevere in the struggle of the proletariat against the bourgeoisie and in the struggle for the socialist road against the capitalist road."[78] The struggle against the people's enemies is ongoing, though

China aims to be "a great and powerful socialist country with modern agriculture, industry, national defense and science and technology by the end of the century."[79] The Cultural Revolution is praised and the dominant tone is one of continuing struggle and ongoing rupture, showing strong vestiges of Mao's militant leftism.

This is not simply history, a recounting of a causal succession of events leading to the constitution. Rather, the event of the constitution is situated within a temporal frame that implies what the current moment means and what must come next. This frame has eschatological characteristics. Eschatology, which will form the subject of chapter 5, is the study of the "last things," the things that take place around an anticipated end. The 1978 preamble invokes an eschatological conception of the flow of time by anticipating a continuing period of violent agitation leading up to an ultimate rupture. In eschatological thinking, that rupture will bring about a period of stable justice and peace expected to last and last. Free from degeneration or decay, this period can be interpreted as a time outside of time, beyond events. Teleology conceives of developmental stages unfolding in predictable patterns, specific to each thing, toward that thing's fruition, its coming into itself. Normally, fruition is followed by degeneration and decay. The telos of the acorn is the oak tree, but that oak will die and rot before long. So one can frame events in time that is not teleological but rather eschatological, culminating in an end that is beyond degeneration and decay because beyond action and event. Eschatology is very specific in its patterning. The period of violent struggle preceding the period of peace takes on a purpose beyond its immediately political goals, incorporating overtones of purification. In a proper eschatology, this purification is a necessary condition for the eschaton's ultimate resistance to decay. Through violent rupture, time-as-we-have-known-it is made to stop and something else, a new era that is qualitatively, temporally different, comes into being.

These elements are evident in the preamble to the 1978 constitution. It situates China in the midst of a moment of violent agitation that precedes the end of struggle in the form of lasting peace and justice. The temporal frame suggests where China "is" in this temporal arc. It communicates when the Chinese people became a people in the relevant sense, where they are now, and where they are going. In the thick of rupture, in the midst of the struggle for purification, the previous temporal era is decisively at an end. Only *after* the break that the struggle represents will a new and permanent era of Communism follow. By virtue of the expectations this conception of the flow of time sets up—lasting peace and justice—current sacrifice is vindicated, legitimated. The frame situates the event of the constitution's promulgation within the narrative structure that eschatology sets up, suggesting what the constitution means and emphasizing its role in bringing about a form of redemption. This becomes clearer in contrast with the constitution that soon followed.

In December 1978, nine months after the constitution was promulgated, Deng marshaled his forces to throw Hua out, moving China into a post-Mao era that would focus on technical and managerial competence, economic growth, and social liberalization.[80] China scholars at the time described this shift as "an ideological crisis" that, if "not backed by clarity and consistency could be very disorienting."[81] The constitution of 1982 marked decided shifts, limiting terms of office, substantially increasing property rights, increasing powers of local governance, and so on. For example, the constitution of 1978, like its 1975 predecessor but unlike the 1954 constitution, did not allow for a right of private property inheritance. But Article 15 in the 1982 constitution restores this right. And while Article 7 of the 1978 constitution stated that "the absolute predominance of the collective economy of the people's commune is ensured," Article 11 of the 1982 version emphasizes individual property rights, which are said to be "a complement to the socialist sector of the economy owned by the public."[82]

The 1982 preamble exhibits radical differences, expressed not just through substance but through temporal form. The 1978 preamble was situated in an eschatologically inflected frame, but the new preamble situates the event of the constitution in progressive time. Critically, the drafters extend the history of the Chinese "we" back millennia. The preamble begins: "China is one of the countries with the longest histories in the world. The people of all nationalities in China have jointly created a splendid culture."[83] This has several effects, particularly in the wake of the Cultural Revolution that attempted to extinguish that culture. First, it shifts focus from the regime, from the People's Republic of China, to China as an entity, a people that exists above and beyond the country's current institutional manifestation. This is a technique similar to the one Augustus Caesar invoked when he shifted the Roman method of event dating from the consular year, characteristic of Rome as a *republic,* to the date *ad urbe condita*—from the city's founding.[84] Drawing attention back to a "we" that predated the current regime emphasizes the continuity of an underlying political entity from the past through the present to the future: in the Roman case, through the new imperial regime, and in the Chinese case, a still socialist but post-radical-revolutionary age. This mode of temporal framing situates the Cultural Revolution, and indeed the radical policies of the fifteen years prior, as a historical blip, a marginal deviation from what is otherwise a gradually advancing path. The new constitution becomes a restoration, not a break. "The Chinese people waged wave upon wave of heroic struggles for national independence and liberation and for democracy and freedom," ultimately achieving victory in the formation of the People's Republic. But progress marches on, the story continues: following China's achievement, "effected step by step," China will now "follow the socialist road, *steadily* improve socialist institutions, develop socialist democracy, improve the socialist legal system and work hard and self-reliantly to modernize industry, agriculture, national defense and science and technology *step by step* to turn China into a socialist country with a high level of culture and democracy."[85] This is no longer a rhetoric of eschatology, with the event of the constitution marking a continuing period of tribulation, not-yet-achieved rupture, nor is it a rhetoric proclaiming the onset of utopia. Rather, the constitution here is framed as a moment in the gradual, ongoing progress of China.

The constitution in this scheme is an event that restores China to a previous path that can be understood as saliently continual, give or take a Cultural Revolution, with the course of the Chinese "we" for millennia. Continuity displaces rupture. This gently progressive narrative creates expectations for what comes next that, in turn, strongly imply the meaning of the constitution as political event. At the same time the frame implies the decisive rejection of the eschatological political narrative Deng wishes to eschew. Thus, the preamble to the Chinese constitution, whatever else it might accomplish, aims to help legitimate and persuade by reconstituting not just Chinese institutions but what counts as China through time.

Zhang Youyu, a constitutional scholar who was assistant secretary of the constitutional drafting committee of the 1982 document, is quite explicit about the pivotal aim of the preamble. He explained, "The reason why we must have a preamble is because we are in a transitional period, some things that should be provided in the Constitution cannot be written into its text. The basic task of the country during the transitional period and the conditions for implementing the Constitution . . . can all not be written into articles, and if they were written into articles, they could not be written as clearly and incisively as if they would have been put into the preamble."[86] And he later notes the preamble's role in signaling the constitution's "progressive orientation, principles and policies, etc."[87]

This is not mere ideology. The progressive temporal frame communicates important nonideological information too. The preamble's frame "keys" the meaning of the innovation, the promulgation of this radical new constitution. It allows Deng's drafters to draw out different underlying ordering assumptions that have the effect of normalizing or naturalizing the innovation. The break from the extremes of Maoism becomes not a rupture but a restoration, a restoration of the Chinese people to their collective purpose. This is where we are in our story as a people at this moment of constitutional refounding. It is because of the shape of our story that we need this constitution—here, now—and the future we offer means you should trust us, your leaders. The temporal frame aligns the innovation with underlying familiar, resonant forms of order. By placing the event of the constitution in a new temporal frame—progressive, not eschatological—the drafters work to legitimize the event of its promulgation and China's new orientation.

Conclusion

This example of China's preambles shows how experience of time can be shaped and reshaped in speech, creating degrees of resonance with underlying self-justifying forms of order. This is possible because time is multiple and malleable. The technologies through which time is shaped, whether found (like the sun rising), constructed (like a clock), or abstracted (like notions of a day or month or of progress or eschatology), relate events in the world to an expected sequence of other, more or less regular events. Each technology, by differently relating events, gives time a distinct shape. Because a variety of time technologies serve a variety of aims, and because there is no organic and objective standard time, we are at home with a variety of experiences of shaped time.

Temporal framing (and reframing), by delineating narrative structure, can imply (and then revise) the meaning of specific events. As we shall see in some detail in the chapters that follow, legitimation of power relies on some order already accepted as legitimate, and temporal framing is one means of facilitating this through frame alignment. And because temporal order enables order keeping more generally, shaping time also contributes to the performance of a capacity to manage contingency.

Temporal-rhetorical framing is often stealthy. Because many marks and measures through which we experience time are found in nature, time seems natural, disguising the frame. And because there is an unbridgeable ambiguity between natural and abstract time, between the time of found and constructed technologies, between the cyclical repetition of patterns and the linear iteration of events, time is always ripe for reshaping, even as it maintains the appearance of objectivity. We turn now to a detailed investigation and illustration of such techniques.

2
Calendars and the Politics of Order Alignment

The Blue Heaven has passed away,
The Yellow Heaven is on his way.
Now see the sixty-year fate replay,
And live the world's heyday.
—*Yellow Scarf Rebellion slogan, Han Dynasty*

Legitimation is a mode of political communication that draws from two wells. One holds claims of capacity. These are made on grounds either of past performance or of some magical or pseudomagical characteristics of the person who claims authority, as with Weberian charisma. Then requiring obedience from the polity is justified because, however the political task is defined, it will be done effectively. The other well holds cosmologies and their corresponding epistemologies, underlying self-justifying forms of order. This chapter and the next show how the puzzle about calendar reform raised in the introduction can be explained with reference to these two forms of legitimation: here the relationship of calendars to these self-justifying orders and in the next chapter the association between calendars and performance. If time can be shaped for political purposes, as the last chapter established, calendars, specifically, accomplish this with flair.

I begin by analyzing those features that make calendars strategic tools of political legitimation. Their Janus-headed structure draws forward familiar features of the old social order and superimposes innovation on these. Because calendars also superimpose cycles of human activity onto natural cycles, they call out both nature and tradition. And because calendars never map neatly onto all natural markers for which we take them as a proxy, they are always available for reform. I illustrate these characteristics through the example of the Julio-Augustan calendar reform.

Calendars enable the invocation of grand historical cycles, invoking the cosmic order of fate or destiny. This frames innovation as inevitable, as part of the order of things. Counting forward from foundings along a projected cycle can frame a violent or radical intervention as the mere servant of grand historical force: a power's rise is destiny, unstoppable. This rhetorical technique is widely evident historically and in contemporary politics. The illustrative cases here are the founding of the Mayan city-state of Copan and the preamble to Hungary's 2012 constitution.

But framing success through the inevitability of an expected cyclical rise means facing the inevitability of decline too. Calendars help manage the resulting question: What is the place of human agency in this structure of inevitability? Polybius and Machiavelli were both engaged with this problem, arguing that pursuit of glory—both as a stalling tactic and for its own sake—is the most appropriate strategy in a regime that will inevitably meet its end. Indeed, the temporal frame through which political events are understood goes some way to determine not just the kinds of goals it is appropriate to pursue in politics but even what is conceived to be possible, the extent of political agency. Machiavelli, in addressing the challenge of inevitable decline, called for "resuming the government," or bringing citizens or subjects back to desirable principles at regular periods. Across a range of political situations, calendars seem to have been made to serve precisely this function. By means of national holidays, rites, and observances of historical events, cyclically brought by the calendar (and thus apparently by the order of nature), states are renewed and reinvigorated. The regular performance of charismatic capacity ostensibly stalls inevitable decline. Through these techniques of frame alignment, the already accepted order coupled with the framed innovation, both the linear and cyclical features of calendars can be harnessed in the service of legitimation.

Janus-Headed Institutions

Truth claims are held in place by supporting webs of beliefs and assumptions that are generally foregrounded only when challenged. This is a commonplace of cognitive science and the naturalist branch of epistemology. For any given belief or claim, sets of neighboring beliefs both help justify and cue meaning. It is by calling out different such sets that alternative frames are constructed. Truth claims, though ultimately situated in a whole cosmology, rest among neighboring specifics. To conclude that the person in the lab coat at the hospital is a doctor, one draws on claims and assumptions about the places one expects to find a doctor as well as about doctors' expected forms of dress, action, and comportment. These drawn-upon features provide the frames within which we understand "person in a lab coat" and they also constitute reasons one might give to justify one's belief that this person is a doctor.

While legitimation claims, like all truth claims, rely on (and are framed by) background assumptions and beliefs, because legitimation pertains to an entire order, claims to legitimate power cannot merely invoke specific neighboring particulars. Someone who claims entitlement to generate and keep order will need to anchor that claim in much more sweeping beliefs: what constitutes a proper order, what shape it takes, how it ought to be enforced and maintained, and so on. In other words, an effective rhetoric of legitimation may draw out entire cosmologies in a move to create frame alignment. The content of the cosmology varies across political cultures, between individuals, and over time. But the structure of this rhetoric, creating frame alignment between an already accepted understanding of order and an innovation, is likely a constant feature of legitimation. What Weber called legal-rational and traditional legitimacy both, ultimately, have this form. Cosmic harmony, conceptions of divine or natural order, and any normative liberal-analytic conception of legitimacy derived from first principles all have this form too. In each case, some accepted version of order is invoked to justify the claim to legitimacy. These are not just claims or beliefs but form part of systems for understanding how the world is and ought to be ordered. These systems may be incomplete, fluid around the edges, and they may be mutually inconsistent. Certainly, belief systems, like systems for measuring time, are often multiple and layered, which accounts for the commonality of persons who hold incongruent beliefs, for instance, about science and religion. But the process of justification is always a process of showing the fit of a given claim with some underlying ordering system.

As a rhetorical tactic, creating frame alignment with one of these already accepted systems of order makes sense because the more novel an innovation, the more substantial the legitimation challenge it may present. The more an innovation is cast instead as a new iteration of the old order or as a novel restoration of what was or what ought to have been, the more that legitimacy challenge is mitigated.

POLITICS OF ORDER ALIGNMENT

The purpose of harnessing a Janus-headed institution is to create pedigree for novelty. Even the most radical of political innovations—the founding of new regimes through revolution or conquest—is often wrapped in a rhetoric of restoration, bound to a preexisting order taken as self-evident, as just. This is so even where a revolution claims to be progressive, not reactionary. For example, the propaganda of a classically reactionary revolution, that of the United States, condemned the trampling of established common law rights to representative government and consent to taxation. The stated aim was the restoration of a putatively preexisting social contract. Other reactionary revolutions go further, claiming to reestablish something originary, how things were at the beginning in some golden age before moral or political corruption set in. Pocock has called this a "strategy of return."[1] In the rhetoric of apparently radical revolutions, like Iran's, radicalism takes on very conservative forms of legitimation, claiming to restore justice, order, or the will of God, either as they once were or as they should always have been.[2] Even the most progressive revolutions are often colored by rhetoric about restoring what is natural or original. Marxist revolutions aim to make whole those whose labor has been alienated. And the French Revolution's obsession with restoring the corrupted authority of nature and reason was everywhere evident: from Rousseau as poster boy to the decimal system of measurement. The radical reforms of Augustus, too, were supported by comparisons between himself and Romulus and by his revival of ancient religious rites.[3]

In part because what is claimed for the point of origin probably never was, every reactionary revolution yields something new. Revolution always goes beyond the restoration of the status quo ante. At a minimum, rules and institutions function differently in new contexts, as an array of recent American constitutional scholarship demonstrates.[4] Institutions may read the same yet be entirely different in substance and effect. This can be termed an institutional recension. By framing legitimacy in already established orders—the order of nature, tradition, moral order, God's law, and the like— as a cosmic rebalance, innovations come already justified. It is because institutions, both in their functionality and in their symbolic power, are always fluid and amenable to recension that such a symbolic shift is plausible. The consequence is that preexisting institutions continue to shape the exercise of power even when radical changes are occurring because they shape the symbolic discourse.

Calendars are Janus-headed institutions, which is to say, they invoke the familiar past in setting the way forward. A politically useful Janus-headed institution should exhibit continuity with things as they have been, preexisting orders, even as it reshapes social and political space. Such institutions should ideally be (1) pervasive and functional—the more they are integrated in daily life the more profound their impact; (2) deeply symbolic—since their function is communicative and frame resonance is among their aims; and (3) comparatively easy to reshape, drawing old symbols forward. Not all Janus-headed institutions conveniently serve legitimation. For example, when the office of the Gentleman Usher of the Black Rod in Canada's Parliament was reformed to reflect gender neutrality, this was symbolically significant and had the correct form, but because this office has a limited function, it had a limited impact also. By contrast, calendars are very effective in this regard, meeting each criterion: they are pervasive and functional, importing any reform into the every day of every person, they are deeply symbolic and resonant and, because they are permanently out of synch with natural cycles, they are always ripe for reform.

Drawing the form of the previous year into the next and superimposing in each new year a new set of tokens on the structured types of weeks and months, seasons and days, calendars are ideal Janus-headed institutions. January is named for this two-faced god of doors and gates for good reason. And calendars can easily be shaped in subtle but profound ways that maintain their essential form. This is one reason why calendars are useful tools for confronting a legitimation challenge.

Cases of failure in calendar reform support the importance of the Janus-headed structure. Both the French decimal calendar and Stalin's reform of the week were radical reconstructions of social space that preserved little of the backward-looking face of Janus, and neither took hold. The French revolutionaries, recognizing how profoundly the seven-day week was bound up with social structures, attempted to replace it with a decimal week. The aim was not only to increase productivity by reducing rest days but also (importantly) to desacralize the cycle of work and rest.[5] The calendar change, like the decimalization of other modes of measuring, was intended to rationalize, naturalize, and hence purify time of church corruption. Consider that the whole world—with the United States, Liberia, and Myanmar the sole exceptions—measures with a base of ten now. But nobody uses the base-ten week or the ten-hour clock. France's calendar reform was a notable failure. While alignment with nature and reason made these other measuring systems seem justified, the calendar revision ignored the all-pervasive character of calendar time in social life and made too radical a break. The new calendar and the new decimal clock were abolished on January 1, 1806, and no one has tried to reinstate them since, despite the mass success of every other kind of decimal measurement.[6] Sacralized rest was so entrenched in social life that people, sometimes at great personal risk, simply ignored the new week. Despite the pointed association of the new calendar with the order of nature, it did not draw strong enough threads from the old calendar into the new. Given the importance of the calendar in social organization

Philibert-Louis Debucourt's French Republican calendar of 1794.

and the necessity of the Janus-faced structure of successful calendar reform, the effort failed.

The Janus-headed structure of calendar reform was again ignored when, a century and a half later, Josef Stalin attempted to institute a five-day week. In 1929, Stalin adopted an idea of Yuri Larin to promote maximum efficiency among the industrialized proletariat. Instead of a universal Sunday, workers were divided into five groups, each with its own "randomly" assigned rest day—five separate cycles of work and rest. Hence, the factories could run 365 (or 366) days a year. Family members no longer had the same rest day and again, religious observance and the sacralization of rest were undermined. The state could, theoretically, dictate who could socialize with whom. This would have had profound ramifications for social cohesion and social control if it had worked, but again, in practice, and despite Stalin's

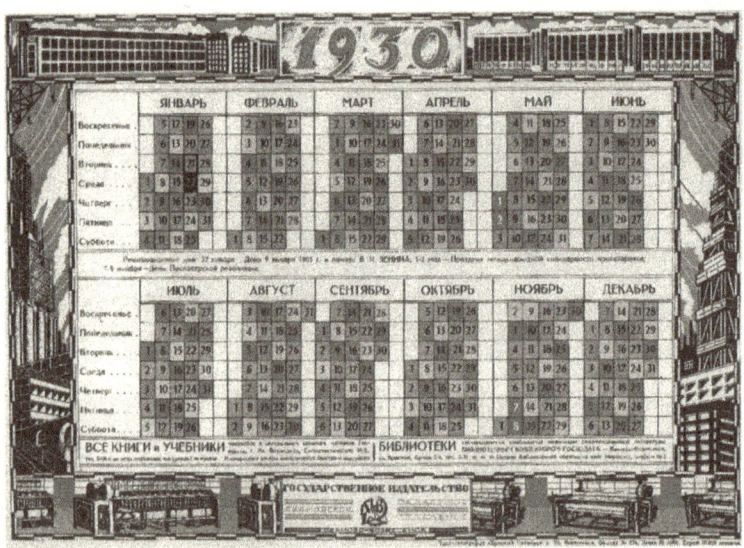

1930 *Soviet calendar showing the five-day week.*

awesome power, the experiment failed. Except in official reports, the five-day week was largely ignored.[7]

There were practical challenges to the five-day week. For example, with no downtime, machines could not be maintained, which actually decreased productivity. But few put the system into practice long enough to discover this drawback in the first place. By failing to maintain the carrying structure, an already accepted order that creates resonance for the new by means of the familiar old, these reforms failed. Frame alignment necessitates an appropriate, already resonant frame. It is noteworthy that attempts to reform the week in particular tend to fail. Perhaps the week, more than any other time unit, gains its profound resonance because it is the cycle most closely bound up with the rhythms of daily life and with the camaraderie of mutual leisure. Reformers ignore this aspect of the backward face of Janus at their peril.

The Constructed and the Natural

Calendars are effective at drawing established order into an innovative future not only because of their inherently repetitious, and thus familiar, character but also because they purport to track, and therefore easily become conflated with, nature. The political work is done not by nature's order as such, but by the way that nature and human activity become intertwined.

With superficial variations, most calendars attempt to combine lunar months with solar years, counting the number of these years with reference to a fixed point—a new reign, the foundation of a city, quadrennial Olympiads, years since the creation of the world or the arrival of a prophet, and so on. Those calendars that are primarily lunar take the cycle of the moon—roughly 29.5 days—as their most fundamental base and often alternate months of 29 and 30 days. The solar year may track the movement of constellations across the sky or use a technique or device to mark the solstices. For example, at Machu Picchu, there is a structure at a cave entrance "designed to admit the light of the rising sun for only a brief period before and after the December solstice."[8] Some other mark—perhaps the arrival of monsoon rains, the migration patterns of birds or animals, or the flooding of a river—may serve as an additional measure of the passing year, alongside of or instead of these constructed technologies. When there is an attempt to align lunar months with the solar year and the seasons, then twelve such months yield a year of 354 days to which, commonly, is added an intercalary period to square it all up.[9] Sometimes, historically, this was done through the annual addition of 11 leap days and sometimes through addition of a leap month. Regardless, the year, whether stellar, lunar, solar, or some combination, is associated with an array of natural cues. The phases of the moon, monsoons and floods, the budding, blooming, and withering of trees and vines, and the apparent movement of the constellations are all naturally occurring technologies for marking and measuring, but they have the effect of making time keeping appear to be a mirror of nature rather than nature a marker of time.

Calendars schedule the rehearsal or repetition of themes and activities associated with natural phenomena. There are harvest festivals and times for planting or setting sail. In this way, it can come to seem as though it is not only nature in the sense of the stars, the rains, and the budding of trees that calendars track but temporal propriety: what is natural for people to do when, or how it is natural to act at various junctures. These temporal habits form our, so to speak, second nature as a community, reflecting not only the rhythms of the seasons and stars but also the rhythms of life that come to be associated with them.

Consider this section from a poem of Claudian: "Happy he who has passed his whole life amid his own fields, he of whose birth and old age the same house is witness. . . . For him the recurring seasons, not the consuls, mark the year; he knows autumn by his fruits and spring by her flowers, measures the day with his own round of toils."[10] The fine life is lived according to the right kind of schedule: laid down by nature, not by (artificial) political cycles, the implication being that these, because constructed, are corrupt.

Like most institutions, calendars hover between what is given in nature and what is sculpted by human intention and activity. The perceived legitimacy of institutions is sometimes bound up with this sense that they are in line with nature understood in this complex way: not just natural phenomena free of human activity but the perception that nature and proper action are imbued with each other; thus the mode of action or institution comes to seem natural itself. Then the legitimacy of that institution and the behaviors it schedules goes beyond notice and beyond question, as we might say of the Gregorian calendar we use today. Nature cannot do this work alone, however. It is the lived confluence of the natural and the social that creates this powerful sense of right order.

It is, finally, important to note that difficulties inherent in intercalation and in accurately tracking the fluctuating values of the solar year and lunar months mean that calendars are permanently in need of reform. Systems of intercalation have varied historically, displaying degrees of complexity. But no such system aligns perfectly, not only because there is no way to make the two periodicities (solar and lunar) map neatly onto one another but also because celestial periodicities change—if only very slightly—over time. This means lunar-solar calendars are permanently "wrong"—and so permanently available as projects of political reform. Calendars are so omnipresent that we may forget how contingent it is that months have irregular numbers of days, or that the year starts in the middle of winter, and not necessarily on a Monday. These features are, of course, not universal. They serve to show that calendars can and have taken a range of forms and been made subject to a range of reforms.

The example of the Julio-Augustan calendar reform, to which we now turn, serves as a dramatic illustration of these three calendar features: their Janus-headed structure, their capacity to superimpose the constructed onto the natural, and their susceptibility to reform.

The Julian Calendar

In the letters of Cicero to Atticus around 50 BCE, while Cicero was away from Rome governing the province of Cilicia, we find a curious series of pleas. "When you know whether there are to be additions to the calendar or not, please," Cicero asks his friend, "write me with positive news."[11] He asks again in a letter written a few days later.[12] Cicero refers to the intercalary or additional month intended to keep the Roman lunar calendar roughly in step with the solar year. The twelve Roman months added up to 355 days, and so periodically an extra 22 days were inserted near the end of February.[13] Years in which an intercalary month had been inserted were either 377 or 378 days long, which Cicero, understandably eager to return to the culture and politics of Rome at this tumultuous time, might well have felt too long. Whether or not he is to expect an intercalary month, and hence a prolongation of his absence, is thus a matter of personal and political importance.[14]

In Rome, intercalation was inherently political. The person deciding Cicero's fate in this respect was an elected priest-politician with nothing more firm to guide him than his own strategic considerations and the influence of his friends. The option of keeping magistrates in

Illustration created from a fragment of a pre-Julian (60 BCE) Roman calendar, known as the *Fasti antiates maiores*. Note the intercalary month at far right and the eight-day week, denoted by the letters A-H. (Museo Nazionale Romano, Rome, Italy. Mondadori Portfolio/Electa/Sergio Anelli/Bridgeman Images)

POLITICS OF ORDER ALIGNMENT

office longer or keeping powerful figures far away in the provinces longer, all by the device of extending the year, proved irresistible to many holders of this office of Pontifex Maximus. Intercalation, though hardly the only abused element in the pre-Julian calendar, was particularly shamelessly abused.[15] So much so that by the time Julius Caesar crossed the Rubicon, not long after Cicero's plea, on January 10 of 49 BCE, the leaves were beginning to turn and the harvests had just come in from the fields. It was early autumn. It was decidedly not January at all, if nature is to be the grounds of the calendar. These were the so-called years of confusion, when the calendar had been literally corrupted. The calendar, like the republic itself, which was fraught with civil conflict, had fallen into disorder. It is in this context that the place of calendar reform among Caesar's urgent projects must be understood.

Caesar arrived in Rome and took the mantle of dictator under the pretense of restoring order. The republic's institutions and the mode of conduct of its citizens would be brought back in line with what was proper and harmonious.[16] This was carried further by Caesar's heir, Augustus, who justified his power on the basis of the restoration of the republic to its moral origins. Both men used symbolic and functional aspects of the calendar to frame the claim that they were servants of both natural and social order, wielding legitimate power.[17]

The Julian reform is familiar because the modern Gregorian calendar is nearly identical, save minor changes to the leap year system. It did away with the discretionary intercalary month and fixed the days of the new months in such a way that no rest days were negatively impacted. Macrobius, in his *Saturnalia,* notes that Caesar was careful not to toy with existing holidays and games, a lesson Stalin and the French republicans should perhaps have taken to heart.[18] The new 365 1/3 day calendar, borrowing from an Egyptian model, restored harmony between the seasons and calendrical time, symbolically purifying corruption while functionally sealing off the possibility of future corruption by removing discretion over intercalation.[19] In so doing, Julius Caesar demonstrates that his power is the servant and defender of nature and science, and of those aspects of human practice that seem naturally associated with these. The calendar draws forward the most immediate and familiar elements in the form of games and holidays, and those elements that are new are cast as the result of the extinction of corruption and the restoration of nature's rightful representation. The new calendar restores the propriety of the social and political with respect to nature's laws. It restores harmony between these realms of order.

The politically brilliant Augustus took advantage of the calendar's open condition to engineer a more profound, if subtle, shift in the calendar's symbolic rhetoric. Augustus begins by fixing an intercalation error—leap years every fourth, not every third year—then he sets to the real work. Denis Feeney notes that first, in the margins of the fasti, Augustus added dates ab urbe condita, from the founding of Rome. Consider the significance of this simple change. The fasti look pretty much the same, but the conception of the year and of the passage of time has subtly shifted. Time in the republic had until then been marked solely by the *consular year.* That is to say, rather than a numerical year—as we might refer to, say, 2018 CE—each year was named for its pair of elected consuls. So the year we know as 320 BCE, for instance, was known as the year that Q. Publilius Philo was consul with Papirius Cursor (for the first time). The fasti listed each pair of consuls in turn. Since the consuls originated with the republic, the implication of fasti that counted consular years was essentially that time—or at least time worth counting—had, in a sense, begun when the republic began.[20] By adding dates ab urbe condita, Feeney argues, consular time is situated in a broader temporal framework, one that stretches back before the republic, with the implication that it could then stretch onward beyond the republic with continuity. So Augustus's new calendar reflects his political strategy as a whole. "They look like Republican *fasti*," Feeney says, "but they are Augustan, imperial *fasti*."[21]

It is worth noting the parallel between Augustus's temporal reframing strategy here and that of Deng and the drafters of the preamble to China's 1982 constitution. Like Augustus, the preamble to the 1982 constitution draws an alternative temporal arc, beginning at a different point, changing what counts as the relevant manifestation of China and creating the impression of continuity. By casting the Cultural Revolution as a mere irregularity along a progressive arc and quieting the eschatological tone, Deng reframes his reforms from a form of treachery to righting a wrong turn. We will see below another contemporary example of this technique in the discussion of Hungary's new Basic Law.

In accordance with the technique of dates ab urbe condita, Augustus was often at pains to associate himself with Romulus, the legendary founder of Rome, and with all things ancient and traditional. The reform thus manages to look conservative in two senses: the change is so small, almost beneath notice, and at the same time fundamental in the sense that it looks back to what is originary. Augustus situates himself in deep traditions while at the same time associating himself with the creation of the new and glorious. He marks himself as profoundly Roman while at the same time shifting what it is to be Roman. He is a founder of the new empire, but he is a *Roman* founder. He uses a new temporal frame to assert both his fundamental connection to the republic (he has "restored" it) and his position as a new founder in the line of Romulus, deeply connected with the originary, and hence legitimate, Roman line. He employs republican modes to establish an imperial order. The dates ab urbe condita quietly assert the importance of Rome's continuity on either side of the republican age. Augustus also gradually "allowed" the Senate to add to the new calendar dates that were significant with respect to the glory of Augustus and his family: birthdays, the dates of significant victories, and the like all became public holidays celebrated with games and other festivities. These, too, gradually reshaped social space and collective memory through important lived elements in Roman public life.[22]

As is true of all reactionary revolutions, what emerged was quite different from the original it purported to revert to, but the symbolic frame it invoked for the sake of legitimacy managed to blur the hazy brightness of a golden age into the sharp glint of something new. Even Augustus's titulature is a list of the republican offices he has held. It looks like a republican titulature, but it's an Augustan, imperial titulature. These are recension institutions. As symbols, the institutions become so familiar in the daily life of the members of a polity that a rereading or reperformance, perhaps through a new context, can make a new meaning at once both familiar and quite new.

The Julio-Augustan calendar reform clearly shows how a calendar can become a proxy for political order, its "purification" and restoration to natural order the symbolic purification of political corruption. The political agent who executes this reform associates himself with natural harmony, framing his claim to power by drawing on underlying self-justifying order to take on the cloak of legitimacy. The calendar's Janus-headed form—its pervasiveness in daily life, its capacity to maintain the traditional and familiar while engineering innovation—makes it particularly useful in this regard.

Harnessing Grand Cycles

The Janus-headed structure of calendars roots innovation in tradition or nature, invoking self-justifying forms of order to frame novel claims of legitimate power. But the epoch-counting function of calendars provides a range of other opportunities for temporal frame alignment by invoking the ordering function of fate, destiny, or inevitability. Political entrepreneurs can harness a rhetoric of grand historical cycles by using the calendar to draw attention to synchronous events. This tactic has been used in the legitimation of political innovations ranging from conquest to the writing of constitutions. It is a function of the linear aspect of calendrical time. Furthermore, because cycles in political contexts often imply the inevitability of decline, political actors who make use of a grand cyclical frame require stalling techniques, and calendars are helpful here also. Because of calendars' cyclical aspect they provide a means of automating the renewal of foundational principles, which Machiavelli called "resuming the government."[23] A political agent can use a calendar to automate and naturalize this function by inscribing the rehearsal of civic religion in the calendar by means of public holidays. Calendars thus give form to a number of kinds of framing cycles, not just cycles of days, weeks, and months that structure everyday and annual activity in politically useful ways but also grand historical cycles that chart the rise and fall of epochs. These cycles frame because they pick out, and then insinuate the inevitability of, a pattern of events, anchoring claims of legitimacy in cosmic order or destiny. Thus calendars do not just chart natural cycles, they themselves constitute cycles, and they do not merely follow the pattern of natural events, they also carry with them desired markers of political events. Both through the harnessing of epochs and through the inscription of those public festivals and holidays that punctuate, and so stall, grand historical cycles, calendars play a range of other legitimation functions.

POLITICS OF ORDER ALIGNMENT

Consider the calendrical inscriptions on the stone monuments that liberally cover the site of Copan. The ruins of this classical Mayan power center lie near what is now the Guatemalan border in Honduras. For nearly four hundred years, a single dynasty held sway there, despite Mayaland's constant warfare and its highly mobile population.[24] In 423 CE, the founder of the dynasty, K'inich Yax K'uk' Mo', made his conquest of this territory shortly before the approach of an important juncture in the Mayan calendar: the turn of a baktun, a cycle of roughly four hundred solar years. Using the calendar to draw out the synchrony between his arrival and this epochal shift, this critical feature of accepted temporal order helped cement dynastic legitimacy.[25]

In classical Mayaland, the calendar was bound up with auspiciousness, luck, the capacity to make use of, through temporal propriety, the favor of the gods, just as it has been in many other civilizations, including ancient Assyria, Egypt, and Rome, and as it continued to be in more recent times in parts of China and the Chinese diaspora and in Ronald Reagan's White House, too.[26] Like most calendars, including our own, the Mayan calendar reflected linear and multicyclical elements: a bipartite cyclical year tracking solar and ritual cycles, and the so-called Long Count, which extends from a creation year into the future with cycling units of a base-twenty counting system.[27] Among these cycles, one of particular importance was a period of twenty katuns—or periods of twenty (360-day) solar years. Twenty times twenty solar years constitutes a baktun, of roughly four hundred solar years. This was an epochal juncture of great resonance for Maya, auspicious and religiously sonorous, and it was shortly before this moment that K'inich Yax K'uk' Mo' arrived with his forces near Copan. Inscriptions on the monument known as Altar Q at Copan record that he arrived already invested with power from a distant source, possibly the rulers in Tikal, and a military victory over warring local lords followed. Having triumphed, K'inich Yax K'uk' Mo' and his heirs used inscriptions and dedications to claim that they would reign through the whole baktun, erecting buildings, temples, and monuments that made reference to the auspiciously timed arrival of the founder.[28] Consistently, the power of each subsequent king is depicted as drawn directly from the founder (rather than, for instance, from that ruler's father), and the founder's power is tied not only to the power of Tikal but to the auspicious turn of the baktun.

Altar Q depicts all the kings of Copan up to the sixteenth, Yax Pasaj Chan Yopat, who is receiving a symbol of power directly from K'inich Yax K'uk' Mo'. He became the symbolic source of legitimacy for every subsequent king of Copan during the classical period. K'inich Yax K'uk' Mo' and his heirs made skillful use of the symbolic significance of the calendar cycle, bolstering fifteen generations of subsequent kings.

While David Stuart has recently argued that it was likely the second ruler, K'inich Popol Huh, who oversaw the celebrations for the turn of the baktun in the company of his father, the contemporary so-called Motmot Marker pictures father and son together.[29] As the dynasty progresses, a number of monuments continue to explicitly connect K'inich Yax K'uk' Mo' to the baktun turn, for example, Stela J, erected by the thirteenth ruler.[30]

Consider how, today, we celebrate a new year, a new century, or a new millennium with fanfare, building projects, the dedication of monuments. For the classical Maya, the turn of a baktun was at least as auspicious and important. The stelae and other monuments still standing throughout Mayan territories are as likely to mark calendrical junctures as military victories or other legitimacy-bolstering events. The Mayans were keen astronomers and astrologers and, like the Chinese, whose almanacs will make an appearance in the next

Altar Q at Copan, Honduras. (Jean-Pierre Courau/Bridgeman Images)

chapter, they maintained detailed celestial books tracking in particular the path of Venus, associated with their war god. Architecture throughout Mayaland seems to have been designed to help mark important points in Venus's path associated with agricultural planning.[31] Temporal propriety here, as elsewhere, was central to political and social order.

Many of the earliest building complexes in Copan celebrate the turning of the baktun and seem to tie it to the founding of the dynasty's destiny to rule through the whole of the new baktun, as do monuments from centuries later.[32] Indeed, Copan has more calendar inscriptions than any other Mayan city. This is at least suggestive of a conscious intention to evoke, in the lived world of Copan, the auspicious coincidence of the dynasty's dawn and that of the new calendrical epoch.

By arriving with the baktun, K'inich Yax K'uk' Mo' may have framed *himself* as an auspice of stability and plenty, a divine gift to the people of the region. Certainly, people flocked from elsewhere to live in Copan until late in this period, suggesting that the regime was successful. Performance bolstered and interacted with the claim to legitimacy on the basis of auspicious timing, divine temporal order. It is noteworthy that the promise of four hundred years' rule seems to have become self-fulfilling through this interaction with performance. It was almost precisely at the end of this baktun that the last king of Copan left the throne. Recent archaeological investigations show that the population of Copan had grown enormously, which seems to have led to soil degradation. That in turn would ultimately have reduced food production.[33] This seems to have led to malnutrition, disease, and eventual depopulation. A stunning military defeat in the eighth century at the hands of Copan's neighbor, Quirigua, led to a period of instability and fractured power, and the last known king of Copan, Ukit Took', came to the throne in 822 CE. It was soon thereafter that the regime appears to have collapsed completely.[34] These are performance failures that would call the legitimacy of any regime into question. But the events of Copan's final century must also have looked to some of its denizens like a confirmation of inevitable decline. The baktun came in with the regime, and the regime would go out with the baktun. If something like a prophecy, reported and repeated everywhere in one's physical environ, ties the legitimacy of a regime to a time-delimited destiny, and if the end of that time corresponds to consistent performance failures—hunger, disease, and war—it would be natural to wonder if the end of the calendar epoch also heralded the end of the regime.

At the dawn of the baktun in Copan, the synchrony of a calendrical juncture of great symbolic importance with a political event of some independent importance was picked out, then repeated again and again, to imply the inevitability and divine sanction of that politi-

POLITICS OF ORDER ALIGNMENT

cal event. The legitimacy of K'inich Yax K'uk' Mo"'s rule is grounded partly in this sense of inevitability and destiny that he and his son cultivated, bound to an irresistible order evident to anyone who would look in the right way. He and his progeny frame their actions in a conception of the flow of time. If time moves in great sweeping cycles in which regimes are born, grow to maturity, perhaps flourish, and eventually decline, the meaning of any specific event in the course of a regime's history derives partly from its synchronic position with respect to a constructed cycle and partly in its sequential place in that cyclic pattern. An arrival is not just an arrival but a beginning, and not just a beginning but the start of something the shape of which we know in advance. It is this frame that casts the event of K'inich Yax K'uk' Mo"'s arrival as destiny; he claims his power is legitimate in part because it is in line with the cosmic order. Without the rhetorical frame provided by this conception of the flow of time, his appearance is no promise of inevitable good, just the arrival of a violent man from the north.

Of course, the rulers of Copan did not rest claims to legitimacy on calendrical framing alone. Maya scholars note a range of sources and techniques through which leaders aimed to bolster their legitimacy. Some are based on performance: Mayan rulers facilitated trade and sometimes organized natural resource provision.[35] They organized and performed religious rituals together with or on behalf of their people and provided them with military security.[36] Then there are other order-based sources of legitimacy, such as rules of descent and title inheritance. A variety of written Maya records note that a king, at particular moments, took on the vital force associated with the divine, and many ceremonies included the virtual presence of divinity in the form of carved effigies, "a set of localized supernatural patrons" who "were invited to participate and sponsor [a] ceremony through the direct solicitation of the ruler."[37] These signs of divinity are legitimating also and are incorporated into royal titles. Notably, K'inich, the first glyph in Copan's founder's name, connotes the Mayan sun god.[38] Like leaders in all times and places, the kings of Copan made use of a variety of performance- and order-based legitimation strategies. Yet the importance of the grand cyclic temporal frame among these strategies is evident, inscribed over and over in the towering stelae that crowd the site of Copan to this day.

Framing with grand historical cycles is no artifact of ancient politics, as the preamble to Hungary's 2012 Basic Law makes evident. In this next case, political leaders used a grand cyclic frame to help legitimate a constitutional framework that departs dramatically from the liberal democratic status quo. The preamble's grand cyclic frame directly and no doubt intentionally clashes with the progressive frame prevalent in European Union rhetoric. Denigrating and de-emphasizing liberal values and democratic procedures, from which the substance of the constitution departs, the grand cyclic frame in the preamble helps construct an alternative source of legitimacy. It emphasizes the continuity of the nation beyond regime type. It asserts a constitutive mandate to rejuvenate that nation, and by means of the grand cyclic frame implies that this rejuvenation will take the form of a new upward arc on a cycle.

Hungary's first written constitution dated from the Soviet occupation (1949) and drew many key features from Stalin's 1936 constitution. After the fall of Communism in 1990, Hungary made do with an amended version of this Soviet-era document for nearly two decades. A landmark election in 2010 saw Viktor Orbán, leader of Hungary's right-populist Fidesz Party, defeat the corruption-mired socialists; he was returned to power with a two-thirds majority. Though Fidesz had made no mention of constitution making in the campaign, it soon became a priority.[39]

Rapidly drafted on the basis of minimal consultation and the exclusion of the opposition, the new Basic Law came into force in 2012. Both the constitution and the process through which it was created and promulgated faced controversy at home and abroad. The new Basic Law was widely understood as a challenge to Hungary's liberal democracy: it limits checks and balances, reduces judicial and central bank independence, and alters institutions in a way that serves to consolidate Fidesz's power and influence, even in the case of a future election loss.[40] At the same time, it focused attention on the Hungarian nation and ethnic Hungarians within and beyond Hungary's political borders. Scholars have called this a move toward illiberal democracy, and Orbán himself was not at all coy about explicitly embracing this label.[41]

Concerns regarding concentration of power and the constitution's treatment of external and internal minorities arose in Europe, and the constitution was referred to the Venice Commission (the European Commission for Democracy through Law) for review. The commission singled out the preamble in particular, claiming that preambles are explicitly political, serving a unifying function particular to each state.[42] And certainly this preamble rewards attention.

> We the Members of the Hungarian Nation, at the beginning of the new millennium, with a sense of responsibility for every Hungarian, declare the following: We are proud that one thousand years ago our king, Saint Stephen, built the Hungarian State on solid foundations, and made our country a part of Christian Europe. . . . We promise to preserve the intellectual and spiritual unity of our nation torn apart in the storms of the past century. . . .
>
> . . . We date the restoration of the self-determination of our State, lost on the nineteenth day of March 1944, from the

second day of May 1990, when the first freely elected popular representation was formed. We shall consider this date to be the beginning of our country's new democracy and constitutional order.

. . . We hold that after the decades of the twentieth century leading to moral decay, a spiritual and intellectual renewal is absolutely necessary. . . . Our children and grandchildren will make Hungary great again. . . . Our Fundamental Law shall be . . . an alliance among Hungarians of the past, present and future. It is a living framework expressing the nation's will. . . .

We, the citizens of Hungary, are ready to found the order of our country.[43]

The new Basic Law is not an illiberal revision of institutional rules or a restatement of principles, values, and rights. It is instead cast as a mechanism of national renewal. As it was at the dawn of the previous millennium, the nation is again on the rise. One thousand years after Saint Stephen, Fidesz, through far-reaching reforms that include this constitution, is regenerating the Hungarian nation. The significance of the new constitution as an event on its own may be interpreted in various ways. But the rhetorical placement of this event in sequential relationship after moral decline and in synchronicity with the start of a previous millennial cycle of glorious rise strongly implies a particular significance. The audience abstracts the shape of time from the sequence of events presented here, and this abstracted shape in turn impacts the substantive meaning of the event of the constitution. The new constitution's significance is framed by the grand cyclic narrative in which the preamble situates it.

How does this serve legitimation? Orbán has a problem: Not only is the constitution illiberal and somewhat undemocratic in its substance, it was drafted and promulgated without the usual procedural (order-based) markers of legitimacy: interparty consultation, plebiscite, a constitutional convention, and so on. Although Fidesz did circulate a dense questionnaire on the document to every voter, only 12 percent returned it, and commentators viewed the questionnaire as essentially theatrics.[44] So to legitimate the constitution both as a substantive document and as an event (that is, to claim both that it was legitimate for him to make a constitution and that the contents of the constitution are just and good), Orbán needs to ground its legitimacy in a form of order that is both *for* the people and *of* the people but that does not claim to be liberal and democratic: not *by* the people. What he needs, then, is a constitutive mandate, a form of power that will allow him to act on behalf of the people not as a democratic representative but as an avatar of the nation in its unity.[45]

The grand cyclic frame supports this constitutive mandate. First, it makes democratic and procedural values, debate and contestation subservient to grand historical themes, displacing attention from the document's, so to speak, *unconventional* mode of production. The contrast is especially stark when the preamble is read together with the preambles to the European Union's founding documents, which are explicitly progressive in their framing, tying progress to mutual interest, universalism, and liberal values.[46] At the point of the 2010 victory, Fidesz MPs' attitudes toward Europe took a dramatic negative turn.[47] Indeed, in 2012, it became an offense for MPs to display the flag of Europe.[48] In the years immediately prior to Orbán's victory, emphasis on a concordance of progress with the left had been a strategy of Ferenc Gyurcsány, prime minister from 2004 to 2009; he even joined forces with Tony Blair at one point to speak of "we, the European progressives."[49] What Orbán offers is not-Europe, not-liberal, and not-progressive. He offers something more than incremental betterment, something better than milquetoast European identity. He offers to represent and restore to glory the Hungarian nation itself.

Second, he needs to establish that there is a political unity of which he is the avatar, independent of institutional structures. The grand cyclic frame creates precisely such a narrative of a unitary Hungarian nation, extending in time back beyond its current institutional structures, back beyond the "colonial power" of the EU, back beyond the Communists.[50] And the nation extends forward not step by step through incremental improvements in the material quality of life but toward glorious renewal.

Finally, Orbán needs to establish that he and his party are the genuine and worthy torchbearers of that glorious renewal. The grand cyclic frame attempts this in a number of ways. It delegitimizes the political opponents of Fidesz, blaming the socialists for Hungary's decline and insinuating their inauthenticity—the socialist period was not a genuinely Hungarian government but a foreign corruption. When he lost power in 2002 Orbán declared that "the nation cannot be in opposition" and after he regained power in 2010 he described the victory as "revolution at the polling booths."[51] Further, the grand cyclic frame enables the by now familiar strategy of Augustus, minimizing the importance of a republican period while invoking the memory of mythic, distant founders to signal rejuvenation. It is certainly worth noting that Fidesz's reforms included ejecting "Republic" from Hungary's official name and bringing the crown of Saint Stephen to the Parliament from its previous home in the National Museum. Finally, the grand cyclic frame also helps in establishing Orbán's ethos by explicitly noting the coincidence between the dawn of the millennium at the moment Saint Stephen founded Hungary and the dawn of the millennium at the constitution's own moment.[52] The grand cyclic frame allows Orbán to take advantage of this temporal felicity, just as K'inich Yax K'uk' Mo' had done sixteen hundred years before on a far continent.

To the extent that Orbán wields legitimate constitutive power rather than simple democratic power, he can consistently claim the authority to make far-reaching changes that reduce the centrality of liberal and democratic values in Hungarian political life. To the extent that there is a unitary Hungarian nation separate from state institutions, there is a demos to represent. And both because the opposition is corrupt and because Orbán takes the place of Saint Stephen at an auspicious moment, he represents that he is the one to play this historic role, the one to set the nation out on a new rise to glory. A progressive frame would entirely preclude this, but a grand cyclic frame is ideal.

Of course, the temporal-rhetorical frame emphasizing Hungary's place at the dawn of a new grand cycle does not achieve this effect alone. Fidesz engages in a variety of other symbolic and substantive tactics that undergird the legitimacy of a unitary political voice, including the politics of external ethnic Hungarian minorities and of immigration. These rest on, but also bolster, the claim of unitary nationhood. The temporal-rhetorical frame in the constitution's preamble does not do the work of legitimation alone, but it makes a substantial contribution to the cause.

This case illustrates how, even in the contemporary world, grand cyclicality can be harnessed to make use of a felicitous temporal synchrony. But it also shows, in a way that might be difficult to observe in a less contemporary case, how directly competing conceptions of the flow of time are deployed to frame and reframe directly competing political positions. Just as pollsters and survey designers know that how they frame the question partly determines the response, temporal-rhetorical framing can be used to cue the meaning of a claim or event in an attempt to solicit a desired response.

Rise and Fall

Grand historical cycles are a common theme in political thought, impacting what is understood as politically possible or desirable. There is high expectation when events are cast as synchronous with the beginning of such a cycle. But cycles come with the assumption that any achievement will face a process of decay and change.[53] Hence, to advance a grand cyclic conception of time is to concede in advance serious limitations on human agency. It makes no sense, on a grand cyclic view, to imagine utopias and less still to engage in utopian schemes. The very notion of utopianism is dependent on the idea of *lasting* happiness and perfection, so it is generally framed instead by notions of temporal rupture—the creation of a regime beyond time and hence beyond the decay otherwise understood as inevitable. Furthermore, different political values seem differently suited to different temporal orders. If one concedes in advance the fleeting nature of a state in the grand scheme of things, it might make less sense to strive for liberty or equality than to strive for glory, since glory has an afterglow that long outlasts the glorious state. But the memory of liberty is sour, the memory of equality dull. To strive for liberty and equality makes more sense in a framework of progress or eschatological permanence.

Latent in talk of grand historical cycles are highly political assumptions about the limited extent of human agency and capacity for control, so this poses a challenge for anyone who would attempt to invoke the order of fate or destiny or natural order to frame legitimation claims. But the inevitability suggested by a grand cyclical temporal frame doesn't necessitate quietism. Within this set structure much is open to determination. Innovation is compatible with grand historical cyclicality—indeed, it is central to the definition of political success within this conception of the flow of time, as the work of Polybius and Machiavelli demonstrates. The idea of cyclicality structures the political questions posed by Polybius and Machiavelli, and the mode of agency with which cyclicality is compatible structures the answers they give.

This is markedly evident in Polybius's account of Rome, which engages explicitly with the role of agency. In his histories, Polybius embraces cyclicality and its source in the natural world. "That to all things . . . which exist there is ordained decay and change I think requires no further arguments to show: for the inexorable course of nature is sufficient to convince us of it."[54] Empires follow this pattern: each reaches a pinnacle, a period of perfection and strength, only to confront a downward slope. But for Polybius, permanence is no part of the perfection of states.

Rome is important to Polybius because it shows that the mutability of empire does not always follow the same pattern. While Rome will ultimately meet the same end as every other empire, Rome is nonetheless different. In fact, its ascendance is "an event for which the past affords no precedent."[55] Rome is special because its period of perfection is marked by constitutional genius that makes that ascendance last and last. At the top is a broad plateau, not a point. For Polybius, the Roman constitution's "peculiar character contributed largely to their success, not only in reducing all Italy to their authority, and in acquiring a supremacy over the Iberians and Gauls besides, but also at last, after their conquest of Carthage, to their conceiving the idea of universal dominion."[56]

Like Sparta, which lasted eight hundred years, Rome had a system of government that did not conform to the usual patterns of kingship/tyranny, aristocracy/oligarchy, democracy/ochlocracy, each containing the seeds of its collapse. Whereas Aristotle had identified the rule of those in "the middle" as the most secure, the genius of Rome was to combine aspects of aristocracy, kingship, and democracy: not an average of the extremes but a combination. Each has its role and each checks the others, which has the dual effect of giving each class what today we might call a sense of ownership and of providing checks on abuses of power. Because of the brilliance of this constitution, to which Polybius devotes an entire book of his histories, "it came about that nearly the whole world fell under the power of Rome in somewhat less than fifty-three years."[57] Even when common enemies are gone and the Romans inevitably "begin to yield to the seduction of ease and plenty," Polybius believed these (mostly customary) checks and balances would preserve the system for some time.[58]

Perfection is not permanence since permanence is against nature. Even the Roman republic, in all its perfection, will come to an end eventually. Perfection means securing Roman ascendancy for as long as possible, not forever. Polybius's aim, ostensibly, is to convince his fellow Greeks that resistance to Rome is futile. To this end he demonstrates that waiting it out is not a feasible option. The rapid regime cycling familiar to, for instance, the Athenians, will not characterize Roman power. Roman ingenuity has found a way to stall the inevitabilities inherent in the order of nature. What we should note here is that the Roman scheme counts as ingenuity only within the rhetorical frame of grand historical cycles to begin with. Without this frame, Rome's success has no touchstone. It is only because the frame suggests that *one should have expected* Rome to fall that its failure to do so is worthy of note. The frame is what gives Rome's success its meaning.

Polybius hopes to inspire quietude among the Greeks by a lesson in how Romans' superior agency would impact what might otherwise seem inevitable. Machiavelli hopes to quash quietude with the same lesson. In the work of Machiavelli, sophisticated new elements of the political use of grand historical cycles emerge because Machiavelli is interested not only in the capacity of agency to impact and alter such cycles but in the techniques one might use to achieve this aim. And here the cyclical aspect of calendars reenters the picture.

By the time Machiavelli writes of republican Rome, it has been dead for a millennium and a half. Machiavelli's model of greatness is a dead city. It is only and precisely under a conception of the flow of time as cyclic that it makes sense to hold up a destroyed regime as an example worthy of emulation. Under some alternative conception, progressive, primitivist, or even eschatological, we might expect the fact of Rome's destruction to stand as a mark of failure. But to begin from the idea that it is the way of things to come into being, rise, decay, and pass out of being again implies no shame in destruction. The question then becomes one of longevity, a capacity to stall, to wrestle not only Fortune but fate to the ground whenever they appear. Like Polybius, Machiavelli is struck by the length of time Rome endured before it met ruin. "Those who read what the beginning was of the city of Rome and by what legislators and how it was ordered will not marvel that so much virtue was maintained for many centuries in that city, and that afterward the empire that the republic attained arose there."[59] It is because Rome makes the most of available time through the pursuit of glory that its great virtue lets it linger as long as it does. It is for this reason that Rome is suitable for emulation. Here, grand cyclicality functions as a rhetorical frame that turns a disaster into a success.

From this perspective, Machiavelli's intensive criticism of Christianity is functionally a critique less of the content of Christianity than of the temporal framework of eschatology within which it rests. Machiavelli's rejection of Christianity is performed largely through a rejection of the framing effects of that conception of the flow of time. The state-sponsored eschatology that dominates political thinking in a religious context results in a quietism that looks forward to a rupture—just far enough in the distance—that removes the state from time entirely, a condition that, among other things, removes the very possibility of glory. It is because Christianity is concerned only with the world to come that it effectively prevents the rise of a glorious new republic in Italy, a cyclic rebirth.

In Machiavelli's writing, a concern with cyclicality and its corresponding political values generates a number of practical techniques. Among these, there is one especially worthy of note in our context because it explains a common and important political use of calendars. While the Copan case illustrates the political potential in harnessing synchrony with calendrical epochs to generate a sense of inevitability, Machiavelli suggests to us a means by which the cycle of the lunar-solar year can serve to perpetuate and renew a regime in order to stall the inevitability of decline. In the introduction to book 3 of the *Discorsi,* Machiavelli discusses how, although all we make must someday crumble, those states that run their full ordained course depend on periodic renewal. The frame of grand historic cyclicality is clear, but so is the potential for agency: while each regime moves eventually toward its demise, a good or lucky regime—or a regime leader skilled at managing luck—can be made to linger longer if power is regularly rejuvenated.

"The means of renewing [regimes]," Machiavelli says, "is to bring them back to their principles," and this can be done in a number of ways.[60] Sometimes an external shock, such as an invasion, does the trick. This is Fortune at work. At other times, a show of great virtue serves as a reminder, as when Junius Brutus executed his own sons for treachery to the republic. It is also possible, Machiavelli tells us, to engineer this renewal through a shocking show of violence, as was done in Florence under the Medici. Violent punishment served to remind the people of the force behind the laws.

Effectively punctuating the cycle at regular junctures can slow inevitable decline, like winding a clock again and again until the spring gives out. But there are other, less bloody and less strenuous ways of periodically reminding citizens and subjects of their civic religion, and one such tool widely—if not universally—used in societies both contemporary and historical is festivals that occur regularly and inexorably, marked on the calendar, seemingly brought by the calendar. While these do not supplant other forms of shock, they occur with more reliability, and political actors, at least, seem to think they are of central importance to legitimation.

Here I want to introduce the concept of agent-punctuated cycles and their relationship to calendars. Fundamentally, this variation on the grand cyclicality of time involves the notion that cycles are not regulated entirely by fate or fortune but can instead be manipulated by a charismatic power, an individual force that changes their prescribed path. An agent can, at a given point in the natural course of things, punctuate that course with the aim of reinvigorating the regime and holding off the inevitable. Cyclical time here is understood to be subject to external force to maintain or disrupt momentum, just as some clocks have movements that require winding. Employing agent-punctuated cycles as a temporal frame presents a range of opportunities for political entrepreneurs because the course of the regime is now understood to be partly dependent on the agency of individuals. Political actors, on this view, can slow the process of decay or give particular impact and force to a regime's emergence. By invoking this conception of the flow of time, political actors can frame their actions in ways that impact the perceived legitimacy of those actions and the political regimes they are designed to alter or protect. This, in turn, frames political actors' own legitimacy within a regime.

Most temporal cycles are what we might call equilibrium cycles: they perpetuate themselves. These would include cyclical aspects of nature like the phases of the moon or the changing of the seasons. Cycles that are punctuated have a distinct point at which they might be said to end or begin. Some cycles in nature are punctuated by our superimposition of form, for example, when we decide that a year will end on December 31 or begin around the spring equinox, as in the traditional Persian calendar. But another conception of the cyclical flow of time requires the active intervention of an agent, whether human or divine. These agent-punctuated cycles are of particular interest politically, both in the history of political thought and in terms of the actions of political innovators.

Agent-punctuated cycles can be used to establish or cement personal legitimacy through at least two mechanisms. First, if an actor either synchronizes his actions with what is portrayed as the natural order of time or ruptures that order, he either casts his actions as mandated by heaven, in the case of synchrony or, if he claims to act on his own initiative to disrupt order, implies that he holds the power to combat the forces of fate, however understood. In either case, this is a claim to power on the basis of charismatic capacity, either borrowed from order or capable of overcoming it.

Second, if it is in an actor's interest *not* to disrupt the existing order by inserting herself charismatically into the course of things (in other words, if it would not be a good idea to violently resume the government, Medici-style), she can employ a strategy of automation to help cement the legitimacy of a regime she founded or supports either by casting a specific innovation/intervention as a process of renewal or by making the regime's periodic renewal automatic. Jean-Jacques Rousseau includes this in his advice to the king of Poland. If regimes need periodic reminders of their patriotic principles and the force of the law, why not make these reminders automatic, ensuring that one's will continues, effortlessly, for years to come? Thus Rousseau tells the king of Poland that he should "establish the custom of celebrating the confederates' deeds every ten years in solemn ceremonies—with the pomp appropriate to a republic: simple and proud . . . with dignity and in language free from exaggeration, let praise be bestowed upon the virtuous citizens who had the honor to suffer for their country in the toils of the enemy."[61] In other words, he should institute a festival that will, thereafter, come about every decade, brought by the calendar as naturally as the calendar seems to bring the spring. The punctuation of the cycle moves from agent-centered to self-perpetuating by means of the calendrical cycle.

Once instituted, the calendar becomes a technology of political renewal, doing that work seemingly automatically, as though nature itself celebrated the regime and its principles. This provides a means of rehearsing a particular conception of history and a means to "bring [citizens or subjects] back to their principles" with no apparent intervention by political actors.[62] To my knowledge, there is no empirically rigorous evidence proving the efficacy of such measures in promoting political health. But a substantial field of evidence demonstrates how widely the truth of this is assumed by political actors; the universality or near universality of such calendrically brought rituals implies the generality of belief among practitioners.

Are there countries or cultures without such regularly occurring festivals that rehearse events of symbolic significance? "Before all," Durkheim insists, "rites are means by which the social group reaffirms itself periodically."[63] Indeed, for Durkheim, not only do such rites always serve this political aim but no political unit can function without them: "There can be no society which does not feel the need of upholding and reaffirming at regular intervals the collective sentiments and the collective ideas which make its unity and personality."[64] Such views are widely echoed in contemporary descriptions and discussions of symbolic political discourse. Kurti asserts in the context of Hungary that "no nation can exist without a multitude of recognized, officially sanctioned public ceremonies."[65] And a great deal of ethnographic literature charts the use of periodic ritual in the affirmation or contestation of political symbols.[66] While several scholars have noted the importance of the rituals themselves, I want to draw attention to the importance of their *periodicity*.

Examples abound. As noted above, Augustus Caesar, once he had made Rome into an empire and himself into emperor in all but name, gradually "allowed" the Senate to add dates to the calendar that were significant with respect to the glory of Augustus and his family: birthdays, the anniversaries of significant victories, and so on all became public holidays celebrated with games and festivals.[67] These reshaped the calendar and the Roman experience of the year, and hence became part of Roman collective memory. The year becomes a cyclical series of celebrations of the glory of Augustus and his family. Once instituted, these festivals come around and around of their own accord. The origins of such political festivals are quickly forgotten, and they come to seem like institutions as old as memory, as natural as the arrival of spring. Both the Ayatollah Khomeini in postrevolutionary Iran and Soviet Russia worked hard to alter traditional patterns of festival observance. This process of naturalization is apparent with respect to the American Thanksgiving. Children are taught that Thanksgiving began with the Pilgrims in the seventeenth century although historians have shown that it was a Civil War–era innovation designed and promoted explicitly and intentionally to unify Americans through a shared day of domesticity, Christian piety, and celebration.[68] The holiday, imbued with useful political values, was made to seem legitimate through the construction of a long pedigree and its association with a very specific (constructed) natural moment: the harvest.

Is it a surprise, then, that the 2012 Hungarian Basic Law, explicitly framed in terms of grand cyclicality and millennial renewal, inscribes in Article J a range of political holidays? Or that it was brought into force on August 20, the feast day of Hungary's founder, Saint Stephen?

Conclusion

Why do powerful political innovators bother with calendars? Regime change and other extreme forms of political upheaval present a substantial legitimation challenge, and calendars are versatile tools in the dynamic game of legitimation. Legitimation has two key elements: claims of correspondence to one or more underlying self-justifying forms of order, some of which this chapter has engaged, and claims to performative capacity, further engaged in the next chapter. Calendars have the capacity to associate political order with diverse self-justifying forms of order that serve as sources for legitimation: the order of nature, of tradition, of fate or destiny. As Janus-headed institutions, calendars bring the form of the old—with the self-justifying capacity of traditional order—into the service of the new, and superimpose the constructed on the natural so that the constructed appears to *be* natural. Through linear counts, a political agent can harness the synchrony of important or auspicious junctures with events of his own choosing. Then, within a rhetorical frame like grand historical cyclicality, he can cast those events as inevitable, fated, and powerfully hopeful. The calendar can then be put to work winding the clock, stalling the inevitability of decline by means of an automatic rehearsal of civic religion.

Sorokin and Merton once argued that the variation in calendars stems from the differing coordination needs of different communities.

Time *must* be social because it often has little or nothing to do with astronomical time.[69] But most calendars in complex polities stubbornly imply their connection to astronomical and natural time, blurring—perhaps intentionally—the natural and the sociopolitical. This association with order—natural, divine, or fated—does some of the work of political legitimation insofar as all claims of legitimate power rest partly on coherence with a background, self-justifying order. Overall, calendars are mechanisms through which temporal propriety is pursued and performed in the service of legitimation. The next chapter shows how calendrical time also works as a tool of performance legitimacy.

3
Khubilai Khan's Calendar and the Politics of Performance

The lord is like a boat; and the common people are like water. The water may support the boat but the water may also overturn the boat.

—*Xunzi*

In 2009, a massive earthquake shook the Italian city of L'Aquila in Abruzzo. The quake, which had been preceded by seismic events of lesser intensity, left more than three hundred dead and wrought destruction on a massive scale. When it comes to earthquakes, this is hardly unique. But in the wake of this earthquake, something novel happened. Six scientists and a public official, members of the National Commission for the Forecast and Prevention of Major Risks, were arrested, convicted of manslaughter, and sentenced to jail.[1] The convictions of the six scientists were ultimately overturned, but the public official, Bernardo De Bernardinis of the Civil Protection Unit, remained in prison. His conviction was upheld because in his capacity as a government figure he had announced on television that while citizens should "remain alert, without panicking," there was "no danger."[2] The responsibility the official had criminally failed to meet was not to *predict* the earthquake, which is scientifically impossible, but rather to adequately forecast the level of risk and communicate this clearly to the public so citizens could prepare accordingly.[3]

Some four years earlier, Hurricane Katrina drowned New Orleans, killing more than eighteen hundred people, displacing hundreds of thousands more, and causing one hundred billion dollars in damage. It took several days for the U.S. federal government to respond, and the extent of the loss of life, damage, and overall chaos showed how radically unprepared all levels of government had been for a foreseeable crisis.[4] Again, the implicit assumption that government ought to forecast, be prepared for, and mitigate risks—even natural risks— became explicit. In the aftermath of the disaster, President George W. Bush's approval rating plummeted to an unprecedented low for any president, and the head of the Federal Emergency Management Agency was forced to resign.[5]

Of course, nobody thought President Bush was responsible for the hurricane itself. But because the government had failed to prepare for a foreseeable contingency by strengthening New Orleans' flood defenses and had subsequently failed to mitigate the disaster or even to maintain law and order, Katrina was perceived as an incidence of state failure, an indication of incompetence and incapacity. People withdrew their trust—if not from the institutions then from the officeholders—accordingly. Government must manage contingency and mitigate risk as part of an overall expectation of security and order. When governments fail in this regard, it is experienced as a performative failure. This chapter shows how, historically, calendars have served as tools to frame claims to performative capacity, to an ability to manage contingency which, in turn, supports claims to legitimacy. I begin by establishing the importance of performance legitimacy generally, particularly with respect to engineering the weak, tacit legitimacy easiest to reach for conquerors and colonizers. While what "performance" will mean in practice is dependent on epistemological and ontological assumptions of wide cultural and epochal variability, the core requirement is constant.

At the mundane level, calendars allow for coordination and planning as well as forecasting natural events for purposes of food production, anticipating weather extremes, resource planning, and so on. This helps mitigate foreseeable risk, preserving order through time. But in many civilizations, managing future contingencies also requires the complex regulation of temporal propriety. Timing is one factor in the triad of elements of order. It matters not just *what* one does but *where* and *when* one does it. In many civilizations, *when* has taken on an outsized importance in influencing fate, fortune, or the will of the gods. In these civilizations, the infrastructure of timing has taken on a correspondingly outsized role in the conduct of statecraft. Timing, here, is a core element of contingency management, which contributes to performance legitimacy.

To achieve the necessary level of detailed forecasting for mitigating risk requires an extensive infrastructure for the maintenance of calendars (and sometimes clocks), and hence, in addition to maintaining order through time, the capacity of a state to actually construct and maintain this infrastructure itself frames claims to legitimacy.

Performance Legitimacy

"Legitimacy," Seymour Lipset once claimed, "involves the capacity of a political system to engender and maintain the belief that existing political institutions are the most appropriate or proper ones for the society."[6] In the previous chapter I argued that what is appropriate and proper is normally delineated by means of one or more self-justifying and often mutually reinforcing background orders. These may take the form of normative principles, traditional or generally accepted procedures, nature, or destiny. For Lipset this contrasts sharply with effectiveness, a distinct element of regime stability. A government's capacity to perform contributes to stability, not legitimacy. Nonetheless, Lipset notes that sufficient stores of legitimacy protect a regime against economic or other shocks, at least temporarily, since "even in legitimate systems, a breakdown of effectiveness, repeatedly or for a long period, will endanger stability."[7] Conversely, a regime that is effective "over a number of generations" gains *legitimacy*.[8] It might, then, be more consistent to describe these factors as interrelated. Both effectiveness and legitimacy can contribute to stability, but stability and effectiveness also contribute to legitimacy: after all, a stable regime, and particularly a high-performing stable regime, becomes a habitual regime that, over time, comes to seem legitimate through familiarity. Effective performance is one element in a complex scheme of legitimating and delegitimating factors.

Lipset's analysis nonetheless suggests a range of hypotheses with respect to the relationship of performance to legitimation. For one, in democratic regimes, ceteris paribus, one might expect length of incumbency and voter attention to record of achievement to hold an inverse relationship, at least until a record of underachievement becomes impossible to ignore. While achieving office through established procedure helps, as does the borrowed legitimacy of dynastic personality, entrenchment through time builds a wider reservoir of legitimation resources on which to draw, and hence more shock resistance. In cases of regime change, colonization, or conquest, where tradition and procedural sources of legitimacy are unavailable, it would be reasonable to expect performance to play an even more substantial role. This may take the form of charisma, which is a proxy for performance capacity. But more generally, one should expect to observe that where innovation and novelty are difficult to pass off as a restoration, leaders will emphasize effective performance in the rhetoric of legitimation. Alternative wells may be too shallow to draw upon.

Many contemporary scholars associate performance legitimacy with authoritarian or authoritative regimes: the term is, for instance, commonly employed in scholarship on post-Deng China or Singapore, which offer to meet some range of needs in return for tolerance of a functional monopoly on power.[9] Conversely, the liberal democratic emphasis on procedure and consent may suggest that performance legitimacy is less important. This is a misperception. Performance legitimacy is in play in a range of regime types of varying complexity. Firmly in the liberal democratic tradition, Joseph Raz has called a claim to authority on the basis of performance capacity a "service conception," and in parliamentary regimes, leaders lose their job and parties their mandate in no-confidence votes when they fail to perform.[10] A version of performance legitimacy is at the heart of current debates surrounding the legitimacy of the European Union's complex federal system too. As Fritz Scharpf has argued, positive policy outcomes create critical "output legitimacy," which is of especial importance where there is a lack of cohesive identity and transparent procedural rules that would lead to "input legitimacy."[11] Beyond complex constitutional regimes, William Reno has documented how warlords ultimately build up political legitimacy from effective capacity.[12] Leaders of steppe Mongols, prior to the emergence of the great khans, were elected partly on the basis of their perceived performance capacity.[13] In historical authoritarian regimes such as Mayaland, city-states that could not ensure food and physical security depopulated.[14] Competence matters for legitimacy. Incompetence can lead to the explicit withdrawal of consent (to regime, institution, or individual) through no-confidence votes or electoral failure, or to implicit legitimacy consequences, such as widespread law breaking, the erosion of compliance with constitutional norms and procedures or, in extreme cases, rebellion or revolution.

A source of this misperception, that performance is for authoritarians, procedure for democrats, may be different conceptions of legitimacy in the comparative history of political thought. From the late Renaissance into modernity, claims to legitimate power were based primarily in divine right or in consent, either of which could confer power with reference to the self-justifying background order. The contract tradition of Hobbes, Locke, and Rousseau arises in the context of the birth of science. Epistemological autonomy is the companion of political autonomy. Descartes, Galileo, and Bacon call for experimental science, for observing and confirming for ourselves. We ought not to submit to anyone else's intellectual authority. Evidence will no longer be drawn solely from the works of Aristotle, as in the Scholastic tradition, nor will the word of God (as contained in the Bible) suffice on its own.[15] Since those who wish to know must rely on the interim evidence of reason, of the senses, of their own inquiries and investigations, charismatic or traditional claims to divine sanction continue to look *strategically* useful—Rousseau still advocates them—but less obviously *authoritative*.[16] Rather, submission to authority depends on actual or hypothetical consent on the grounds that consent is rational. Reason becomes, at least in theory, the ultimate self-justifying background order. The threshold for disobedience or rebellion may, after consent, be extremely high: only an existential threat justifies resistance in many accounts. So performance is put aside in theory but never in the practice of democratic legitimation. This focus on consent, a consequence of the epistemological move toward autonomy, has clouded attention to *why* people give their consent in democratic and other contexts (as opposed to why philosophers think they ought to). Consent marks a judgment of legitimacy on the part of those who give their consent, but on the basis of which substantive criteria do people make this judgment?

By contrast, performance legitimacy is at the center of normative political thought in imperial China from the ascendance of the Western Zhou (eleventh century BCE) onward. The Zhou defeat of the Shang was improbable, given their relatively small population. They faced dissension in their own ranks and challenges from surviving Shang aristocrats (it being some twenty-five hundred years too early to benefit from Machiavelli's brutal advice on *that* subject). To address this legitimation crisis, the Zhou invented the Mandate of Heaven (*tian ming,* 天命) which served both as a means of legitimation and as a way to promote internal discipline. The Mandate of Heaven is, most simply, an entitlement to rule based on virtue and skill. Zhou documents are rife with citations of the mandate. In the *Shang Shu*, or Book of Documents, words attributed to the Duke of Zhou forcefully underline the centrality of performative responsibility entailed by the mandate: "Heaven [removed] the mandate from the Shang state and passed it to us, . . . but I cannot count on the mandate resting with us and will respect the heavenly mandate and our people forever. It is all contingent upon human conduct whether mistakes and evils will occur. . . . Heaven cannot be trusted. Heaven will [allow us to keep] the mandate that King Wen had received only if we carry on his virtuous conduct."[17] The good conduct of rulers pleases heaven, and heaven protects China. When rulers do not perform or are not virtuous, heaven sends signs of displeasure in the form of disasters: earthquakes, floods, famine. Legitimacy is signaled from heaven by good fortune on earth, and legitimacy is granted by heaven on the basis of the ruler's performance. Within this legitimation equation, the emperor must take responsibility for everything that goes wrong, from crop pests to bureaucratic failure, and this generates a rhetorical trope of self-blame in imperial penitential proclamations (*xia zui ji zhao,* 下罪己诏), which is perhaps related to the self-criticism practice in more recent Chinese political history.[18] The necessity of performance through the demands of the tian ming has remained a cornerstone of legitimation in the Chinese political tradition, even as it has slowly come to explicit recognition in the West.

But what kind of performance do people expect? Doubtless, this varies from time to time, place to place, and perhaps person to person. Certainly residents of extensive welfare states like contemporary Sweden have different expectations than a denizen of thirteenth-century China. However, it may be that these expectations differ more profoundly in scale and modulation than in fundamental kind. Themes that underlie performance expectations across regimes are physical and economic security and just order.[19] For example, Miguel La Serna, in his study of why some Peruvian peasants acquiesced to the demands of the rebel group Sendero Luminoso while others took arms against it, found that where the state had failed to keep order through just enforcement, people were likely to support Sendero. But where people perceived that the state was doing a fine job of justly keeping order, they would resist the rebels.[20] There is evidence of similar dynamics among peasants in other states.[21] Even anarchists see a capacity to maintain order—even if an order in flux—as a critical element of the normative legitimacy of a nonstate. As Proudhon argued, in an anarchist community, "each citizen's sphere of activity is delineated by his choice of profession and the natural division of labor, and this mode of combining social functions produces a harmonious effect; *order results from the free activity of all men.*"[22]

Though there may be variable levels of tolerance for insecurity, some kind of security (not only order but something approximating just order and hence predictability) is a near-universal expectation of government, and the provision of security is an element in any ongoing campaign of legitimation.

In part because legitimation is an ongoing process, and in part because security depends on order achieved through time, a regime that taps the reservoir of performance legitimacy must have not only the matters of the moment in hand, it must have considered likely sources of future risk and planned for a variety of contingencies. It is the failure to mitigate foreseeable risk that damaged FEMA and the Bush administration after Katrina, and imprisoned Bernardo De Bernardinis in the wake of the L'Aquila earthquake. And it is this same failure, albeit through an alternative ontological and epistemological lens, that caused Chinese emperors to make a show of cowering for the peoples' forgiveness after a crop failure. Performance through time is a necessary condition of claims to legitimacy, and that requires contingency management, forecasting, and mitigation.

Risk has become a loaded term in the social and political theory of the last twenty years as a substantial literature has grown around the concept of a risk society, developed by Ulrich Beck, Anthony Giddens, and others. Giddens has defined risk society as "a society increasingly preoccupied with the future (and also with safety), which generates the notion of risk."[23] The risk society contributes to a distinct and systematic mode of political interaction grounded in pervasive fear of the global manufactured hazards specific to modernity.[24] Giddens writes: "Risk is not, as such, the same as hazard or danger. A risk society is not intrinsically more dangerous or hazardous than pre-existing forms of social order. . . . Life in the Middle Ages was hazardous; but there was no notion of risk and *there doesn't seem in fact to be a notion of risk in any traditional culture. The reason for this is that dangers are experienced as given.* Either they come from God, or they come simply from a world which one takes for granted. The idea of risk [by contrast] is bound up with the aspiration to control and particularly with the idea of controlling the future."[25] This statement directly contradicts China's mandate tradition and the Duke of Zhou's claim to be solely responsible for events, which would, predictably, go wrong if he did not rule skillfully or maintain his own virtuous conduct. Nonetheless, Giddens follows Beck in erroneously claiming that premodern society was at the mercy of *natural* hazards that were exogenous, local, and time-limited. Modern industrial society, by contrast, thrived on attempts to predict risk and gain active control, while now in the risk society, these scholars claim, we recognize that this may not be possible. We do not and perhaps cannot know the extent and source of the risks we might face. Modernity is a condition of reflexivity and a push for control: we think about and try to confront or alter risk. But risk now, in postmodernity, is global, potentially unlimited temporally, beyond prediction, and beyond regulation.[26]

Certainly, we face novel kinds of risk, representing a fundamental shift in the epistemological characterization of risk and its ontological character also. But the contrast with and between previous risk-mitigation regimes may be overdrawn. Novel forms of risk and of the calculation of risk have not extinguished attention to more traditional concerns, nor is it correct to claim that in premodern societies danger is experienced as given. The expectation that risk is to be anticipated and mitigated is as much premodern as it is modern, and it has not been extinguished by the novel global and unpredictable forms of risk that characterize the postmodern age. It may be apt to attribute these shifts to ontological and epistemological characterizations of risk, while the underlying expectation that governments should do their utmost to forecast and mitigate risk, even when this is near impossible (as it arguably was in the L'Aquila case), remains a constant.

In summary, part of the necessary repertoire of the rhetoric of legitimation are claims of performative capacity. To effectively make such claims, it is necessary, if not sufficient, that a regime maintain some kind of order and honor some reasonable conception of justice. When these conditions are met, they contribute to something like a basic, subjective experience of security for those living under a regime and constitute a state that has not-failed.[27] If Machiavelli is right that the mass of people are less interested in power than in a nondominating form of security, then a regime skilled at justly maintaining order would be likely to generate at least a grudging acceptance, however it had come to rule. Because this reduces the cost of governing (by minimizing policing and violence), it would also be reasonable to assume that some leaders happily cultivate the perception of legitimacy by actually acting in a way that yields performative satisfaction, even where, for instance, tax farming constitutes the core motive. This will require that regimes anticipate, attempt to prevent, and mitigate threat, promoting more predictable physical security and a more predictable order through time. Ceteris paribus, leaders of a regime successful in this regard are more likely to secure weak legitimacy both for their regime as such and for any activity or innovation they introduce that may be understood to contribute to this aim.

Like all sources of legitimacy, such capacity is partly performed, but not only in the theatrical sense. According to one line of thought, power, regardless of its institutional grounding, is always trying to hide behind display. As Geertz put it, a Hobbesian state aims to perform "a dark noise to impress the impressionable and to induce in them a trembling awe," while Marxist readings emphasize how "state ceremony" serves only "mystification . . . spiritualizing of material interests and the fogging over of material conflicts."[28] Even liberal and pluralist conceptions of the state are engaged in mystification as state ritual "trumpets [the popular] will's immensity" or "clothe[s] received procedures in moral legitimacy."[29] All of Geertz's examples of state power as mere display draw on a unidirectional form of communication aimed at shrouding the truth. Here, performance is mere theater, pomp and pageantry intended to legitimize through dazzle or awe. But effective power does not hide behind performance so much as manifest in it. And where display is dissimulation only, it runs the risk of incurring disdain. This is clear from George Orwell's account of performing power in his essay "Shooting an Elephant." The narrator had been called to wrangle an elephant that had stampeded in a Burmese market, killing a man. He writes: "Suddenly I realized that I should have to shoot the [now calm] elephant after all. The people expected it of me and I had got to do it; I could feel their two thousand wills pressing me forward, irresistibly.... I perceived in this moment that when the white man turns tyrant it is his own freedom that he destroys.... For it is a condition of his rule that he shall spend his life trying to impress the 'natives.' ... My whole life, every white man's life in the East was one long struggle not to be laughed at."[30]

Not being laughed at is no joke. In the USSR of the 1940s and 1950s, purveyors of political jokes that highlighted the discrepancies between official and lived versions of social life were sent to the gulag.[31] Dissimulation is dangerous because it presents opportunities for derision. And derision is the death of power.

While a theatrical performance is paradigmatically not reality, there is an element of show in the performance of capacity.[32] The thing must in fact be done, but people need to see it done also. In *The Prince,* Machiavelli recounts how after the death of Cesare Borgia's brutal henchman Remirro de Orco, his usefulness in purging enemies at an end, the two pieces of his body were left in the piazza for all to see. Machiavelli reports that "the ferocity of this spectacle left the people at once satisfied and stupefied."[33] This is a blunt communication of restoration of just order, but it is not just a telling and showing of what this power that claims obedience *can* do. It is also a performance in the sense of an intrinsic accomplishment of a constitutive task. In executing the henchman, Cesare executes justice, and that is the role of competent authority. He is the bona fide occupant, in good standing, of the role that generates the duty to execute justice. Every state does this in more or less spectacular fashion. Bagehot notes of the fussier elements of English procedure that they "attract [the government's] motive power. . . . They raise the army, though they do not win the battle."[34] Doing the things that legitimate power does simultaneously shows that one can and actuates or instantiates the claimed role. Performance of the act is simultaneously proof of capacity to act and proof that one is the actor whose duty it is to act in that way. To communicate this in words is precisely to fail to communicate it because it is the instantiation that has semiotic power.[35]

Performance legitimacy, then, is concerned not only with outcomes but with the substantive and symbolic modes of conduct associated with legitimate power. A political actor must do what legitimate powers do, and in meeting the duties of legitimate power, she simultaneously actualizes and communicates capacity.

Calendars, Capacity, and Contingency

Historically, several threads bind performative legitimacy with calendars. To mitigate risk, calendars provide first-order systems to coordinate natural phenomena and human activity such as food production and storage or readying for periods of flooding. Accompanied by an almanac, calendars provide second-order systems for guiding the temporal propriety of individual and public action. At the third order, the provision of a fine calendar performs a regime's capacity because its production reflects control over technical skill, the production of knowledge, and the resources necessary to each of these. At the fourth order, the smooth coordination of all these elements is a mark of, for example, Mandate of Heaven in imperial China or cosmic order in Assyria, which provides material for the order-based well of legitimation claims. A king or emperor needs an excellent calendar to ensure temporal propriety and good planning, and when things do go well, this implies, in circular fashion, that he *must* have got the calendar right, which in turn suggests both his control of knowledge and technical skill and heaven's favor. These four strands of performative legitimation are key tactics in the imperial strategies of history's longest-lasting regimes, but dressed in different ontological and epistemological clothing, they are not so distant from contemporary strategies of performative legitimation too. Let us turn to some examples.

In explaining the original verdict in the L'Aquila earthquake case, the judge stated that citizens are entitled to risk mitigation by the technical experts employed by government: "The task of the accused . . . was certainly not to predict the earthquake and indicate the month, day, hour and magnitude, but rather, more realistically, to go ahead . . . with the 'prediction and prevention of the risk.'"[36] This was precisely what, in a distinct epistemological and ontological context, was expected of the king in Assyria. The Assyrians, who governed a substantial empire for the better part of a millennium, were profoundly concerned with the production and management of technical expertise in risk management, bound up with temporal propriety. We know how seriously this task was taken both from extant letters between technocrats and royals and because of the lengths Assyrians went to gather and secure expertise. In 1215 BCE, for example, the Assyrians staged a raid on a library in Babylon, and we have evidence of similar episodes throughout the Middle and Neo-Assyrian kingdoms: in 675 BCE, King Esarhaddon expanded this "booknapping" tradi-

POLITICS OF PERFORMANCE

tion to kidnapping.[37] Scholars "were held hostage at Nineveh and, when not put in irons, forced to copy cuneiform texts."[38] This seems to have been common enough in the region, and is even reflected in the book of Daniel. Daniel and his aristocratic peers are captured and then employed as slave-scholars by King Nebuchadnezzar of Babylon.[39] On another occasion, in 647 BCE, King Assurbanipal captured a large number of clay tablets from the library of his brother, then king of Babylon.[40] These tablets, and the scholars who could interpret them, were concerned with timing and planning, with the stars and the calendar, with divination.

This Late Babylonian clay cuneiform tablet provides a table stipulating the amount of water to be used in a water clock in order to measure out the length of a night watch at different times of the year. The tablet is signed by the scribe Nabu-aapla-iddin. (British Museum)

The god secured the state from harm at his pleasure, and ensuring he was pleased was a key aspect, in this epistemological and cosmological context, of anticipating and managing risk. Determining what the god wanted done, when, and under what circumstances was a serious business. The responsibility fell profoundly to the king personally because, for the Assyrians, the universe was a mirror image of the god and the king his earthly representative. Addad-Sumu-Usur, exorcist to one Assyrian king, wrote to him, "The king is the perfect likeness of the god."[41] For the Assyrians, this meant maintaining "absolute perfection and mental balance," judging with exquisite insight, perfectly balancing justice with mercy, and behaving with utmost purity.[42] This is importantly distinct from the idea that the king is God's chosen or anointed. To be chosen or anointed is to be given a license or charter. Who holds it is sanctioned to do as he wishes, a divine *right,* even if within certain boundaries. But a representative, by contrast, is tasked with a principal/agent relationship. The king who acts as God's representative must act as God would act. As Parpola explained, "The king who would not conform to the role of the Perfect Man . . . would automatically, willingly or unwillingly, disrupt the cosmic harmony, and with it the stability of the empire he was commissioned to maintain."[43] The management of contingency, securing the Assyrian order through time, required that the king be a good king, whose legitimacy was signaled by his success. Success in maintaining this cosmic harmony, by consistently acting in a god-willed fashion, yielded imperial success, and each of these served to perform legitimacy in this ontological-epistemological context.[44]

It is quickly evident from the letters between Assyrian kings and their army of scholars that for the Assyrians, perfect behavior was as closely tied to the question of *when* as *what.*[45] It fell to the king's scholars to give advice on the timing of all sorts of minutiae as well as great affairs of state, and they were consulted on the timing of such matters with parallel earnestness: ranging from the appropriate time for a royal social visit to auspicious timing for warfare. But to determine this precise timing required an army of astronomers to track the movements of the constellations and the phases of the moon, the years, the months, and the days. Performance was a pillar of the legitimation of Assyrian kings, and this performance was tightly bound up with temporal propriety. This critical determination of the right action at the right time required technical experts—astronomers, diviners, astrologers—and Assyrian kings devoted enormous resources to securing this expertise in the service of cultivating performance legitimacy.

This suggests that expertise, its development, recruitment, and management, is permanently wedded to political power not only in the Foucauldian sense of power/knowledge in a modern carceral archipelago but also through this negotiation of capacity in the service of legitimation. Power must expend resources on the production of knowledge, knowledge that it can then perform as evidence of capacity, if it is to maintain itself.

The Assyrian case shows the basic workings of the interrelationship of calendar politics and performance legitimacy. In a second case, that of Khubilai Khan's calendar reform at the dawn of the Yuan, the legitimation challenge was far more substantial and Khubilai's response more multifaceted. Khubilai's was one of the great historical calendar reforms, and here the hypotheses generated by Lipset's analysis with respect to the interrelationship of performance and other forms of legitimation come alive. Khubilai used his calendar reform to legitimize his very presence in China, framing his claim that he was qualified to take his place in the line of Chinese dynastic rulers as a legitimate holder of Heaven's Mandate.

Empire without Letters: The Case of Khubilai Khan's Calendar

To understand the profound legitimacy challenge Khubilai confronted requires attention to the clash of cultures he faced in China and thus some historical context. When the young nomad Temujin—later Khubilai's grandfather—unified the tribes of the Mongolian steppe and began his military conquest of Asia, not only was he illiterate but the language he spoke had no written form. It was among his early priorities to amend this so he hired a Uyghur scholar to adapt the script of that language for use with Mongolian.[46] Genghis Khan, as Temujin came to be known, thereby recognized a core problem that would continue to face his progeny: how to govern a huge and culturally diverse empire with technologies and traditions that had been developed to suit a nomadic way of life. In his approach to written script, the first great khan set the pattern for a strategy that would continue to shape the imperial policies of his son and grandsons thereafter. Each strove to import and adapt the knowledge and expertise of other cultures in overcoming the gap between sedentary and nomadic technologies.[47]

Like the Assyrians two millennia before, the Mongols were entrepreneurial in seeking an ecumenical-eclectic approach to knowledge: technical-scientific, religious, and otherwise. Indeed, once Genghis's son Ögedei had taken the reins (1229), the range of foreign experts, scholars, and wise men the Mongols had collected from across the world had become so large that it had become necessary for this nomadic people to provide a proper walled city, Karakorum, to house them. Persian astronomers, in the lofty tradition of their neoclassical Assyrian forebears, were not accustomed to life in a yurt, and they were an asset worth cultivating and protecting.

By the time Khubilai came to prominence, initially under the rule of his brother Möngke, the importation and adaptation of practical knowledge from other cultures had become well-established practice. This, combined with the practice of keeping subservient local rulers in place and a remarkable religious cosmopolitanism, served as the key elements in the Mongols' strategy for holding the empire they had won through extraordinary violence.[48] The empire itself had grown to be the largest yet amassed, surpassing the territory of Alexander and that of Rome, stretching from Hungary to China, Siberia to Korea. So this was no small task.

But the most striking technical contrast faced the Mongols in China. China's elaborate bureaucracy, highly developed literary culture, and national pride meant that it posed some special legitimation challenges.[49] The Chinese considered the Mongols barbarians. They were not only not Han, they were also nomads. The apparatus of the imperial state Khubilai eventually inherited, with its huge ministries and elaborate public works, surpassed in complexity anything the Mongols would have managed elsewhere. The techniques that had allowed Genghis to pacify the rest of Asia would not be enough to hold large, powerful, and strategically important China.[50] Generic tax farming backed up by force would simply not work here, at least not for long.[51] To hold China required that the Chinese somehow come to see the Mongols as legitimate rulers: a substantial challenge.

So Khubilai built a capital, Ta-tu, on the site of modern Beijing, deep in China. He went to live there, attempting to navigate the intricacies of domestic Chinese politics. But at the same time he faced the challenge of cementing and legitimizing his claim to rule among the Mongols in a splintering empire beyond China. He consistently fought with his brother, Ariq Boke, who also claimed the title of great khan. This meant that Khubilai had to maintain an image of the appropriate kind of strength and his association with Mongolian culture too.[52] If it appeared that he had been sinicized, this would have greatly weakened his position among the Mongolians who followed him.

The marks of legitimacy among the Chinese and those recognized by the Mongols—who had long *elected* their leaders on the basis of skill, intelligence, and strength—would be quite different.[53] These audiences expected different kinds of performance.

Khubilai chose to cast himself both as khagan (khan of khans) in the Mongolian tradition founded by Genghis and as emperor and dynastic founder in the Chinese tradition. He made decisive shifts in administration in China. He rejected the culturally important but by then corrupt system of Confucian examinations in favor of a system of personal recommendations. Later restored to prominence during the Ming Dynasty, this system had long structured access to elite civil service positions.[54] This reform provided advantages with respect both to assuring loyalty and to securing the best pragmatic talent. And while the bureaucracy remained in place, Khubilai added a layer of authority—Mongolian and foreign but definitely non-Han—above this staff to make concrete decisions.[55]

But Khubilai also worked to secure his legitimacy through normative mechanisms: he attempted to rule well. He cultivated the support of the Chinese peasantry through measures aimed at increasing agricultural output and instituted a more predictable taxation system, showing himself capable of helping peasants manage contingency. He worked to secure the support of what might be understood as a middle class of doctors, scientists, artists, artisans, and merchants by raising the status of those professions, providing tax incentives, and facilitating trade through the active development of transportation and communication infrastructure. This, in turn, secured his tax base.[56] Khubilai had what can aptly be described as an economic policy. Putting a pragmatic spin on the lessons of his Confucian tutors, he saw the practical advantages of ruling justly, improving the lives of his subjects, and the wealth of the Chinese state. He skillfully quelled

China's sometimes violent religious divisions and cultivated the friendship of religious leaders and scholars from all denominations. When Marco Polo's father and uncle first visited Khubilai in the early 1260s, Khubilai sent them back to the pope with a request for one hundred wise Christians to add to his ecumenical entourage.[57]

Economic, infrastructure, and agricultural policy and planning are important ingredients for the actual management of contingency, first-order performance legitimacy. But Chinese people were accustomed to further evidence of legitimacy from their emperor. The emperor must show signs of heavenly sanction, of a special and especially communicative relationship with heaven, that could reveal the temporal propriety of day-to-day conduct. An emperor's own conduct must be seemly and *timely* also, including—profoundly—the timing of his religious observance and his political and military engagements. This in particular was crucial to Khubilai's relationship with political elites, which was much less comfortable, particularly after he abolished the civil service examinations that had, historically, benefited them disproportionately.

So here Khubilai made new conciliatory moves. In particular, he followed traditional imperial court etiquette and ceremony, imitating important actions of his predecessors in dynastic transition. Khubilai realized, with the help of his most trusted Han advisor, Liu Ping-Chung, that his best hope for stability (and hence an enduring tax base) was to have his rule understood as part of the legitimate line of Chinese dynasties: he did those actions that traditionally marked transition from one dynasty to the next, thereby framing his rule as a new iteration in the pattern denoting legitimacy, in line with traditional and legal-rational expectations. In this vein, not only did Khubilai proclaim the Yuan, marking a new birth of the old form of the regime, he commissioned the histories of the Song, Chin, and Liao, whose dynasties had preceded China's reunification. Dynastic histories were typically undertaken at the start of any new dynasty.⁵⁸ He also reformed the calendar.

Calendar reform, like dynastic histories, was traditional in new dynasties. But Khubilai's was unusually elaborate and expensive; he devoted more resources to this project than had any of his predecessors.⁵⁹ The idea to undertake it belonged to Khubilai's close advisor Liu Ping-Chung, who died two years before Khubilai finally authorized the project. Liu, who had organized a substantial and highly successful administrative reform for his Mongolian masters while Khubilai was still a young man, had prepared a sort of memo on desirable reforms, ceremonies, and actions to be undertaken were Khubilai to become great khan. Among these, he underlined that "it will be desirable, on the accession of a new ruler, to promulgate an astronomical system and a new epoch."⁶⁰ Khubilai's annals give the reason for the reform in this way: "On 23 July 1276, because of the cumulative errors in the Great Enlightenment system [the astronomical system employed by the previous dynasties to reckon the calendar], the Admonisher Wang Hsun was commanded to work with astrologers from southern China to set up a bureau and make a new astronomical system."⁶¹ The old calendar sponsored by the old regime was not reliable, and therefore not respectable. A legitimate and well-ordered regime would surely aim to amend this, particularly because of the calendar's significance for planning and temporal propriety.

Wang, a mathematical prodigy whom Liu brought to Khubilai's attention while Wang was still a boy, put together a team of engineers, mathematicians, and astronomer/astrologers. A new observatory, completed in 1286, was built in Ta-tu with newly designed and carefully constructed equipment, employing novel Chinese and advanced Arabic techniques.⁶² The chief engineer, Guo Shou-Ching, had been brought to the project from his post as chief of waterworks. He was apparently a highly gifted and innovative engineer, and it was he who was responsible for many of the innovative instruments and technologies that would allow Khubilai to take credit for this new, superior calendar. The staff of the observatory formed three bureaus, concerned with computation, observation, and water clocks (the last-named, of course, necessary to the accuracy of the first).[63] All of this came at enormous expense, not just in funds but also in diverted human capital.[64]

At the end of the project, Guo presented the emperor with a new "season granting system" that boasted substantial improvements in accuracy over the previous system with respect to tracking lunar and solar movements, coordinating vernacular months with an effective system of intercalation, and prediction of eclipses of various kinds. The improvements were made possible not only because of the excellent new instruments and innovative computational techniques but also because of observations of polar altitudes taken from across the empire. All of this contributed to greater precision with respect to the solstice, the lengths of the tropical year, day, and night, and solar and lunar motions.[65] Guo himself described this range of innovations and their contribution to the accuracy of astronomy, borne out by comparison with other contemporary calculations. These advances and innovations, in turn, allowed for the production of a calendar and almanac of great precision and presumptive stability that Khubilai could provide to his subjects.

Given the resource priority Khubilai accorded to calendar reform, the extant written evidence, and Khubilai's non-Sinic roots, the effort was evidently purposeful and strategic. That this reform was a pillar supporting Khubilai's legitimation project is evident. First, the practice of reforming calendars is what legitimate, dynasty-founding emperors of China did, historically. So, in doing as they did, Khubilai casts himself

Abridged armillary sphere after the design of Guo Shou-Ching at the Imperial Observatory in Beijing. (Illustration by Godard and Smeeton Tilly from *L'illustration, journal universel*, September 18, 1875. De Agostini/Biblioteca Ambrosiana/Getty Images)

as one in their line. It is the emperor who grants the seasons, and so, if it is Khubilai who has granted the seasons, it must be he who is emperor. Furthermore, Khubilai does not just do as previous emperors had done, he does it *best*. The notably superior technical resources of the new regime, its capacity to produce an almanac that more accurately reflected celestial phenomena, help establish performative capacity. This calendar reform makes a symbolic statement about the performative failures of previous regimes; it is an improvement on the "corruption" of the older system, as noted explicitly in Khubilai's annals.[66]

Furthermore, attention to temporal propriety served as a signal of Khubilai's appropriate concern with the Mandate of Heaven characteristic of an emperor, not a conqueror. How could the people of China know if Khubilai had the Mandate of Heaven? Only by inferring what must be the case in order for apparent conditions to obtain, that is, by noting manifestations in the world: successful ventures of individuals and the state, healthy crops, and even good weather are signs of Heaven's Mandate.[67] This shows the substantive, not just symbolic, importance of the calendar and almanac. This kind of success depends partly on temporal propriety, which relies on these tools of timing. Timing and contingency management dominated the day-to-day lives of Chinese people as profoundly as these things dominate our own lives, but in a distinct way. People in China used—and sometimes still use—an almanac's instruction on auspicious and inauspicious days for planting, harvesting, building, conducting business and family affairs, and for festival and ritual timing. If the new calendar is more accurate, then the new almanacs are more accurate. The almanacs, in turn, enable temporal propriety, doing the right action at the right time. Temporal propriety, in turn, is necessary to the success of any endeavor. Heaven smiles on endeavors undertaken not just in the right way but at the right time. And the success of an endeavor is, in this scheme, evidence that one has got temporal propriety right. The calendar and almanac thus constitute elements of infrastructure. Their improvement, like the improvement of roads and the post, is a public service Khubilai performs well. The reform constitutes a substantive performance of capacity and also signals Khubilai's understanding of and respect for domestic conceptions of right order.

It is worth noting that the almanac may also have contributed to a common identity through simultaneity. Far and wide, north and south, from the former kingdoms of the Jurchen to those of Xie

(Western) Xia and the Southern Song, the blueprint for living provided by the almanac was now, under Khubilai, the *same* blueprint. And this almanac provided a mode of simultaneity that was not only identity-molding but in line with nature and uniform across China.[68]

All of this is particularly meaningful in light of the non-Han origins of this new emperor. Sivin has argued that the incorporation of this reform into the orthodox history of China shows that the occupation thereby came to be seen *not* as an occupation but as a legitimate dynasty among other dynasties.[69] Khubilai's new calendar serves as a symbolic refounding, suitable for the actual refounding of a newly unified China. The new calendar associated Khubilai's Yuan not only with the authority of nature but with the human technical skill required to capture and interpret it, appropriate to the figure whose job it was to mediate between heaven and earth. The emperor performs the role of emperor, but he also performs his capacity as emperor, tapping the well of performative legitimation.

For Khubilai as a Mongolian outsider, participation in this tradition signaled his sinophilia while making evident both his adherence to continuity and tradition and the decisive break required for a legitimate new dynasty. By participating so lavishly in this tradition, he establishes his bona fides as emperor of China, a sufficiently Chinese emperor to help legitimate his rule. That Khubilai thought massive expenditure worthwhile for his observatory and the calendar and almanacs it produced now makes sense: it is an investment in legitimacy.

Conclusion

Because we have no access to time-as-such, our experience of time is always mediated by shaped time, time shaped by the technologies we use to mark and measure it. Time *must* be actively shaped if it is to be of any use to us. Different technologies shape time differently, and we simultaneously use a range of technologies to meet our range of temporal aims. We are thus open to diverse conceptions of time, to accepting new technologies that provide new shapes for time. Which time technology a political actor employs for a specific task has important secondary effects, however, because time technologies differently order social and political space, enable the management of contingency more or less effectively, and frame political thought and political action in ways that impact the reception of politically charged claims. So in addition to their first-order usefulness, time technologies play a range of second-order political roles. They are particularly effective in this regard because we perceive time as natural, and our modes of marking and measuring time often take on this naturalness. Therefore, time technologies can be used to naturalize and hence institutionalize and legitimize political innovations and political orders. In this light, it makes sense that the reform of time technologies is so common—and so commonly beneath notice—at times of political change.

Calendars in particular have historically played a critical role in the infrastructure of risk management found in many complex civilizations, as critical to the production of performance legitimacy as economic growth or raising levees is in democracies today. In imperial political cultures like those of China and Assyria/Babylonia, maintaining order through time involved the cultivation of a substantial body of technical knowledge and the support of a cultivated bureaucracy devoted to this task. The temporal propriety of religious and other practices, including the minutiae of daily life, was important for the management of risk, and a great many experts—priests and scholars—and substantial material resources were devoted to the preservation and interpretation of the requisite scientific and esoteric knowledge.

Together, an infrastructure devoted to managing risk developed, which itself became a *performance* of capacity, a symbolic politics of strength and capacity. A critical tool in the arsenal of such technical experts is an accurate calendar. Through its role in this infrastructure of contingency management, the calendar becomes both a practical and a symbolic element of framing legitimation.

Through advances in mathematics and through changes, however uneven, in our ontological and epistemological environment, we have become better at forecasting some kinds of events, with consequential effects for modernity.[70] This skill is specific to the way in which the problem of risk and probability was recast in the Renaissance and early modernity. But the requirement that political leaders attempt to anticipate contingencies, to plan for and thus ideally prevent or mitigate them, is likely as old as effective power. Any leader who hopes for obedience, or at least to avoid open rebellion, and aims to economize on the use of force will have to establish, at least weakly, that she ought to have power. No matter how effectively she frames her rule as in conformity with a self-justifying underlying order, if she cannot maintain basic security in an order perceived as basically just, sooner or later, people will reject those claims to conformity, seeing in her failure a mark of discordance. Doubtless, bias confirmation comes into play here too: where a regime benefits people, they will be receptive to order-based legitimation claims, and where a regime harms them, they will not.

We now have an answer to the first question motivating this book: why are calendar reforms so commonly paired with political innovations? It is by now evident that this is due to their capacity to frame claims of political legitimacy: first, by creating frame alignment with forms of order already accepted as legitimate and second, by performing performative capacity. Having explored some ways in which conceptions of the flow of time and calendar technologies can be used to help legitimize regimes and regime change, we turn in the next chapters to exploring how other conceptions of the flow of time—first primitivism, then eschatology—can be used to legitimate calls to resist order and the power that maintains it, inverting these techniques.

4

The Primitivist's Lament

> Everything which is against nature deserves to be branded as monstrous.
>
> —*Tertullian, De Corona*

I have shown how shaping time aids contingency management and highlights capacity. And I have shown how time can be shaped to evoke forms of accepted order, normalizing innovation. Shaped time continually reentrenches forms of order too. In the absence of renewed conflict, temporal order grows familiar and may pass beyond notice. In these and other ways, techniques of shaping time take their place among the tools available to political leaders who seek to legitimate political innovations or to reinforce and reinvigorate a political order.

But familiarity may breed not complacency but contempt, and time talk frames the politics of delegitimation too. All human order requires constraint and all constraint is achieved through domination, a threat or exertion of force. For some, political order, because always ultimately reliant on force, can never be just. If structured time can aid the legitimation of order, those who reject the justice of enforced order may find, in time, a rhetorical opportunity of their own. Where order is shored up and legitimated by structured time, undermining structured time may help undermine human order. Where shaped time naturalizes order, its subversion may denaturalize order. To achieve this, a political actor may seek to uncouple the experience of political order from underlying self-justifying orders, and invert or destroy claims to capacity. If time is a stealth carrier of order, and hence domination, then one ought to seek freedom in the destruction of time-itself, destroying the illusions of legitimacy that time talk helps to construct. In the radical rhetoric of those who seek the destruction of political order, such inverted temporal techniques are common.

Twin conceptions of the flow of time, primitivism and eschatology, are used to create the illusion of an escape from time, which serves as a proxy for an escape from order, domination, and alienation. Primitivism glances back to a time before time, and eschatology longs for a time coming, when time will come to an end. These may not be coherent elements of a substantive argument or ideology. But they work as rhetorical frames that increase the power of arguments and ideologies to spark or quell political behavior. The aim of this and the next chapter is to illuminate these rhetorical techniques.

Generic Indians

Early in 1992, *Brother Eagle, Sister Sky*, a children's book advocating environmental stewardship, spent seventeen weeks on the *New York Times* bestseller list. The book features illustrations of radiant Plains Indians accompanied by words that the illustrator, Susan Jeffers, claimed she adapted and abridged from a speech of Chief Seattle (more properly "Sealth") of the Squamish and Duwamish Nations (1797–1866). Jeffers describes him as "one of the bravest and most respected chiefs of the Northwest Nations."[1] According to Jeffers, at a poignant moment in a land-treaty negotiation with the government, "with a commanding presence and eyes that mirrored the great soul that lived within, the Chief rose to speak . . . in a resounding voice." He asked, "How can you buy the sky? . . . How can you own the rain and the wind? . . . Hear my voice and the voice of my ancestors. . . . What will happen when the buffalo are all slaughtered?"[2]

On May 3, 1992, the book was removed from the bestseller list and reclassified from "Nonfiction" to "Advice, How-to and Miscellaneous."[3] The reclassification came in the wake of a *New York Times* report that the speech on which Jeffers based her text was in fact the work of a Hollywood screenwriter. In the screenwriter's improbable version, Sealth says, "I have seen a thousand rotting buffaloes on the prairie, left by the white man who shot them from a passing train. I am a savage and do not understand how the smoking iron horse can be made more important than the buffalo that we kill only to stay alive."[4] While we know Sealth did give a speech, historians concur there is no reliable evidence of what he said. The screenwriter had himself drawn on a speech attributed to Sealth by a Dr. Henry Smith, who claimed to have transcribed and translated it from decades-old notes taken at the treaty talk. The time lag and other details raise accuracy questions, but more significantly, nothing supports the doctor's contention that he was even present at the negotiation. On these bases, scholars have concluded that the speech is likely an entire fabrication, embellished and repeated by generations of non-Native Americans.[5] Yet, the assumption that it is genuine stubbornly persists in the face of the by now often published and reiterated facts.[6] In her defense, Jeffers claimed that what was important was that "Native American people lived this philosophy."[7] And of course the message of environmental conservation is a sound one, but what purpose is served, if the message is sound on its own merits, by placing the words in Sealth's mouth?

This case is peculiar, but by no means isolated. Consider Keep America Beautiful's famous Crying Indian ad campaign from 1971. In the television version, an Indian paddles a canoe up a choked and polluted river toward a group of factories belching smoke in the distance. The camera zooms in from this scene of environmental devastation to show the man's tear-stained face, as we can see in the poster version printed on the next page. The Ad Council cites the Crying Indian campaign as "one of the most memorable and successful campaigns in advertising history."[8] But again, there is no notable relationship between actual Native Americans and the campaign. Even the actor, known as Iron Eyes Cody, was Sicilian by birth. He simply liked to dress up as a Native American.

On the face of it, the deployment of these generic figures serves the rhetorical construction of ethos. But the mechanism is not straightforward. In communicating an environmental message, why would aboriginal voices be more compelling than the voices of, for instance, European-, African-, or Asian-American environmentalists? True, environmental holism features prominently among the sacred beliefs and practices of many Native American cultures, creating a perception of spiritual bona fides, but spiritual or religious practice gives no such authority in parallel cases. It is inconceivable, for instance, that a secular food bank would use an actor dressed up as a Mormon bishop in its ads. While tithing and storehouse provision for the poor and needy feature prominently among Mormon sacred practices and, like care for the environment, present a wholesome practice on their own merits, nobody beyond his congregation thinks the Mormon bishop commands a special ethos with respect to support of the poor on that account. A bishop and an elder may both advocate the spiritual wisdom of a universally sound practice and claim special knowledge with respect to the importance of that practice. But the

Some people have a deep, abiding respect for the natural beauty that was once this country.

And some people don't.

An ad from Keep America Beautiful's Crying Indian campaign, 1971.
(Courtesy of Keep America Beautiful and the Ad Council Archives, University of Illinois)

sort of ethotic representation we see in the case of generic aboriginality seems absurd in the case of a generic Mormon bishop. Spiritual insight cannot, on its own, be the source of this ethotic power.

There is also the matter of these Indian figures' genericism. As one reviewer described Jeffers's work, the illustrations feature "a stock of characters . . . from Sioux Central Casting, complete with Plains ponies and tipis (and one incongruous birchbark canoe lifted from the Algonquians)."[9] And Sealth, in the Pacific Northwest, probably never saw a buffalo, never mind witnessed their slaughter. Sealth has been stripped of his particularity. Many actual environmentalists are aboriginal: why employ fakes? Such work uses not only aboriginality but specifically *generic*—and hence necessarily fake—aboriginality. Not just despite but because of the generic nobility deployed, the practice perpetuates stereotypes that prevent individuals and groups from constructing and reconstructing their own narrative identities.

The ethotic power of these strange and unsettling stereotypes, I contend, stems not from their aboriginality per se but rather from the invocation of a primitivist temporal frame. *Primitivism* names a cluster of views that associate proximity to nature with moral purity while, conversely, increasing order and civilization is associated with corruption. Human essence, human *nature* is that which precedes interference or development. It follows that development is corruption because it draws us out of our natural or original condition. Primitivism thus trades on a conflation of "nature" in the sense of true character and "nature" in the sense of an environment unbuilt or unstructured.[10] In drawing us away from nature, from the native condition, civilization and the order on which it rests draw us away from our essential being. To be clear, the word *primitive* in this context refers to the historical subjects of the doctrine of primitivism, those whose mode of life is conducted in a less built environment. Strictly speaking, by this definition, no person and no actual culture could accurately be described as "primitive" because every cluster of humanity is highly built socially, politically, culturally, and in terms of conceptual scaffolding. Hence, when I refer to "primitive" or "civilized" (by which I will mean a society whose mode of life is conducted in a highly built environment), I will always mean the words in inferred quotation marks. The primitive is always an imagined generic type, never an actual particular person or culture.

As a doctrine in the history of ideas, the notion that a peak of perfection, moral or otherwise, characterizes human beings at their origin, in communities unbuilt and in harmony with their natural surroundings, is widespread. Versions of primitivism were central to the doctrines of the Cynics of Greece and the Stoics of Rome. Other versions appear in Vedic texts, in imperial Chinese philosophy, and throughout ancient Mesopotamia.[11] For the Assyrians, a long, gradual loss of knowledge had accompanied the rise of their civilization.[12] In the Judeo-Christian tradition, it is the acquisition of knowledge that, suddenly, precipitates a moral fall when Adam and Eve taste the forbidden fruit. In the Europe of the Middle Ages, stories of earthly Edens, like those of the country of Prester John, inevitably emphasize simplicity and goodness rather than technological, political, or intellectual sophistication. Rousseau framed his argument for the inverse connection between civilization and peace, morality, and happiness in primitivist terms. Related notions engaged artists of the late nineteenth and early twentieth century like Gauguin and Picasso. Where there is a highly built environment there is often primitivism, which continues to frame a variety of contemporary political agendas, and not just on the fringes.[13]

Lovejoy and Boas, in their monumental studies of ancient and medieval forms of primitivism, catalogue variants of two key types, often conflated: chronological and cultural. Chronological primitivism is the view that "the most excellent condition of human life or best state of the world in general" occurred sometime in the past.[14] This time may have been at the beginning, somewhere along an undulating wave, or at a point along a predictable cycle that may or may not repeat. Cultural primitivism, by contrast, is a claim about the (lack of) moral quality of civilization in general. All such views rest on a conception of the flow of time that is in this respect entropic: whether things unravel in a spiral or linear fashion, the more we have advanced in the trappings of civilization, the lower we have sunk.

I contend that, in the political sphere, primitivism's ultimate function is to associate political order with domination and alienation, and hence to associate order with loss. Primitivist rhetoric does this by implying that our natural condition is a generic condition, free of particularities. Any determination that brings us out of this condition entails loss and alienation. A set of determinations that result from human choice or action constitute a human order that negates, by its very existence, every alternative order. So primitivism stands opposed to any nonnatural or nonspontaneous order. In parallel, the primitive is also fundamentally opposed to politics: what is generic has no capacity for agency or action because action is choice, and choice both relies upon particularity and, in turn, creates determinations. Without action and agency, there is no politics. Since any order in the primitive condition is natural and self-enforcing, domination is unknown. Without action, without politics, the primitive remains not just free of domination but stalled or undulating in slow time, that is, a time opposed to event-oriented or chronotic time.

The enemy of the primitive is the intrusion of chronotic time, of mechanisms of human order. An external, violent intervention imposes a constraining temporal-physical environment, alienating people from nature and its rhythms. Through constraint, human order generates domination. Only in the condition of abstraction is there freedom from domination, from politics. But order is constraint and necessitates more constraint. There is only one rule in the Garden of Eden, but countless laws in the Torah.

Genericism and Nature

The importance of genericism to the primitivist frame is evident from its reliance on abstraction. This becomes clear in contrast with an Aristotelian perspective on development. For Aristotle, the highest form of human personality is to become a person of virtue and sound judgment, engaged in a measured way in politics and philosophy. This is achieved after years of careful self-cultivation and exercising the faculty of judgment: choosing and acting. From this teleological perspective, commonality of characteristics among those who achieve this florescence grows from diverse practical and particular experiences. These continue to animate and modulate the exercise of those characteristics. All will share in good judgment, but each will exercise it in her own way, growing from her own particular experiences. Without particularity, no judgment could be cultivated, and this fruition takes place uniquely for each individual by means of an interactive flow of events and actions.

But primitivism invokes a pseudo-Platonic sense of essence. Rather than a path through particularity to achieve human fruition, primitivism implies that human nature is a pure instantiation of formality that, other than its specific extension, has no particular characteristics. A stable human essence is human nature, and that essence is what we have in common, in abstraction, not what we are able to become through self-cultivation. We are true to ourselves at the point of origin. It is in this way that the generic comes to be conflated with the natural. If pure humanity is found in this condition of instantiated abstraction (that is, a physical instance of the generic), then any determination or particularity is corruption of that essential condition. So to maintain this purity requires that we remain in a condition of temporal and developmental suspension. Both the generic and the primitive therefore must exist in a mode of temporality in which nothing, or hardly anything, happens. As an abstraction with no singular features, what is primitive can have neither agency nor the capacity for change. It intervenes in the actually existing world only through the deployment of its *semiotic* power by an actually existing particular agent. The primitive can be made to exhort, but it cannot act.

By virtue of its abstraction, actualized in its genericism, what is primitive is subject neither to development nor to degeneration. It thus becomes important not only that the primitive be generic but that the natural environment in which primitive figures dwell remain in a condition of possibility too. From a conceptual perspective, how could something generic *construct* without thereby becoming particular? From a rhetorical perspective, the rhetor who deploys a primitivist frame conflates this natural figure with his savage environment, his habitat, of which he is very much a constituent part, not just an inhabitant. To build that environment in any permanent or semi-permanent way would be to develop and therefore corrupt it. To be drawn out of the natural and into the built environment is precisely corruption. What was once a space and a condition of potentiality would then be straitjacketed by its determinate boundaries.

So the true primitive resists politics because there can be no internally generated event that does not, at the same time, corrupt and destroy. The moment the primitive emerges into politics as an agent, beyond the semiotic power of its sheer idea, it ceases to be primitive because it ceases to be generic, pure. The primitive is impervious to physical development, too, because this is a corruption of the physical space of which the primitive is a natural element. A corruption of space is a corruption of the inhabitants of that space also.

This combination of benign presence, resistance to events, and slow temporality is a feature of both the generic and the primitive, which reflected (and perhaps fed into) elements of early anthropologists' descriptions of the lives of "primitive" people: in slow time, bound to the undulating cycles of nature. Anthropologists described cultures as existing in a state of suspension in a chronic condition of cultural (and sometimes individual) lethargy. In Evans-Pritchard's description, for the Nuer, "the distance between the beginning of the world and the present day remains unalterable."[15] Lévi-Strauss describes "cold" societies for which history and events are alien: "Nothing has been going on since the appearance of the ancestors," he claims, "except events whose recurrence periodically effaces their particularity."[16] And Gurvich, as I noted above, attributes to the French peasantry an "inclination to move in retarded time turned in on itself," while Geertz once described Balinese time as "a motionless present, a vectorless now."[17] Rites and ceremonies have been interpreted as means of reinhabiting sacred, stopped time.[18] Some, including Lévi-Strauss and Evans-Pritchard, have explicitly associated this condition of freedom from events or freedom from history with a condition of freedom more generally. "Nuer," Evans-Pritchard tells us, "are fortunate."[19]

To maintain this luck necessitates ferocious resistance to the incursion of events. To resist events is to resist degeneration and decay, and this means that the continuation of an existence in stalled or slow, cyclic time is crucial. Indeed, here is the crux of the moral confrontation captured in the deployment of generic aboriginality in these examples of popular environmental politics. The passage of linear chronotic time is the intrusion of the particular—particular action, particular events—into the course of what is natural, cyclic, suspended. The linear and chronotic is the bringer of decay and death. Hence, the primitivist temporal frame does its semiotic work not merely by reference to the generic abstraction of aboriginality or of the primitive, but specifically through the contrast of this abstraction with the intrusion of the chronotic and degenerative, objects associated with machines and with speed but also with rust and dirt. Consider, in this light, the juxtaposition of the Crying Indian with the factory, Chief Sealth with the train.

This is how the primitive comes to represent the radically free, the space of nondomination that does rhetorical work. Any form of particularity is always and necessarily a form of negation and loss: whether it is the individual's choice of a path of action, the shape of the collective (political) order that necessitates maintenance, or the particularity of the construction of a physical space in a specific shape (the layout of buildings and roads). Any nonnatural or nonspontaneous order, and any determinate path or action, necessarily involves closing off every other possibility. Any actuality is loss—loss of freedom, loss of potential. And any constructed order necessitates domination for its preservation, ruling out alternatives, normally by force. Freedom exists only in a condition of abstraction, on this view, only in the primitive or original condition.

Ultimately, *loss* drives primitivism, the loss of the freedom of abstraction, the freedom of space to move and be without being in particular. As Spinoza wrote to his friend Jarigh Jelles, "Determinatio est negatio."[20] Whenever there is order—physical, conceptual, political, or psychical—there is determination, and order instantiates a shape, a set of boundaries, that negates whatever it is not, but could have been. Determination is always the negation of possibility. In giving shape, providing the instantiation of boundaries, physical or psychical, we necessarily constrain. All functioning human societies are necessarily ordered and constraining, and all must use the ultimate threat of force to maintain order and promote (self-)constraint. And so every order is, necessarily, ultimately, a dominating order, despite tacit or even explicit consent. Primitivist framing appeals to the sense that physically-psychically open space, a space that is all potential, without negation, is the space of *real* freedom, where the whole of our needs and experience of the world is immediate.

Thus the purpose of primitivist rhetoric is not insight or knowledge—it rests on a genericism that is necessarily false. Rather, primitivism frames a mirror of shame. The mirror is held up by a generic entity true to human essence and uncorrupted by civilization. Gaze at the "noble savage," uncorrupted, true to his essential self, and see, in the mirror he holds, how ignoble you are. Glancing between the degenerate reflection in that mirror and the exotic, primitive other who holds it emphasizes the deformity of the civilized. And so it does not ultimately matter, for rhetorical purposes, whether or not these humans are generic, or whether or not they accurately reflect a mode of life. Their function is only to show, by contrast with the generic ideal, our own degeneracy. This is what makes the facts irrelevant to the success of the primitivist temporal frame.

The peculiar cases of the Crying Indian and Chief Sealth's speech now make sense. The generic aboriginals featured are not the protagonists, nor are they the subjects. Rather, these constructions carry the *frame* of the environmental message. While legitimation worked in part through frame alignment with an already accepted form of order, here primitivism frames the corruption of order as such. Both genericism and the form of aboriginality exploited by what we can call (with some violence) the white imagination here are mutually reinforced by their situation in primitivism's particular kind of temporality: both the generic and this constructed aboriginality exist outside of regular chronotic time. These are evocative metaphors, not people. The Crying Indian constructed for the Keep America Beautiful campaign exhorts by means of his very presence; he does not even speak. Chief Sealth's words at a time and place, at a specific political event, are erased in favor of generic words that do not belong to him particularly.

Radical Primitivism

The examples above use primitivism the way advertisers use depictions of luxurious surroundings to make a brand of scotch look desirable. Everyone knows it is not luxury itself on offer but a feeling of luxury-by-proxy—at a fraction of the cost. Messages of environmental responsibility in a primitivist frame often have a parallel structure. While nobody is called by the tactics described above to reestablish a primitive bucolic idyll, the emotional experience of righteous purity implied by the frame comes at low personal cost: pick up your litter, don't waste. These examples, restricted to localized marketing techniques, help illustrate the theoretical structure that makes primitivism work rhetorically. This structure can now be put to work in analyzing forms of radical politics that deploy a primitivist frame by unsettling the very idea of a self-justifying order.

In previous chapters, I argued that time technologies laden with political messaging are found in the toolbox of legitimation. They order every aspect of daily life while carrying innovation concealed in the familiar. To delegitimate, one can invert this technique, drawing attention to how mechanical time technologies create and normalize a corrupted order alien to nature and its rhythms. Nature's mechanical antagonist is revealed, in this political landscape, not just as an invader—a train or factory with noise and smoke—but as a colonizer. This machine serves a human order that is corrupt and intolerable. The juxtaposition is emotive, not rational, but it aptly serves its rhetorical purpose.

To generate this frame, a political agent can replace the intrusion of industrial machines in nature with the intrusion of the mechanical clock in nature's rhythms. Clocks, in this narrative, create order by synchronizing and disciplining the work of bodies, rendering those bodies optimally productive. In this extreme form of dominating order, humans as extensions of machines are reduced to their productive capacity per unit of time. As Marx said, under capitalism, "Time is everything, man is nothing: he is no more than the carcass of time."[21] The clock, as itself a machine, not only intrudes in natural rhythms, is the very mechanism that, by means of imposing order, negates freedom. As the carcass of time, we become the literal embodiment of disciplined order. No longer a virtual association, the radical psychic and physical freedom primitivism laments seems to demand a more substantial response. In this way, primitivism can be put to work as a frame that gestures ultimately toward eschatology and revolution. To illustrate how this frame can work in strategies of delegitimation and how this impacts debates of the radical and progressive left, we turn to the Marxist social historian E. P. Thompson.[22]

In his important essay "Time, Work Discipline, and Industrial Capitalism," Thompson argued that the ascendance of the mechanical clock tracked the ascendance of the industrial revolution. Thompson juxtaposed a slow, bucolic time of task-oriented peasant work with the mechanized, disciplined, time-oriented work of the factory. Mechanical, alien rhythms replaced natural ones, and synchronization and discipline meant work was less intertwined with leisure and sociality. With the aid of a Puritan work ethic, which Thompson argues paved the way for mass acceptance of these changes, clock time fundamentally changed not just the essence of work but the souls of workers too.[23] But while it is incontestable that industrial work discipline is degrading, Thompson's claim that a new "time sense" arose from the diffusion of clocks alongside the rise of industrialization rests on consequential errors. Nonetheless, the aspersions on clock time play an important role in Thompson's argument. Clocks, because they appear to oppose nature and "natural time," aid in the construction of a primitivist frame. That frame creates a powerful lament for the loss of a mode of life in which only nature, not other people, constrains us. As with the deployments of localized primitivism in the earlier examples, empirical and normative concerns do not detract from the power of his argument, framed in primitivist rhetoric, and it is ultimately the eminent rhetorical power of Thompson's work that is of interest here. The primitivist frame, because it associates nature with freedom and order with domination, challenges the bona fides of any progressive narrative that would attempt to harness political order (and indeed clock time) in the service of incremental improvement. But primitivism can offer no way back, leaving a choice between the rejection of enforced order in the form of eschatological revolution or else lament.

For Thompson, task-oriented work is the delineation of a day's work by the tasks that must be accomplished. Because it is the task and not the hour that defines the workday, "there is no great sense of conflict between labour and 'passing the time of day'" and no great sense of urgency, either, so task orientation is "more humanly comprehensible" and lends itself to a fluid movement between "'work' and 'life.'"[24] Time-oriented work, by contrast, delimits the workday by means of the hour. It aims to wring maximum work from the worker within set hours, since the worker's labor is purchased in units of time. Time-oriented work means one's hours become interchangeable, become a unit of exchange. Nature and natural necessity are no longer relevant, replaced by a clock-regimented mechanical work rhythm. Task orientation is "natural," marked out by natural phenomena: the tides in fishing communities, the rising and setting of the sun in farming communities: these are the rhythms of daily life in the countryside or by the sea, natural rhythms. Task-oriented work is irregular and varied, characterized by intense bursts of activity followed by stretches of idleness, illustrated in the workday a farmer-weaver recorded in his journal (1782–83). The farmer notes how much and when he is engaged in harvesting and threshing, and when and how much he is able to weave. These activities are punctuated by, for instance, helping a cow birth a calf, walking to town to get medicine for the cow, mending clothing, and so on. What this man does each day is determined by what needs to be done, and in particular, by what nature demands and allows.[25]

Time-oriented work, by contrast, is detached from its natural meaning and context. It becomes susceptible to commodification.[26] To enable commodification, labor needs to be separable into time units. Hence, Thompson claims, time-oriented work went hand in hand with the diffusion of clocks. But chronotic time, which removes the peasant from the necessities of nature and subjects him to the necessities of other men, deforms him, ultimately rendering him a means, an extension of the machines with which he works. Working according to the clock, Thompson claims, instituted "a new human nature."[27] The change in the way working people understood work and leisure was internalized, resulting in a "radical restructuring of man's social nature and working habits."[28] The move to clock time becomes a site of conflict and contestation, as the capitalist attempts to instill a sense of proper order on those whose labor feeds his profits.[29] The intrusion of chronotic time, here literally embodied by the clock, alienates the peasant from natural work in nature's own time. This new form of work is characterized by subjection to human domination. Hence, this alienation from nature enables a permanent denigration of human beings. That denigration is made possible by the more rigid order, which facilitates external domination by naturalizing it, just as calendars were used to naturalize and so legitimize political change. Thompson points out how we hardly think to question clock time, it has so successfully colonized our mode of being in the world.[30] Calling out the clock as an agent of domination frames Thompson's message that subjection to order imposed by other people, as opposed to the order of nature, deforms humanity.

Thompson's is a powerful narrative that "has been taken as *the* standard account of the history of clock time, [and] in the academic community at large, ["Time, Work Discipline, and Industrial Capitalism"] has been taken by non-historians as *the* historical account . . . not just as an intellectual baseline for further research but as something approaching the fact of the matter."[31] Yet a mass of empirical evidence raises grave doubts about his work's accuracy and it faces conceptual and normative difficulties too. But these challenges barely impact the power of Thompson's argument because of its brilliant primitivist framing. A look at these normative and empirical charges helps illuminate how the frame works as a mechanism of delegitimating enforced order while also illuminating what is at stake between radical or primitivist and, for example, progressive rhetorical frames in leftist politics.

It would be silly to dispute that industrial and wage work can be oppressive and dehumanizing or that productive work for oneself can be deeply satisfying. And it may certainly be true that a healthy relationship with leisure has been undermined by the moral demonizing of idleness. But is Thompson right about the central role of the diffusion of the mechanical clock in these processes? The mass of empirical evidence suggests not. Clock time was widespread among all social classes prior to industrialization, and the diffusion of mechanical time pieces met a preexisting need. The clock was neither necessary to nor sufficient for the changes in work rhythm he describes.

As I argued in chapter 1, there always exists a multiplicity of times and time senses that people use depending on their aims. Though one conception of time may dominate in a particular context, it need not replace other conceptions useful in other contexts. A conception of time aptly captured by a mechanical clock easily coexists with one oriented toward nature-driven tasks. The sundown at the new moon may govern the meetings of a star-watching club whose members may use atomic clock time in a lab and a mechanical watch to catch a bus home. The notion that we have a "time sense," a unified orientation toward time, is not sustainable. Hence neither is the claim that one replaced the other.

Thompson claimed industrialization, by means of the mechanical clock, changed what it means to be human, bringing the loss of natural rhythms of work and rest.[32] But he inverted the permeation of clock time and the rise of industry. Clock time, he asserted, "belonged in the mid-[eighteenth]century still to the gentry, the masters, the farmers and the tradesmen," and time-keeping devices were markers of affluence; "the intricacy of design, and the preference for precious metal, were in deliberate accentuation of [this]."[33] A widening range of scholarship on the dissemination of clock time contests this: people of all classes and in all lines of work, rural and urban, were regularly in the company of clocks, coveting and owning them long before industrialization.[34] We know this from the dating of public clocks in Europe, which were widespread as early as 1300, and from the frequency with which clocks are mentioned in literature, in court testimony, and in parish records, which establish the urgency of their repair.[35] Notably, this urgency was explicitly tied, as early as 1620, to "the keeping of fit hours for . . . apprentices, servants, and workmen."[36] Work by the clock was no innovation of industrial production, even in the countryside, and private clock ownership, Lorna Weatherill and Peter King have demonstrated, was widespread among the laboring classes well before industrialization was entrenched. In a study of the spread of consumer goods in the very early modern period (1670–1720) based

THE PRIMITIVIST'S LAMENT

on probate inventories, Weatherill found that clocks were widely preferred to other goods, even when more expensive. This was true of rich and poor, of city dwellers and the denizens of small villages alike.[37] While Thompson notes, "Even labourers, once or twice in their lives, might have an unexpected windfall, and blow it on a watch," he maintains that it was at the turn of the nineteenth century that "the general diffusion of clocks and watches is occurring . . . at the exact moment when the industrial revolution demanded a greater synchronization of labour."[38] Yet it was a full century earlier, between 1675 and 1715, that private clock ownership tripled, with roughly one-third of households sampled across England owning a clock by 1715, and some 90 percent of wealthy London households having one.[39] King's study of pauper inventories showed that already in the early eighteenth century, 20 percent of the very poorest Britons owned a time-keeping device.[40] Clocks were so generally pervasive that, as Glennie and Thrift have painstakingly demonstrated in gathering this evidence, "it is emphatically *not* the case that 'clock time' was created by . . . industrial work discipline in the late eighteenth century."[41] Cheap, precision clocks were invented because there was already demand for them; they did not reshape notions of time but rather served to fill a preexisting desire for an affordable, convenient device that could measure time as it was, for certain specific purposes, already understood.[42]

The idea of measuring time in regular, somewhat artificial subunits long precedes the diffusion of mechanical clocks. When people need to coordinate, or time, or measure equal shares—for instance, in cooking or experimenting, in a court or legislature, or in preindustrial forms of shift work—they find or create a suitable device to meet these aims: a human pulse, hourglasses, water clocks, sundials, oil clocks, or candle clocks. All of these devices use something in nature

THE PRIMITIVIST'S LAMENT

to mark the passing of time—whether fire or water, sand or sun—just as atomic or pendulum clocks use natural oscillations. But they each use elements of nature to measure out units in temporal abstraction. Sundials use the sun, true, but they use it to measure off artificial hours of human invention. Such devices serve coordination, equality, punctuality, and synchronization, all of which have their origins prior to the diffusion of mechanical clocks, even if their use is intensified with increased industrialization and urbanization.

Coordination, synchronization, and measurement needs precede the diffusion of mechanical clocks and were, before that diffusion, met by a variety of more or less mechanical solutions, using more or less abstract units to mark and measure. But mechanical clocks meet these needs dramatically better than these previous technologies, and it is this, not a novel time sense, that must account for their rapid diffusion. Of course people will prefer a mechanical clock, once within reach, because it works when it is cloudy, unlike sundials; it is lightweight and portable, unlike water clocks; it is less fragile than an hourglass; and it is more reliable than the candle clocks sometimes used historically to measure out shift work, and apt to blow out. The measurement of time in regular semi-abstract units for purposes such as synchronization is already in use wherever it is useful. The mechanical clock is simply a better technology for these purposes.

In several Late Antique mosaics found near Antakya, we find men glancing worriedly at a sundial. On one such mosaic, the inscription reads, "The ninth hour has caught up," while a figure on another sundial mosaic says, "Run to dinner."[43] Would these satirical figures not have snapped up a pocket watch if one had been available in the fourth century CE? Imagine the delight of Galileo had he been able to conduct his experiments with a mechanical stopwatch instead of his own pulse. People had notions of punctuality, abstract regularity, and

THE PRIMITIVIST'S LAMENT

Sundial mosaic found near Antioch (now Antakya, Turkey). The caption reads, "The ninth hour has caught up." (De Agostini Picture Library/Bridgeman Images)

(context-dependent) efficiency well before the diffusion of the mechanical clock. There are so many uses for such a technology beyond the context of labor, never mind factory labor, that its rapid diffusion should not be surprising. That abstract time keeping was already an integral if intermittent part of peoples' lives explains, as Glennie and Thrift argue convincingly, "the otherwise puzzlingly rapid diffusion of clocks and watches between 1660 and 1730."[44]

THE PRIMITIVIST'S LAMENT

It would be hard to deny that clock time was, and continues to be, a companion of work discipline, as anyone who has ever "clocked in" will confirm. But mechanical clock time is neither necessary to nor sufficient for changes to labor discipline. That a time sense oriented toward mechanical measurement is not sufficient to account for changes to labor discipline is evident from the fact that this time sense—and indeed the widespread ownership of the means of effectively measuring it—existed long before labor discipline became pervasive. Furthermore, work traditionally aligned with natural time markers is still aligned this way, despite the diffusion of clocks. Just having a mechanical clock around is not sufficient to prompt a shift in comportment toward leisure and efficiency.

The key driver in labor discipline may be instead the very fact of selling units of labor, which is to say *employment*. Thompson notes that whenever someone is employed by someone else, there is a distinction between the time that has been purchased by the employer and the time the employee still "owns." This is why Thompson is speaking only of a transition pertinent to a very specific group of people: "the independent peasant or craftsman," excluding even his wife or children, whose time already belongs to the head of household and whose efficiency is already *his* concern.[45] Thompson is speaking about those men who used to farm or fish for subsistence (close to nature) but who now sell their labor in time units. It seems plausible that it is a shift into mass employment and away from ownership of one's own means of production that ultimately drives labor discipline, not mechanical time keeping.

Could one still say, though, that mechanical time keeping, if not sufficient, is at least necessary for achieving the dominating effects of labor discipline? But time units of labor for sale can be measured in any one of a number of other ways, using any one of a number of other time-keeping devices. Indeed, as Thompson himself claims, "the timing of work can be done independently of any [mechanical] time-piece."[46] Even the need for greater synchronization of labor as industrialization progresses can be accomplished without *mechanical* clocks. So long as there is some means of coordinating start time, synchronization can take place in accordance with markers internal to the factory, even by means of the regular movements of machines themselves, without a mechanical clock. This is true at least until Ford and Taylorism hit the scene much later, at the beginning of the twentieth century, and even then it is more the stopwatch than the mechanical clock that comes into play.

One can exploit labor without mechanical clocks. Nor is a mechanical clock necessary for the development of "mercantilist doctrines as to the necessity for holding down wages as a preventative against idleness."[47] One does not need a mechanical clock to divide labor into units of time for sale, and one does not need a mechanical clock to observe and rail against "idleness" or to promote "time-thrift" or even punctuality.[48] Thompson concedes that "there was [nothing] radically new in preaching industry or in the moral critique of idleness," and to claim that there may be "a new insistence, a firmer accent" on such things bears no intrinsic connection to the diffusion of clocks.[49] None of these changes in the moral conditions of work, however terrible, is distinctly related to mechanical clocks. Though clocks came to be present everywhere, the connection between their diffusion and changes to work discipline is contingent.[50] Their rapid diffusion is on account of their expansive usefulness, even prior to industrialization. It shows that mechanical clocks marked time in a way many people already found familiar and useful.

Thompson is surely right that the move from self-employment and family management of the means of domestic production toward mass employment and wage labor, coupled with a heightened sense of the immorality of idleness, led to a changed relationship to leisure and an increase in alienation from nature. And of course wage labor leaves one vulnerable to domination and exploitation. But the role of the mechanical clock in this process is not established.

There is one more critical element to observe before we can draw the pieces together in the context of primitivism, and this is the moral demotion of fairness. Thompson's association of task- and time-oriented work with natural and clock time respectively hides salient justice-related considerations. Arguably, all work is ultimately task-oriented: it involves doing some specified thing, some task or tasks. But some tasks come to a close of themselves while others do not, and in Thompson's essay, task work seems sometimes to slip too easily into self-delimited work, and then into work necessitated by nature.[51] These things do not necessarily go together. Building a wall is not a nature-driven task, although it has a discrete end point. Caring for infants is a nature-driven task without an end point, at least in the medium term. Nor is one form of work preindustrial and the other industrial, though the relative proportions of people primarily engaged in bounded versus unbounded tasks may change with economic forms. Certainly, there were preindustrial but unbounded modes of work, such as being in service, keeping a military watch or being a soldier at war, entrepreneurship of various sorts, and politics. And self-delimiting tasks, such as masonry or tax accounting, may be natural or artificial, pre- or postindustrial. Many forms of work combine elements of both. The key distinction is not whether the work is task- or time-oriented but rather whether the task has an evident end point. This is because where work is not self-delimiting, some form of clock—and for purposes of delimitation, it does not matter whether it is the setting sun or a mechanical variety—calls out the line between work and rest.

Here the issue of fairness arises. Thompson suggests that work and leisure were interspersed in a way that was "more humanly comprehensible" prior to industrialization, but he already concedes that he is talking only about male heads of peasant households here.[52] In a fascinating passage, Thompson cites the washerwoman turned poet Mary Collier, whom I cite at greater length here to illustrate the case. Collier addresses a lament to menfolk, describing the unequal burden peasant women carry, not only through what we now call the second and third shift but through the day's work in the field:

> But in the Work we freely bear a Part,
> And what we can, perform with all our Heart.
> To get a Living we so willing are,
> Our tender Babes into the Field we bear,
> And wrap them in our Cloaths to keep them warm,
> While round about we gather up the Corn;
> And often unto them our Course do bend,
> To keep them safe, that nothing them offend:
> Our Children that are able, bear a Share
> In gleaning Corn, such is our frugal Care.
> When Night comes on, unto our Home we go,
> Our Corn we carry, and our Infant too;
> Weary, alas! but 'tis not worth our while
> Once to complain, or *rest at ev'ry Stile*;
> We must make haste, for when we Home are come,
> Alas! we find our Work but just begun;
> So many Things for our Attendance call,
> Had we ten Hands, we could employ them all.
> Our Children put to Bed, with greatest Care
> We all Things for your coming Home prepare:

You sup, and go to Bed without delay,
And rest yourselves till the ensuing Day;
While we, alas! but little Sleep can have,
Because our froward Children cry and rave;
Yet, without fail, soon as Day-light doth spring,
We in the Field again our Work begin
And there, with all our Strength, our Toil renew,
Till *Titan*'s golden Rays have dry'd the Dew;
Then home we go unto our Children dear,
Dress, feed, and bring them to the Field with care.
Were this your Case, you justly might complain
That Day nor Night you are secure from Pain;

Our Toil and Labour's daily so extreme,
That we have hardly ever *Time to dream*.[53]

Collier describes task-oriented work that does not come to a close of itself, and that certainly does not allow for the easy intermingling of work and leisure activities Thompson valorizes. But Thompson finds nothing wrong here. It is tolerable to women, he claims, because caring work is "necessary and inevitable."[54] That is to say, nature, not the ordering impositions of other people, makes peasant women work much harder. And because this is "natural," uneven access to leisure and sleep is not domination.

This was clearly of no comfort to Collier herself, nor to a mother testifying to a commission on industrial work conditions in 1844: "Then when I came home in the evening everything was to do after the day's labour, and I was so tired I had no heart for it."[55] Rather, Collier emphasizes the injustice of this unequal burden of work and thereby illustrates the ease with which systemic inequality and domination

THE PRIMITIVIST'S LAMENT

can come to seem natural to those who benefit from it. I have argued above that all work is task-oriented but that some is self-delimiting and some not. Non-self-delimiting work is often the work of caring, and this work falls disproportionately to women, who disproportionately lack leisure time as a consequence.[56] As Oriel Sullivan has argued, it is the clock's limitation of work that enables the enforcement of leisure.[57] The clock serves two justice-oriented purposes in this frame. First, clocks can be used to construct a line, on one side of which waits leisure, where tasks are not self-delimited. Hence, throughout the nineteenth and twentieth centuries, as Thompson himself notes, the clock was a contested ally in labor relations on the shop floor, the mechanism by which shorter and shorter workdays were historically achieved. Second, with respect to labor relations around the kitchen floor, because the clock, deployed in time/work studies, provides a neutral measure, it has become a contested ally in the pursuit of gender equality. Where the workday ends with the clock, leisure begins with the clock. Where the workday ends with a second and third shift of care work, the clock can be used to document, contest, and ideally redistribute this unfair burden. Clocks thus become a key mechanism in establishing objective parameters for claims to equality. Measurement mechanisms are the champion of incremental improvements in equality: they allow for apportioning equal shares of unbounded tasks and hence more equal shares of leisure. Hence, Glennie and Thrift argue that "'clock time' has been as much a liberating as an oppressive force. It has allowed as much [as] it has disciplined. New entities, capacities, and experiences have become possible which did not exist before and there is no reason to believe that all of these have been negative."[58]

The clock now reveals itself as the ally of fairness and equal shares, but it is still the villain of Thompson's story, and this brings us back to temporal-rhetorical frames, legitimation and delegitimation.

Thompson could make his arguments about changes in orientation to leisure and about domination in wage labor without reference to the mechanical clock. And evidently there are empirical and normative concerns with his use of clock time. But by invoking the clock in association with domination, his argument gains rhetorical power. The use of the mechanical clock specifically—which is to say, of a form of timing that Thompson is at pains to show is not "natural"—serves the construction of a primitivist rhetorical frame. Like the other machines to which I make reference earlier in the chapter, in Thompson's narrative, the clock intrudes in nature, it *colonizes* the lives of those who live close to nature, facilitating capitalist domination, enforced human socioeconomic order, and therefore moral and spiritual decline. This is supported by Thompson's appeal to natural necessity as a necessity with which we are supposedly at home, in contrast to the necessities generated by industrial development.[59] Right and wholesome kinds of work are subject to nature's own compulsion, not the dominating compulsion of other people. Freedom consists in harmony with the order of nature, not the economic order of human beings. Machines that disrupt that harmony and are against nature are "monstrous," to use Tertullian's word.

This is a classic instance of primitivism: a bucolic idyll is interrupted by a machine that draws people out of natural, spontaneous order and into a new artificial condition characterized by insupportable domination and suffering. The primitivist frame conjures up a sense of loss exacerbated by Thompson's claims that human nature has been changed, which suggests there is no way back. Then the next step, whether implicit or explicit, is either to be resigned to lament or to actively pursue a different world.

But note how such a pursuit could not, within the primitivist frame, invoke fairness or recommend reforms. What good is an improvement in factory working conditions or more equal access to leisure if clock-ordered labor, alienated from nature, is domination as such? No redemption can be hoped from better policies, calls for justice and fairness, or crusades of reform. Ultimately, the entire system must be rooted out. The use of the mechanical clock in constructing the primitivist frame thus brings to light what is at stake in contests between primitivist and progressive temporal-rhetorical frames in leftist politics. Within a progressive frame, the normative critique of Thompson's work on the basis of fairness shows how clocks have improved lives, shortening workdays and providing a neutral counterforce to prevent exploitation at home as well as at work. Clocks bring hidden inequalities to light, serving justice. In a progressive frame, these are victories, resting on the assumption that fairness, that justice between individual members of distinct groups, is a key moral imperative. Any incremental improvement along these lines is to be applauded. One ought to reject the less in favor of the more fair, the less in favor of the more just.

But these same claims about incremental improvements in justice and fairness, when situated in a primitivist frame, insulate Thompson's argument from the normative critique. For incrementalism, which in a progressive frame looks like victory, is from another vantage a technique of dissimulation. Incremental improvement at best misses the point: more equal domination, more equal corruption, is still domination and corruption. At worst, incrementalism acts actively at cross-purposes as a distraction that undermines the genericism, sometimes cast as universalism, that is central both to the primitivist lament and to the radical eschatological politics to which it sometimes ultimately gives rise. Here is a fine example of how temporal-rhetorical framing fundamentally changes the political reception of a set of facts.

Thompson cannot establish as a matter of fact that clock time, as a mechanism of industrial domination, changed human nature. But the primitivist frame does the work as a matter of feeling. That is, what matters is not what the clock has actually done to human nature but the emotional resonance the clock conjures through the primitivist frame. This partly accounts for the article's continued power, just as people cannot seem to let go of the certainty that it must have been Sealth, not a Hollywood screenwriter, who worried about the fate of the buffalo from a train. An assault against freedom and purity has taken place, the frame aligns with existing assumptions, and so the details are of little consequence. As a moral cri de coeur in which the clock is cast as a force of capitalist exploitation, Thompson's work generates precisely that powerful sense of loss that is the hallmark of effective primitivist framing. The mechanical clock carries the idea of artificiality, alienation, and the intolerability of subjection to human order. That the machine in question is not just a carrier of order but specifically of *temporal* order is surely relevant, recalling to mind that we live in the time of events, of decay, between the event-free time of the primitive and of the eschaton. Then there is the pervasiveness of clock time: it is not just a symbol of imposed order, it is insidious, infusing everything. The very effectiveness of calendar politics at legitimation demonstrates the potential of clock politics with respect to delegitimation. Calendar politics imply the order-based bona fides of regimes. Clock politics claim to expose the fraud of human order and in the process generate a sense of loss—loss of freedom, of orientation, of meaning, of harmony with nature. But what is the purpose of this disposition? Can primitivist rhetoric support some constructive political activity? Or are we left merely with lament?

The Consequences of Lament

Justice in the sense of fairness can be no concern of the primitivist because justice is always dependent on enforced order. Injustice is deviation from a standard, and justice is the meeting or enforcing of right standards. Order is delineated by means of the shape marked out by limits, and just social order is one in which those limits are demarcated by right standards. But even the most just order is reliant on limits and, to the extent anyone actively seeks to breach them, on domination to enforce them. So it may seem at first that a primitivist perspective, which generates a lament for a condition of spontaneous or natural order through abstraction and genericism, must reject justice. Indeed, it is common for primitivists to claim that there was no need for justice in the primitive condition. Many early (and some contemporary) anthropologists claimed, for instance, that "warfare is virtually non-existent among many primitive tribes."[60] A similar bias inflected the archaeology and anthropology of Neolithic sites, where fortifications and smashed skulls were explained away as anything but evidence of pervasive violence. War and injustice are diseases of civilization, of a temporality characterized by action, event, and politics, on this view, a view that often stubbornly resists evidence to the contrary.[61] Like all primitivism, this is dehumanizing. It denies those cultures it co-opts their full humanity, implying that only some aspects of human agency and experience are open to them. As Keeley notes, "The proponents of the pacified past disclaim the idea that all peoples share a common human nature by denying that all societies are capable of using violence to advance their interests."[62]

Even if one were to accept, for the moment, the primitivist assumption that justice was unnecessary in the original condition, what then? No primitivist believes we are still in that condition, and only

THE PRIMITIVIST'S LAMENT

the most extreme imagine we could somehow go back. Perfectibility means that not only the conditions of human life but the condition of human being has changed. In this case, either the nature of living together needs to change fundamentally, or else (or as well) the condition of human being must change again too. Rejecting progressive, incremental politics and the enforced order on which it relies leaves only those options—if they are options—or lament.

Consider, in this regard, Jean-Jacques Rousseau. Rousseau claimed that all of his work was animated by the "great principle that nature made man happy and good, but that society depraves him and makes him miserable.... Vice and error, foreign to his constitution, enter it from outside and insensibly change him."[63] As Rousseau argued in his *Discourse on the Origins of Inequality*, through social intercourse *amour de soi*, or a natural desire for self-preservation, transforms into *amour propre*, or something like self-regard, leading some to dominate others—with devastating results. For Rousseau, we could not regain our lost natural condition since we are *changed*. Perhaps this, rather than our individual, literal birth, is how we ought to understand Rousseau's claim in the opening lines of the *Social Contract* that we are born free yet are everywhere in chains. How, then, could we live in society without domination? Rousseau endeavors through a range of thought experiments to solve this puzzle generated by the primitivist's lament. Can we change sociopolitical life to restore freedom? The *Social Contract* considers this question, designing a republic in which people effectively substitute a collective or public self for their individual selves, the public interest for their individual interest.[64] No one dominates anyone because they are all *one*. Yet this republic's origin lies in deception and manipulation by the lawgiver. And Rousseau says, "Il faudrait des dieux pour donner des lois aux hommes," which is not encouraging.[65] And the result is a society in which social and intellectual life remain tightly constrained. The citizens must live apart, they must be provincial and simple, and they must overcome and reject their individuality and individual interests.[66] Is it still freedom if this mode of living together, because its origin involved deception, was not freely chosen? "In Genoa," Rousseau tells us with approval, "the word *libertas* can be read on the front of prisons and on the chains of galley-slaves."[67] Do Rousseau's citizens, because tricked for their collective good, throw off their chains, just as those in the prisons and galleys are symbols of freedom because they are imprisoned for the good of a collective of which they form a part? Certainly this form of domination is not arbitrary or capricious. But because it relies on so much constraint it seems a weak substitute for the radical freedom of the primitive. And anyway, Rousseau admits that any experiment in republican freedom will ultimately dissolve in a renewal of domination: "Sooner or later the prince must finally oppress the sovereign and break the social treaty. That is the inherent vice which, from the birth of the body politic, tends unceasingly to destroy it, just as old age and death destroy the human body."[68] Setting off from primitivist assumptions down this path with Rousseau, we return to the relentlessness of decay brought by time, and hence arrive at lament.

Rousseau tries another option in *Émile*. Could freedom from domination be restored by the most meticulous upbringing, by standing apart from the polis in a posture of care, being willing to serve others when called but separate nonetheless? To achieve this, every detail of young Émile's upbringing aims to construct a person who has no desire to dominate and who experiences psychic freedom even in the midst of physical constraint. But even were the project of raising Émile sound in itself—and elements of the tutor Jean-Jacques's devotion and control of Émile may generate discomfort—at best, because of the intensity of this approach, only a wealthy few could benefit.[69] It serves the needs of an isolated individual and prepares that individual for a life of social isolation. Fraistat has argued that the lessons of Rousseau's *Émile* could be applied more broadly: "Educating ourselves in caring values and virtues would . . . nurture core capacities essential to freedom as non-domination and robust republican citizenship."[70] But this aim is incremental and progressive. If it were enough to compensate for the loss of a universal, open freedom of the primitive, *Émile* would have been a much shorter book.

Rousseau's designs for an order without domination, or else for a person at home with himself in a world of domination, would apply at best to rare communities or individuals. These designs cannot do without dissimulation nor escape decay. Through a primitivist frame, there is no collective freedom because institutions rely on constraint for their preservation through time and breed forms of domination as they go. Civilization is simply not compatible with radical freedom. Hence, primitivism can never serve a constructive social function: there is no way to build a way of living together that conforms to primitivist normative assumptions. Any attempt to build without constraint and domination will necessarily move that constraint elsewhere, for example, deeper into the psyche.

Moving forward, there are three alternatives. First, one could, with liberal thinkers like Kant and Locke, admit that constraint is not inherently bad so long as we see and recognize it for what it is. Indeed, submission to reasonable constraint and self-constraint is precisely the mark of maturity on these men's views.[71] One could then take the incrementalist route in pursuit of fairness, advocating as much freedom as is compatible with the freedom of others. If, from within the primitivist frame, this is thought (or felt?) an impossible compromise, then one can lament. And if, regardless, one feels compelled not just to lament but to *act*, then primitivist rhetoric may develop into its opposite number, eschatology.

THE PRIMITIVIST'S LAMENT

Once enforced human order itself is characterized as the villain and we recognize that there is no way back to a bucolic past, then we must imagine some means of order's constructive destruction. Some massive force with the capacity to stop time, and to stop those events in time that bring degeneration and decay, must be marshaled for this purpose. Only this massive force can enable a condition of grace, spontaneous order without constraint of any kind. We enter the sphere of a politics of redemption, a politics that promises to restore the condition of slow time, the event-free time of the primitive, while lending satisfying meaning to the suffering that characterized the meantime, the time of events. So politics framed by primitivism often yields to politics framed by eschatology, and a politics framed by the rejection of order yields to a politics framed by the promise of a force that explodes all future need and hence the need for any future capacity. If the only freedom is in the sublation of law and force in love and grace, then the only political response to primitivism is radical revolution framed by eschatology.

5
A Dead End?

The time is near.

—*Revelation* 1:3

Two conceptions of the flow of time dominate the rhetoric of radical politics: primitivism and eschatology. Primitivism casts corruption as the natural florescence of order: order imposes and enforces constraint, limiting freedom and drawing humanity away from nature. Order brought humanity to its present degraded condition, a claim the primitivist supports through the contrasting vision of free, noble, and "natural" humanity in an unbuilt, unsullied environment. Order itself, with chronological time its sometime proxy, is the villain. Any claim to legitimacy built upon and enforced through an order other than that of nature itself is thus undermined. But time marches on; there is no return to a primitive free condition. So primitivism is the rhetoric of lament, not liberation. It serves as an advance party for politics framed in the rhetoric of eschatology, a conception of the flow of time focused on the last things, on bringing time to an end.

This chapter identifies a rhetorical structure of eschatology and examines how and why it works to challenge political legitimacy. As doctrine, eschatologies are theologically and ideologically diverse. Some, which Eric Voegelin once characterized derisively as gnostic,

A DEAD END?

speak of heaven on earth as an immanent culmination that human beings can bring about in history, while others insist on a purely transcendent end.[1] For some that end is truly eternal while for others it lasts for a pseudo-eternity, eons beyond our comprehension. Some are more or less secular, others more or less religious. But despite this diversity in doctrine, wherever we find eschatological rhetoric framing political communication it tends to share common structures.

The political actor who uses eschatological rhetoric to delegitimate order may confront the problem of order-as-corruption with a call for the violent escape from order by means of a violent escape from time. While vastly improbable, in an eschatological frame, this escape is cast as inevitable. Inevitability rests on the combined force of three rhetorical elements: some conception of history that moves of itself, some variation of promised divine intervention or recognition, and a call for appropriate submission to these forces, to the *compulsion* of inevitability. So long as we submit to the mode of participation the tenor of the times requires—either to act or to wait—the chronotic time of events, of suffering and domination, will be brought to a halt, with infinite peace in its wake. Then there will be no more need for the political state, its claims to legitimacy on grounds of capacity now irrelevant. A call to reject the legitimacy of human order can be used to encourage active participation in violence. A call for patient submission can serve as a placeholder to substitute for legitimacy when an eschatological movement achieves political power. Both active and patient participation figure in both sacred and mundane eschatologies.

The patient/active modulation is central to eschatological politics because while eschatology makes for powerful talk, it is a dubious prognosis of actual future events. Historically, when movements sold through eschatological talk have failed politically, leaders have fallen back on revising the timing of the inevitable. The calculations were wrong, the time was not ripe, or the movement's followers did not submit in the right way. Perhaps they were active when they should have been patient, or vice versa. Regardless, the outcome remains *inevitable*. This strategy is well documented by scholars of millennial and apocalyptic movements and has met with varying success.[2] But even in those cases where eschatologically framed movements have succeeded politically, for example, with the Christian Church after Constantine or in some Communist regimes of the twentieth century, they remain a spiritual failure. After all, these movements promised not regime change but an ultimate *end* to regimes. They began not by asserting their own superior claim to legitimacy but by rejecting the ultimate need for performative capacity or enforced order in the first place. Leaders must explain the continuing presence of order and domination in the wake of victory too. Again, this challenge is met by shifting the timing of the inevitable: a call for action becomes a call for patient submission not on the grounds of an authority's legitimacy but on the grounds that that authority will ultimately render itself superfluous.

Historically, this has been a precarious strategy. It secured the ready—if neither consistent nor universal—submission of medieval Christians to mundane power while apparently bypassing the need for legitimation. But medieval Europe was shaken by intermittent peasant uprisings and explosions of active, eschatologically motivated violence. Since attention to mundane justice is not only diminished in importance but becomes a mark of insubordination to the cause, deployment of an eschatological frame not only delegitimates but subverts mundane legitimation. With no well of legitimation for a regime that has sold itself through eschatological talk to fall back upon, legitimation and eschatology have a permanently tense relationship. In China, as we saw in chapter 1, the renewed focus on performance under Deng was accompanied by a move away from eschatological framing. It is possible that the rise of consent theories in early modern European political thought served a similar purpose there.

In every case, a core requirement of successful eschatological rhetoric is the compulsion of inevitability. Inevitability helps to generate an appetite for violence or martyrdom that radical movements may require. It helps to generate patient submission in the absence of legitimacy, whether or not such movements succeed politically, because it guarantees that patient endurance is worthwhile.

If a primitivist frame leads only to lament, then an active radical politics will favor eschatology. Because eschatology necessitates the promise of inevitability, inevitability may be a necessary condition of any really radical politics. On the right, there are many contemporary examples of politics framed in eschatological talk. Here, mass death, sometimes sought actively, is a necessary station on the road to ultimate redemption. In the United States and Europe, Christian Dispensationalism as well as a variety of far-right and neo-Nazi movements make use of this rhetoric.[3] Worldwide, the Islamic State has taken a similar approach. But this chapter concludes by investigating what has happened to the radical politics of the left after postmodernism and the reconstruction of Marxism have made inevitability implausible. Could it be that, on the left, eschatology is, for now, a dead end?

Movement

In 1985, the journalist Gustavo Gorriti attended a large rally of Sendero Luminoso, a faction of the Peruvian Communist Party. For five years, Sendero and government forces had been locked in armed struggle, with bloodshed on both sides. Gorriti describes a vast crowd of hardened operatives and new recruits there to hear the words of the faction's normally secretive leader, Abimael Guzmán. It was a pivotal moment for Sendero both because of the intense level of political activity it had achieved and because a progressive leftist movement had come to power in Lima. Now that Peruvian democracy would be more inclusive of other Communist factions and more responsive to labor concerns, sympathy for radical factions would diminish. This specter—the specter of partial justice—haunted these most radical Peruvian Communists, threatening the conditions for the inversion for which Sendero stood. Political order is constraint, and enforced constraint is domination. The only possible justice, on this view, a justice that can ultimately persist without enforcement, requires a sublation of human capacity and human order. In this light, no half measures, no capitulation to that order was conceivable. It was thus crucial to the movement that the moment not be lost, momentum not be stalled.

Guzmán had been a professor at the University of San Cristobal of Huamanga, which from the late 1960s through the 1970s was dominated by competing factions of the Communist Party. Guzmán's Sendero faction ultimately intimidated the university's administration to such a degree that it effectively took over. Guzmán built a following of young college students, left the university, and went underground under the nom de guerre Presidente Gonzalo, calling his followers to armed struggle through a series of speeches and writings that are collectively known as Gonzalo Thought. His strategy began with the obstruction of elections, which are, after all, competing claims to capacity and thus to legitimate power. The Sendero Luminoso ultimately took over rural areas in the center and south of Peru as well as in regions close to Lima.

A DEAD END?

That day in 1985, Guzmán framed his call to action in the rhetoric of eschatology. To the assembled crowd he issued a clarion call:

> The trumpets begin to sound, the roar of the masses grows.... It will take us into a powerful vortex.... There will be a great rupture and we will be the makers of a definitive dawn.... This we shall do, this is the rebirth. Comrades, we are reborn!
>
> We have learned to manipulate history, law, contradictions.... The progress of the world, the country, and the party are pages in the same book. That is why our future is assured.[4]
>
> We are the initiators.... Comrades the hour has come, there is nothing further to discuss, debate has ended. It is time to act, it is the moment of rupture, and we will not carry it out with the slow meditation that comes too late, or in halls or silent rooms. We will make it in the heat of battle.... All of the great actions of the centuries have culminated here at this moment in history. The promise unfolds, the future unfurls.[5]

Gorriti, the journalist in attendance, records that the "ecstatic gathering felt fervently that they were the messengers of the millennium, and signed on."[6] These young people were signing on not just to a movement but to "the Quota," a policy that required each Senderista to swear an oath of self-sacrifice and valorizing blood. The Senderistas tortured and publicly executed. The final report of Peru's Commission on Truth and Reconciliation found that more than 69,280 people died in the violence between Sendero and government forces and a majority of the dead were indigenous Peruvians, killed by Sendero itself.[7] Despite Guzmán's rhetoric of peasant liberation, people were divided both in their self-identification as oppressed "peasants" and—understandably, given the violence—in perceptions of their self-proclaimed liberators.[8] While there were poor and indigenous supporters, the core of the movement was educated, affluent young people who had converged around Guzmán at the university.

We should ask ourselves: How were these young people, hardly in desperate circumstances, brought to torture and kill those they understood themselves to be liberating? Extreme violence does not come naturally to most people. The followers of revolutionary leaders are sometimes, in the tradition of Weber, said to accept authority on the basis of charisma, but charisma grows partly from rhetorical skill. And, as David Apter has noted, most people need to be *talked into killing*.[9] Talk that transforms mass death into new life is talk framed by eschatology.

Eschatology—literally, the study of the last things—refers to speculations or theories of what will happen at the end of time. These, in their variety, span major cultural traditions, East and West, North and South. They are found in Judeo-Christian religious texts, including the book of Daniel and the New Testament book of Revelation. They are found in Vedic texts of great age and in records of Chinese peasant rebellions of more recent vintage.[10]

Eschatological speculations share a common structure. An eschatological conception of the flow of time is linear both in its directionality and because it begins and ends at distinct points. It is also inertial. At both ends of eschatology's temporal spectrum, a massive force either generates or stops the time of events. In a moment, the world-as-we-know-it is forced into being out of a bucolic primitive past. Adam and Eve fall from Eden because willful action and moral knowledge initiate degeneration and decay. God throws them out, wrenching the earth into motion. In other accounts an invader, a foreign technology or way of life, or the force of the colonial or capitalist oppressor and her machines does the work. Imposing this alien will corrupts the denizens of the pseudo-Eden, as we saw in chapter 4. Out from bucolic, event-free, slow time, human beings experience alienation, suffering, and injustice. They are forced into the ever-churning world of action and politics in a fruitless attempt to ameliorate their condition. Time-itself is the conduit of degeneration. So for the eschaton to come about, eradicating suffering and any need for politics, time must stop. Time must end to establish lasting freedom, equal but opposite to the timeless condition of the primitive. The sublated form of order is engendered spontaneously through love, not law, so harmony can be preserved without further domination or constraint. There will be no more events, no more politics, so that there will be no more degeneration.

But how does one stop time and create the conditions necessary for a regime of love, not law? Eschatology promises implicitly or explicitly a wave of purifying violence, a massive force that will be the means of shaking the world free, disrupting the causal flow of events, restoring harmony. The violent force of the eschaton that ends the time of events is a massive capacity to end all capacity, a massive performance to end all performance. And because the eschaton brings harmony, peace, and an end to suffering, it ultimately obviates the need for any further power or capacity, and hence for political legitimation. Want and desire—including the desire to dominate—are gone, and each receives according to his need.

How does this seemingly abstract and implausible narrative lead to mass action? Eschatology, like other conceptions of the flow of time, is not an account of the facts, since there is no objective shape of time's flow. Time is experienced through the marks and measures—natural or constructed—we pick out for specific purposes. The value of eschatology, then, like the value of all shaped time, is its use-value, not its truth-value. Eschatology's use-value is supported by its structure. The linear-inertial shape of eschatological rhetoric scaffolds a particularly compelling form of narrative: an existential conflict boils to a crisis, it is resolved at a ripe and decisive point by a benevolent strength that purifies and transforms, the protagonists are redeemed, and harmony is restored.[11] Bringing an end to the time of events, the time of domination and suffering casts the listener in a key participatory role: it is not just a good story to hear but an exciting story to live. The force driving this process promises redemption. It generates excitement partly through narrative pacing. It constructs compulsion, inevitability, and sometimes immediacy through talk of kairos, the right or ripe moment, the moment by means of which the force of change, against which no one can stand, demands submission in the form of active participation.

As John Smith describes, kairos is "*the time when* a constellation of events presents a crisis to which a response must be made; it means *the time when* an opportunity is given for creative action or for achieving some special result that is possible only at 'this' time."[12] This sense of a ripe moment is not just intellectually but physically compelling: we must live up to the task that has been put in our way to complete. We are the agents of opportunity who must not but also cannot fail because the advent of this end-time is inevitable. Events will unfold toward a ripe moment. A divine or pseudo-divine figure will either prepare for and recognize or else create that moment. But to bring about the end always also requires a certain kind of mass agency, submission to the demands of inevitability either actively, in the moment, or else through an energetic patience that calls for a form of withdrawal and work on the self. Active and patient participation thus constitute two appropriate modes of comportment toward the eschaton, each with its proper time.

A DEAD END?

For the political entrepreneur who wishes to offer more than a glimpse of the crisis moment but also an account of the motive force that will bring that crisis to its highest tension and release, there are two apparent paradoxes with which she must contend. First, there is the apparent paradox of time that is forced to end. Second, there is the apparent paradox of an inevitable outcome that must nonetheless be brought about by human agency. These two paradoxes are bound up with, and always awkwardly resolved by, a trio of sources of motive force that vary from eschatology to eschatology, overlapping in different configurations as the political entrepreneur seeks to address this question of the mechanism of crisis and the reality of its denouement. There is, first, the divine: it is the hand of God himself that grabs the earth and stops it spinning. This fulfills a promise that, since it is God's own promise, listeners know to be trustworthy. Second, there is a preordained course of events in time, perhaps a purposive conception of history, that will unfold in the way it is meant to and must, whether according to Vedic cosmology, according to a pattern of dispensations we find by correct interpretation of the Bible, or perhaps according to the logic inherent in dialectical materialism. Third, there is human agency, which must submit to its assigned task, to prepare the world, to "look forward to the day of God and speed its coming" or, to use Marx's metaphor, to play the part of midwife in easing the new era into life by means of revolution.[13] But the midwife does not decide when labor will begin, nor does the Christian who speeds it decide the moment of Christ's return. The forces of inevitability, whether divine, historical, or both, combine with a call to recognize the form of participation—active or patient—proper to the kairotic moment. Time will come to an end because that is in the nature of time. One is called to aid what is anyway inevitable because submission to that calling is part of the process of the event's unfolding.

A DEAD END?

Everything, in eschatological rhetoric, depends on the correct understanding of the times and the timing, and the forms of participation appropriate to each.

Kairotic rhetoric, the rhetoric of right timing, is charismatic. Political entrepreneurs claim special insight into the ripe moment. At the same time, constructions of inevitability lower risk and render participants agents of destiny, lending a sense of world-historical importance to the activist and his actions. Moreover, eschatological rhetoric provides an avenue to realize fantasies of vengeance, those hidden transcripts James Scott has argued characterize relations of domination, with neither risk nor moral qualms.[14] Together with the promise of a permanent condition of freedom and harmony, born from participation of the right kind, whether active or patient, the force of this narrative structure partly explains the willingness of young people to sacrifice themselves and their neighbors. Not everyone, of course, is susceptible to this kind of rhetoric, and surely, as with all rhetoric, there are temperamental or experiential characteristics that modulate its resonance for specific individuals. But for those who are susceptible, this divine-historical/kairotic-human structure of inevitability, combined with the narrative of a crisis that leads to the highest possible resolution, a crisis to end all crises, might make Guzmán's Quota or Christian martyrdom perfectly rational. Thus, eschatology reframes violent action that, within any other frame, can appear violently irrational.

I have cited Christian martyrdom and Guzmán's Quota in the same breath. For some this may be a jarring juxtaposition as one seeks life in heaven and the other heaven on earth, one awaits God's hand and the other depends on the work of human hands. But while eschatological theologies and ideologies are diverse, eschatological politics exhibit a notable continuity in the rhetorical forms and narrative structures political leaders use to promote or quell action.

Development

It may be tempting to look to the motive triad I have identified—a ripe moment brought by the fullness of time or history, divine or pseudo-divine intervention that either makes ready for, recognizes, or brings about that ripe moment, and individual patient or active participation—and seek there a developmental story. This story would distinguish the transcendent from its degeneration into the immanent, distinctly separating human from divine. This is what Eric Voegelin does in his influential account of so-called gnostic eschatology in *The New Science of Politics* and later works. Voegelin argues that eschatology began as a sacred and transcendent matter in Judeo-Christianity. The early church, notably through the agency of Saint Augustine's *Civitas Dei,* places the eschaton securely beyond human influence. Saint Augustine "boldly declared the realm of the thousand years to be the reign of Christ in his church in the present saeculum that would continue until the Last Judgment and the advent of the eternal realm in the beyond."[15] This sufficed, Voegelin claimed, to limit any more active conception of eschatology until the twelfth-century development of a tripartite structure in history that moves of itself. This initiated the process of making the eschaton immanent in history.[16] No longer is eschatology a purely sacred matter with hopes for redemption placed on divine intervention. This pure religious eschatology is now infected with the notion that redemption may take place *within* history, which has its own force and pace and unfolds in the earthly realm. This twelfth-century innovation, attributed to Joachim of Fiore, is just a way station along the developmental path. History will not yet have an "immanent eruption," but rather the eschaton would come about through the irruption of a transcendent spirit *into* history.[17] But this preservation of the role of the transcendent doesn't last because once the events of the eschaton are immanent, they can be affected by human action. There arise a number of dangerous eschatological movements that cloak their gnostic and secular elements through the highly selective use of scripture, as, for instance, the Puritan revolution.[18] These gnostic eschatologies usurp God's role in bringing about the end in, not beyond, history. As Voegelin argues, Puritan rhetoric, however graced with scripture, "has nothing to do with Christianity. The scriptural camouflage cannot veil the drawing of God into man. The Saint is a Gnostic who will not leave the transfiguration to the grace of God beyond history but will do the work of God himself, right here and now, in history."[19] Finally, "only in the 18th century with the idea of progress the increase of meaning in history [became] completely intramundane, without transcendental irruptions," and this new phase in history Voegelin calls "secularization."[20]

For Voegelin, immanent or gnostic eschatology that is understood to come about either through the unfolding of history or through the intervention of human beings is dangerous and displaces the important but uncomfortable activities of faith and philosophy in the open soul. But more immediately, he notes with some justice, such movements "disregard the structure of reality" and are often "morally insane."[21] And this moral insanity is contained in an "inner logic of . . . Western political development" from the twelfth century through the humanists, the Enlightenment, and positivism: each is "one step on the road to Marxism" and ultimately to Nazism and the Third Reich.[22] For Voegelin, equally, progressive liberalism is a dangerous, purely secular gnosticism. And all this means, he argues, that we are due for an imminent "explosion" because the gnosticism pervasive in twentieth-century politics tries but will necessarily fail to repress the truth of the soul in the experience of Christianity and philosophy and hence "contains a self-defeating factor."[23]

A DEAD END?

In this account, first eschatology is sacred and transcendent. Then, beginning with Joachim, it becomes increasingly secularized and (because it centers the role of human agency in the coming of the end) gnostic. This develops toward moral insanity, which stamps out and negates the proper patient activity of the soul, leading ultimately to imminent and immanent destruction.

At least with respect to eschatological rhetoric in politics, this developmental story is questionable, as Voegelin himself recognized late in his life.[24] Any eschatology that is politically engaged—and arguably, every eschatology is directly or indirectly politically engaged—makes use of the compulsion of inevitability to generate desired forms of behavior. That compulsion in turn always rests on some combination of historical force, divine power, and individual comportment, however different the emphases. The claim that there is a developmental path of increasing secularization and immanence does not fit the evidence.

Let's begin with the claim that it was with Joachim in the twelfth century that history, immanence, and hence the possibility that human action might aid the coming of the eschaton enters the picture. In *Meaning in History* Karl Löwith claims, "There have occurred and recurred apocalyptic speculations and expectations of an imminent consummation, but never until Joachim of Floris have they been elaborated into a consistent system of historico-allegorical interpretation."[25] Löwith, like Voegelin, who likely draws upon his work, is referring to the influential twelfth-century Calabrian Abbot Joachim of Fiore, who claimed to have discovered, through a combination of divine inspiration and esoteric reading, a pattern inherent in the Testaments that Joachim's followers used to predict what would come next. His prophecy was based in interpretation, not personal revelation: a theory of history proper, itself structured by an eschatological conception of the flow of time. Jesus, for Joachim, is a sort of divine mechanism of history. The patterns Joachim claimed to find in the Bible were projected forward by his followers to mark out a succession of "dispensations," or eras, corresponding to three "statuses" and to the three parts of the Trinity. The age of God the Father, which lasted from Abraham until the birth of Christ, was the age of law and punishment. The age of Christ, in which Joachim lived, was the age of filial duty and faith. And Joachim calculated that the third age, the age of the Spirit, would arrive around 1260 CE, a speculation with important political consequences.[26] Joachim was particularly beloved of the Franciscan spiritualists, some of whom held that Francis himself, in founding his mendicant order, was the bringer of Joachim's third age. In this third age, on earth, the church and its organizational structures would no longer be needed, making way for an earthly, self-ordering monasticism governed neither by law nor duty but instead by love. This would be the end-time before the eschaton. As in later theories of history, some of which are directly and sometimes explicitly indebted to him, Joachim argued that each period contains within it the incubating seeds of the next, which begin to oppose the existing condition until the new one flowers.[27] For example, the second age began its rumblings in the time of Elijah.[28]

Yet, while Joachim's system of dispensations has been uniquely influential, the idea that history moves according to its own internal logic from stage to stage toward a point of fruition dates back much further, both in the Christian tradition and in traditions that were, at least in classical times, in conversation with the Western classical tradition. The Hindu Vedas provide early written evidence of immanent historical movement in eschatological thinking, and extensive evidence supports the movement not only of goods but of ideas back and

A DEAD END?

forth across the Indian Ocean from as early as 2000 BCE.[29] Time in the Vedic tradition is divided into a succession of progressively shorter epochs that collapse into one another at a designated moment, culminating in an eschaton. The end of the last and shortest age, the corrupt and violent age of Kali, builds toward an explosion of violence chastising the unjust and corrupt, and bringing time to an end. But this end is succeeded by a renewed age, the Satya Yuga, which lasts exponentially longer than any other age. This conception of the flow of time is evident in texts including the *Mahabharata,* which dates from somewhere between 300 BCE and 300 CE. The interaction between events that move toward a ripe moment, divine intervention, and individual comportment is clearly evident in this passage from the *Vishnu Purana*:

> When the practices taught by the Vedas and the institutes of law shall nearly have ceased, and the close of the Kali age shall be nigh, a portion of that divine being who exists of his own spiritual nature in the character of Brahma, and who is the beginning and the end, and who comprehends all things, shall descend upon earth: he will be born . . . as Kalki [an avatar of Vishnu], endowed with the eight superhuman faculties. By his irresistible might he will destroy all the . . . thieves, and all whose minds are devoted to iniquity. He will then reestablish righteousness upon earth; and the minds of those who live at the end of the Kali age shall be awakened, and shall be as pellucid as crystal. The men who are thus changed by virtue of that peculiar time shall be as the seeds of human beings, and shall give birth to a race who shall follow the laws of the . . . age of purity.[30]

A DEAD END?

Indeed, the notion of structured, historical movement is found in Hesiod and Horace, and Virgil praises Augustus as a prince who brings a new golden age.[31] Then there are the persistently popular Sibylline texts, like the late seventh-century CE *Pseudo-Methodius,* which sometimes extended an account of the past into a prediction for a future immanent heaven brought about by a person's actions on earth in the lead-up to the final judgment.[32] That events have a motive shape that manifests through a succession of periods in time and that these events are sometimes brought about or catalyzed by human beings is neither an Enlightenment innovation nor even a Joachimite innovation.

It is evident from the Vedic and Sibylline texts that the interpretation of historical events as a motive force within eschatology is nothing novel, even by the time of Joachim. Conversely, the force of historical events has never fully displaced the divine. Leaders of some Marxist and pseudo-Marxist movements have not been shy about making use of the ethotic power of their kairotic claims. A person who claims the capacity to help stop time, or else the knowledge of the point when time will stop, also claims a charismatic legitimacy through close proximity to ultimate power or cosmological wisdom. This may take the form of proximity to God and a knowledge of his intentions, a special insight into scripture or, as in the case of Guzmán, a vision of the time and the times. By intervening in the normal causal sequence of worldly events, divine-inspired power is manifested and, in the same moment, sanctified by means of the delegitimation of earthly order. Leaders of activist eschatological movements may imply or directly claim that they are God-like, God-chosen, or indeed—as in the case of Jesus or Hong Xiuquan, the leader of China's Taiping Rebellion—elements of God himself.[33] Those who follow eschatological entrepreneurs believe them on the basis partly of charisma, but the kairotic rhetoric itself generates charisma.

Sendero Luminoso propaganda poster, 2009.

Stefan Lochner, Last Judgment, c. 1435. (Wallraf-Richartz Museum, Cologne)

Furthermore, the properly divine motive element in eschatological politics has not been displaced. It has continued, to the present day, to animate a variety of monotheistic sects and movements. America's 30 million Christian Dispensationalists, for instance, whose creed is a nineteenth-century reconstruction of Joachimism, expect a very imminent rapture of the faithful.[34] Pew polling data shows that 41 percent of all Americans believe Jesus Christ will return by 2050, and among white Evangelicals, this number increases to 58 percent.[35] Moreover, 23 percent of all American Christians thought they could impact the timing of Jesus's return.[36] The biblical translation preferred by Evangelicals (New International Version) reads in 2 Peter 3:12 "Look forward to the day of God *and speed its coming,*" while the King James Bible reads, "Looking for and hasting unto the coming of the day of God," which has a somewhat different connotation.[37] Several scholars have established the very active political role Dispensationalists play: to return Israel to its historical borders, a catalyzing condition for Jesus's return, some bankroll West Bank settlements.[38] And some work against environmental and other medium-term policies, which would limit short-term gain or comfort for the sake of a medium-term future they do not expect. James Watt, interior secretary under Ronald Reagan, once responded to a question about care of the environment with "I do not know how many future generations we can count on before the Lord returns."[39] And this is no isolated perspective. In polls, Evangelicals in the United States show substantially lower levels of concern about medium-term policy issues than non-Evangelicals, who consider these issues very serious.[40] The imminent but also immanent intervention of the divine and of charismatic leaders who imply their proximity to the divine continues to have an impact on politics. We must also note in this context the important twentieth-century liberation theology movement that continues to sustain and support adherents within the Catholic Church.[41]

Whether or not Voegelin is right that political movements that both employ sacred texts and save a role for human action "ha[ve] nothing to do with Christianity," the persistent use of scripture in eschatological politics to the present day shows the continuing rhetorical power of divine intervention. Whatever development eschatology may have undergone in theology or philosophy, whenever eschatological rhetoric is deployed in *politics* it has structural commonalities not only with respect to the eschatological shape of time but also with respect to the three elements of motive force. These commonalities belie the appearance of development. If the object of interest is earthly, political behavior, as it is here, then whether the promised heaven is on earth or beyond and how precisely the forces of the divine, historical, and human combine are secondary to the fact that *heaven is promised, so long as individuals comport themselves as required.* Whether eschatology calls for people to act on the world or for people to act on themselves, this call rests on a construction of inevitability that relies on some combination of this triad of motive elements. They perform eschatology's rhetorical work by constructing the compulsion of inevitability.

The Compulsion of Inevitability

It is this promise of success that makes active participation in violence or withdrawal into a sect reasonable. The promise of inevitability also enables members of failed eschatological movements to cope with the disappointment of an end that does not arrive as scheduled, as Landes and others have demonstrated.[42] Even where an eschatological movement finds political success, it cannot forego this continued commitment to inevitability. For every politically successful eschatological regime is still a spiritual failure insofar as enforced human order and domination remain. Worse, such a regime can offer no grounds for a legitimate claim to more than temporary authority. This is revealing with respect to the relationship of eschatology to legitimation and delegitimation.

To review, why is eschatology inherently opposed to political legitimacy? The lure of eschatology is release from domination. All human political order, which is to say all order in time, is both inherently constraining and requires domination to maintain itself. It is constraining because all order, necessarily taking a determinate shape, is a negation of freedom to live and be in alternative ways. It requires domination because of the assumption of decay through time. The threat of force delays the entropy of order. This is particularly important because the condition promised in the eschaton is one of perfect harmony, an end to suffering. Any change in a condition of perfection is by definition decay. So time, or more strictly events in time, must stop.

It follows that all grounds for political legitimacy are subverted. If legitimation claims are based either on correspondence with already accepted order or on performance, and if enforced order, beyond a transition period, is rejected, then long-term legitimacy could be based only on performance. But an eschatological frame precludes performance both because it dismisses the importance of the here and now and because it frames a focus on improvement in immediate circumstances as traitorous to the ultimate cause of order's inversion. Eschatology is thus a mode of rhetorical framing that destroys any basis for the settled legitimation of human order. So how can political regimes that are sold on the basis of eschatological narratives hope to function?

A DEAD END?

A necessary feature of eschatological expectation is a kairotic modulation between active and patient participation. Both are modes of submission to the superhuman forces compelling time to end, but the timing of time's end demands different postures. It becomes possible, in the space Paul identified between "the present time" and the moment of salvation, to call believers to live as though obedient to earthly power for the sake of what is to come.[43] This is a powerful but highly precarious tool for social control that attempts to bypass legitimacy and legitimation entirely.

Eschatology inverts performance legitimacy by forcefully eradicating the need for performance, since worldly things are of base importance and ultimately all needs will be met. While rhetorics of legitimation persuade people to obedience on the basis of claims to capacity and correspondence with order, eschatology promotes submission to the inevitable—as well as *participation* in it. It may be a call for active participation in an immanent project of destruction or it may be a call for patient participation, a kind of alert and active waiting, a collective, conscious biding for the right or ripe time. But obedience here is never on account of the legitimacy of earthly power but instead is submission to the force that will ultimately bring the eschaton, a sign of devotion to the cause through, for example, virtuous conduct. Engaged in patient participation, one ought to devote oneself actively to the care of one's soul or to ideological purity in the hope or expectation of election, of resurrection and grace.

The promotion of patient participation leading up to the eschaton may make strategic sense. If a regime came to power on an eschatological platform, there is a strong incentive to put off not only the last dawn itself, so earthly power can be enjoyed, but also the dangerous resurgence of speculation about its imminence. While it might ultimately be safer to attempt to disarm eschatological rhetoric entirely, its negation of the conditions of robust legitimacy provides a convenient means of skirting the demands of performance while still commanding submission. Eschatology demotes the ordered world of events to unreality or inconsequence in expectation of redemption. If redemption is effectively put off long into the future and tied specifically to patient forbearance now, injustice becomes a worldly concern of little consequence, and attention to it, beyond the relief of local, immediate suffering, is a sign of disloyalty or a lack of commitment to the cause of the eschaton.

This may generate submissiveness, but it would be an error to understand this submission as a recognition of political legitimacy. Certainly, there is truth in the trope—important to Machiavelli and Marx alike—that the promise of an otherworldly eschaton demotes the importance of present political action. But calling for patient submission as a sign of worthiness of grace is not a legitimation strategy but rather a means of maintaining power while skirting the need for legitimacy entirely. One should not conflate this justification of the use of power with a claim to political legitimacy. Regimes that hold earthly political power under an otherworldly eschatological promise are placeholders during the biding time. Subjection to the power of others results from human sinfulness. It guides us toward grace, through humility and discipline, and works to settle or prevent conflict that could interfere with the provision of basic human needs.[44] It does not ultimately matter *who* holds this power either, as Augustine notes: "As far as this life of mortals is concerned, which is spent and ended in a few days, what does it matter under whose dominion a dying man lives if they who govern do not force him to impiety or iniquity?"[45] The question of legitimacy simply does not arise in this context.

But while the rewards of such a strategy are clear, the risks are substantial too. If the strategy succeeds, submission is uncoupled from an expectation of effective government: high benefit, low cost. But stark reality and competition over power mean such a rhetorical strategy is unlikely to be consistently effective, and the availability of such volatile narratives presents an invitation to political challengers. Indeed, volatility has been the constant companion of establishment eschatologies. Both Norman Cohn and Richard Landes have documented how ruthlessly the church stamped out constantly reemerging claims of eschatological imminence and how relentlessly they continued to reemerge.[46] This pattern began almost as soon as Christianity was established and was exacerbated wherever poverty and oppression came together with upheaval in modes of life and social organization.[47]

It is worth considering the rhetorical interplay between active and patient participation in eschatological politics for at least three reasons. First, it provides critical nuance to the function of eschatological rhetoric. Second, it illuminates strands in the history of political thought that have been largely ignored until recently, and finally, it illuminates a contemporary crisis of the political-intellectual left in Europe.

Patience

After Constantine, the church had to manage the paradox of an order sold on the promise of a destruction of order, mundane power grounded in its own eventual, just sublation. Given that eschatology diminishes the value of one's own physical persistence and the violent potential inherent in its narrative structure, and given its availability where it is part of established power's own creed, this is no small concern. It is already evident with visceral clarity in narratives of early sainthood and also in the contests of early church fathers like Origen and Irenaeus.[48] After Constantine, it was important to discredit those who had spoken aloud about imminence. The church forcefully designates the timing of the eschaton as a mystery and the province of God alone. No predictions and none of those calculations found in the book of Daniel can be permitted. In his history of the church, Eusebius of Caesarea argued against a literal interpretation of Revelation, and even against its authenticity.[49] Saint Augustine, too, strongly advised against any efforts to predict apocalyptic or millennial events. With respect to further persecution by the Antichrist in the form of an earthly king, a form of eschatological rhetoric that continues to crop up basically unchanged to the present day, he calls "upon both sides to abstain from the presumption of making any assertion on the matter."[50] Augustine took a similarly stark view of any attempts to determine the time of the final persecution at the hands of the Antichrist. "Truly, Christ commands all who make such calculations on this subject to relax their fingers and let them rest."[51] As he points out, Christ himself said in Acts 1:7, "It is not for you to know the times or the seasons, which the Father hath put in His own power." One should instead prepare oneself for the millennium through patient obedience and constant virtue. While the book of Revelation, the most apocalyptic of biblical texts, won its place, it was with the important proviso, in Catholic dogma, that it be understood as allegorical, not future-historical.

Yet Christian leaders never entirely succeeded in quelling the resurgence of kairotic speculation, as the history of millennial and apocalyptic politics in Europe confirms. In the mid-thirteenth century, there was a burst of Joachimism that cast the ambitious Hohenstaufen emperor Frederick II as the Antichrist and the wars with his secular army as a harbinger of the end, forecast by Joachim for the year 1260. The death of Frederick in 1250 did little to settle these eschatological speculations, as some among the newly founded Franciscan mendicant order came to understand Saint Francis himself as the bringer of the new dawn. In this context, we find Saint Thomas Aquinas in Paris when, in 1254, Fra Gerard Borgo San Donnino published a text drawing Joachim's arguments to their logical political conclusion. While Joachim himself was both careful and sincerely mindful of papal authority, Gerard argued that the third age was at hand, and with it the supersession of the authority of both the Old and New Testaments, with Joachim's own testament the evangel of the third.[52] In the context of the tense political situation with the new mendicant orders, Gerard's text grew into a renowned scandal that reverberated well beyond Paris. Gerard's, and ultimately Joachim's, work was condemned.[53] Bearing this in mind, it becomes evident that the threat of a Joachimism that overthrows human order on earth forms both a subtext and explicit target of Thomas's political thought. Thomas calls out Joachim only once in the *Summa Theologica,* but on at least three occasions elsewhere he rails against Joachimism, casting aspersions on a dangerous and questionable reconstruction of the gospel, finding in the claims of imminence it sparked a menace to orthodoxy.[54] But beyond these explicit engagements, Thomas imparts through his theology a consistent and clearly intended bulwark against the political dangers of immanent eschatological thinking. Eschatology places political power in a precarious position with respect to legitimacy, and Saint Thomas's political thought addresses itself directly to this problem.

Thomas begins from the subordination of everything to the telos of achieving grace in the end-times. Obedience to law and submission to power are justified by this ultimate end, though not, we should note, on the grounds of power's inherent legitimacy. But Saint Thomas is also at pains to explain the nature of time and events as such that the human contribution to achieving this temporal fruition is patient participation, not action. Human beings have no active role in a causal chain that will bring about the end; they can only conform their action to what comports with the requirements of eventual rupture and subsequent grace. Patience requires rejection even of speculation about the timing of the end. For Thomas, any discussion of politics and law is ultimately driven by the preconditions for grace in the eschaton. In the *Summa*, he concludes that "happiness is the perfect good, which lulls the appetite altogether; else it would not be the last end, if something yet remained to be desired. Now the object of the will, i.e. of man's appetite, is the universal good; just as the object of the intellect is the universal true. Hence it is evident that naught can lull man's will, save the universal good. This is to be found, not in any creature, but in God alone; because every creature has goodness by participation.... Therefore God alone constitutes man's happiness."[55]

It is through the achievement of blessedness, proximity to God, participating in his goodness, that human beings know happiness. "It is evident that the proper effect of law is to lead its subjects to their proper virtue": and since virtue is "that which makes its subject good," it follows that the proper effect of law is to make those to whom it is given good.[56] For the most part, Thomas follows Aristotle in claiming that goodness comes from training, particularly of the young, in virtue. Those who are virtuous are inclined to be good for its own sake or for the sake of blessedness. But for those who are depraved or wicked or who lack such training, human law provides a means of compelling them to behave as though they were good through fear of punishment. By habituation, even the wicked may become virtuous.[57]

Happiness comes only after the resurrection. The purpose of submission is not primarily to honor the legitimate power of the ruler; rather, the ruler's power exists to serve the aim of blessedness. When eschatology reframes obedience as patient participation, it creates the appearance of imminent freedom while indefinitely forestalling performative demands on power. Rebellion—except in extreme cases of injustice—is a mortal sin because obedience is a virtue—obedience to God in the highest instance but also to our superiors in the existing order.[58] We obey not because power is legitimate but because obedience is a performance of virtue, of patient participation, keeping the peace by the management of bodies until the time of bodies is at an end. Despite negating expectations of performance, earthly power nonetheless maintains its call for functional obedience. If this delicate balance can be made to hold, then legitimacy becomes superfluous.

Augustine saw that a necessary safeguard in this scenario is to associate any speculation with respect to the eschaton and any action to hasten it with disobedience. There is *no* appropriate time for political intervention, for action aimed at anything other than promoting or defending virtue for the end of blessedness. Except in the most extreme cases, we can neither reject power on the grounds of poor performance nor work to hasten the eschaton. From a political perspective, it is evident that any work in the service of hastening the eschaton would imply performative capacity that is vitally dangerous to existing power. Eschatological prognostications can only lead to instability. So Thomas, too, is very clear that only God can bring about apocalypse and only God knows when. Thomas argues:

> God is the cause of things by His knowledge. Now He communicates both these things to His creatures, since He both endows some with the power of action on others whereof they are the cause, and bestows on some the knowledge of things. But in both cases He reserves something to

Himself, for He operates certain things wherein no creature co-operates with Him, and again He knows certain things which are unknown to any mere creature. Now this should apply to none more than to those things which are subject to the Divine power alone, and in which no creature co-operates with Him. Such is the end of the world when the Day of Judgment will come. For the world will come to an end by no created cause, even as it derived its existence immediately from God. Wherefore the knowledge of the end of the world is fittingly reserved to God. Indeed our Lord seems to assign this very reason when He said (Acts 1:7): "It is not for you to know the times or moments which the Father hath put in His own power," as though He were to say, "which are reserved to His power alone."[59]

To look for signs is to look for intrusions in the causal order, and this is for God alone. Those who claim to make or recognize signs claim a special kind of divine sanction. This has not been lost on centuries of rebels and revolutionary leaders, or on those who have taken an interest in their strategies. Machiavelli, for instance, mindful of eschatological politics in the wake of Savonarola, notes the strategic use of pseudo-miracles in legitimating inversions of power and warns against the dangers wrought against the credulous by tricksters.[60] Hobbes, too, warned of these dangers when he describes how "it belongeth to the nature of a miracle that it be wrought for the procuring of credit to God's messengers, ministers, and prophets, that thereby men may know they are called, sent, and employed by God, and thereby be the better inclined to obey them. . . . For how admirable soever any work be, the admiration consisteth not in that it could be done, because men naturally believe the Almighty can do all things, but because He does it at the prayer or word of a man."[61] The rupture of time is the prerogative of power and a sign of power, the manifestation of the most potent conceivable capacity.[62] At all costs, established power must both fervently reject the importance of performance in the mundane world and discredit any claim to a capacity animated by imminent eschatological expectation. Claims to capacity must be suppressed, reserving *only* to the divine, as sanctioned by established authority, the capacity to explode the causal chain in time, to bring about the eschaton.

Thomas's concern with this matter is also evident from the large section of the *Summa* devoted to metaphysical aspects of the question of intervention in time.[63] God is eternal, outside of time and the creator of time, without beginning or end, and without change. Angels and our souls were created and hence had a beginning but will have no ending—that is to say, they are unchanging in their substance; they are aeveternal. Everything that comes into being, changes, decays, and passes out of being is less perfect and is strictly temporal.[64] Perfection in this ontology is what is constant, uncreated, and unchanging but has *capacity* to intervene in the course of change: God himself.[65]

Thomas contests any human claim to impact the flow of time, to a capacity to influence, encourage, or even have knowledge of the timing of the eschaton. The Messiah must be understood as, for now, an abstraction, a spiritual condition of separation from mundane matters, to maintain the illusion produced by a reframing of obedience as patient participation. This is necessary to avert the violent catastrophe generated by imminent expectation. At the same time, without the absolute assurance that the Messiah *will* come, inevitably, with certainty, the political enterprise comes apart with no available source of legitimacy to brace it, as we shall now see.

A Dead End

Modern and contemporary political movements have continued to employ a classic eschatological rhetorical frame with its emphasis on inevitability. Pocock, for example, has shown how Hobbes's political writings must be understood not just as a response to disorder and war as such but to the especially violent and dangerous form of disorder enabled by the English Civil War's pervasive rhetoric of an imminent eschaton.[66] Even in the contemporary American context, eschatological talk animates the politics and policy preferences of America's Christian Dispensationalists, and it has also framed the recruitment propaganda of the Islamic State (ISIS). The English-language ISIS magazine, called *Dabiq* after the Syrian town where, according to a hadith, the final conflagration is supposed to occur, is full of familiar eschatological tropes: for instance, the association of the military enemy with the Antichrist (issue 14) and the firm promise that victory is inevitable because of divine will (issue 10).[67] This eschatological frame aligns with a sense of imminent threat and imminent promise. Submission to destiny demands action, and escape from mundane constraints and concerns, coupled with inevitability, makes this demand attractive. Both Christian and Islamic eschatological movements aim to hasten the eschaton by preparing its necessary conditions: returning Israel or a caliphate to its necessary borders, sparking a final purifying conflagration. These ends overrule all other considerations of legitimate power or obedience. Eschatology, in its classic form maintaining the tripartite motivational structure, remains a vibrant rhetorical force of the religious right.

But on the secular left, the use of eschatological framing is now difficult. In the early 1990s eschatological narratives were early victims of postmodernism. At the moment when critiques of grand narrative, progress, and teleology reached their highest pitch, scholars of the

A DEAD END?

radical left were forced also to confront the altered global landscape of Communism. Many leftist scholars turned to rooting out more localized forms of domination through sophisticated forms of identity politics, yielding substantial but incremental dividends within a progressive frame. Identity politics, because it appeals to the existing order in demanding an ever more robust equality, works neither to uproot and invert human order nor to overcome law. But those radical-left scholars who reject a progressive frame have had, in the wake of postmodernism, to construct rhetoric that would promote active participation in a context of spontaneous, thus dissatisfying, meaning. With no grounds to claim inevitability, eschatological rhetoric is no longer compelling. Rejecting progress too, radical-left thinkers may find themselves stuck in a stalled present, an intolerable now with no way forward and no way back. Since they have rejected the resources for political legitimacy too, what's left may be a politics of paralysis, or else of nihilism.

This new leftist politics is exemplified in the work of European scholars who have returned to the apostle Paul. The aim is to construct a form of rhetoric with the appeal of eschatology that is not reliant on discredited theories of history or divine intervention but does not rest on progressive incrementalism either. The resulting call for patient participation recalls the conservative eschatological politics of the medieval church but without the steadying promise of inevitability.

These scholars construct a post-secular Paul centered around the critique of law. Law here generates strained and constrained individual subjects and represents a proxy for order and domination in the political field. For Badiou, for instance, law is bound up with sin, with particularity, and with a living death. Drawing on Paul, he claims law does not so much regulate as actually create sin through the creation of limits that produce desire.[68] This desire in turn serves to reiterate the limit. If desire is outlawed, it is not eliminated but suppressed and re-created. The law sets the limit and the law creates and compels sin by means of that limit. And because the limit, ultimately, is death, both in the sense of the penalty imposed for sin/law breaking and in the sense that death is the ultimate limit, the individual who is compelled to dwell constantly in psychic proximity to the limit (because of the compulsion of sin the law itself creates) dwells constantly in proximity to death. To live with law is a living death, life lived in the environs of death. This condition creates a *particular* subject in constant struggle with the liminal space of death that law signifies. Law, as the generator of compulsion and (self)-coercion, also negates thought.[69] Real life, then, may be had only through an inversion, a reversal that in the Christian tradition resurrection makes possible: life in death rather than death in life. It is redemption through a grace that is universal and noncontingent that negates the particularity the law generates. The means to redemption is thus the destruction of the law that creates sin by "giving life to desire."[70] The law is the limit but also the center of things, the liminal space *around* which desire, sin, and particularity hover.

In *The Time That Remains,* Agamben, too, looks to Paul with the aim of superseding law and its force. But in part because Agamben's understanding of the nature of law remains more Schmittian than psychoanalytic, what counts as the limit to be destroyed here is not the limit that creates desire—though Agamben, too, cites Romans 3:20—but instead the limit that conceals law's force. According to Agamben, Carl Schmitt had demonstrated that there is no "outside" the law, no limit, because the sovereign exercise of power through the state of exception means that whatever the sovereign does, however law is used (or not used), is just what "coincides with reality itself."[71]

A DEAD END?

But this separation, this ever-present potential exception, provides the means of maintaining law's force while negating its meaning so that everything and anything comes to be subject to the force of law. This is the reason, for Agamben, that the state must die. Without also escaping law, we cannot escape sovereignty, and where there is sovereignty we are all homo sacer, available to be sacrificed at the sovereign's whim. Law is not just contingent domination and subjection, on this view, but domination and subjection as such. So what we need is to open up the possibility of "non-statal nonjuridical politics and human life."[72] This would enable a politics of love, not law. Messianic time for Agamben provides the means of conceptualizing this new nonjuridical politics as what he calls a "messianic community."

From Paul, Agamben builds a fleeting image of this messianic community. It is universal in the sense that all are called to a messianic vocation, and for those who take up that call, this messianic vocation is a condition of being what we are as though not what we are.[73] This creates what Agamben somewhat cryptically describes as "a zone of absolute indiscernibility between immanence and transcendence, between this world and the future world."[74] More concretely, this community shares important commonalities with the Franciscans, for whom, Agamben claims, "what mattered was to create a space that escaped the grasp of power and its laws, without entering into conflict with them yet rendering them inoperative."[75] In this universal community, the law of Moses, which is to say propagated, spoken law, is inoperative in favor of a law of faith and love. The law of justice remains when the spoken/written law is rendered inoperative—God's promise is to Abraham, before the law, not to Moses—and it is by means of the negation of law that justice achieves its fulfillment.[76] Citing John Chrysostom, Agamben states that by taking law out of action, so to speak, its vital energy is preserved for its fruition as justice.⁷⁷ The messianic community exists in a state of grace, of gratuitousness, because this is the excess when faith and law combine and break apart.⁷⁸ What Agamben hopes for is a conception of a community that has overcome the necessity for enforced law, overcome conflict, redeemed what has been negated by bringing it to its fruition, and overcome the need for action in the world and responsibility for it. Short on constructive detail, Agamben's community takes on the rough outline of a Joachimite or Franciscan monastic community of the third age, a possibility his most recent work has begun to address extensively and explicitly.⁷⁹

Žižek's Pauline musings overlap substantially with those of Badiou and Agamben, though with characteristic marks of Hegel and Lacan.⁸⁰ Ultimately, the sublation of law in love is made possible in the Christian story because "Christ's statements . . . *suspend* the circular logic of revenge or punishment . . . the logic of . . . legal or ethical retribution, of 'settling accounts,' by bringing it to the point of self-relating. . . . Love, at its most elementary, is nothing but such a paradoxical gesture of breaking the chain of retribution."⁸¹ For Žižek, love itself is the means of rupture and can be exercised in the absence of divine intervention. Love, here, is what creates the Christian community beyond the reach of order. It is the means of escape from the force of law, enabling the self-ordering community that is defined by its shared commitment, "by fidelity to a Cause."⁸² Žižek says, "The key dimension of Paul's gesture is thus his break with any form of communitarianism: his universe is no longer that of the multitude of groups that want to 'find their voice,' and assert their particular identify, their 'way of life,' but that of a fighting collective grounded in the reference to an unconditional universalism."⁸³

What, exactly, do these post-secularists want? For what end is Paul put to work? Žižek says: "The saddest thing to happen in the

A DEAD END?

last thirty years is the loss of the belief that we had in communism. . . . This belief that some blind fate does not control us, that it is possible, through human collective action, to steer development, is gone. . . . The only question is, Will you accommodate yourself to [global capitalism], or will you be dismissed and excluded? A certain type of question, and it needn't be put in the old-fashioned Marxist way as class struggle, but the general anticapitalist question, basically has disappeared."[84]

Each of these thinkers seeks the end that Paul offers, a condition of order effected by universal love, which negates or sublates law-governed order: the dignity of the human person restored, the negation of sovereignty through spontaneous justice, the sublation of capitalism's alienation, the destruction of a legal-human order that is domination, and in particular the obliteration of liberal self-domination, self-government, which, because it is not self-honest, is worse. Paul, these thinkers hold, provides a means of continuing to imagine an alternative way of being in the world together, without law and its enforcement and hence without the need for the legitimation of power. This would be an eschaton, a time beyond law and politics, beyond events.

How precisely is the law to be overcome and freedom achieved? What motive force can animate this narrative? Badiou says, "The Christ-event is essentially the abolition of the law, which was nothing but the Empire of Death."[85] The abolition of law and the resurrection are one and the same: the law is death; the resurrection is its abolition. The law is then sublated into a condition of universality where law is now love. This universalism may be understood as its own spontaneous and self-enforcing law, where freedom comes not from the constraint of each but from the rendering whole of all. The Christ-event serves as a model for a secular truth-event, a rupture in the causal flow that can bring about redemption, releasing us from hovering in suppressed desire around the law. Truth-events open the space of revolution. But in the absence of an actual Christ, what does the work of a Christ-event? For Badiou, the event should be understood as a sort of secular miracle, an intervention in the causal chain, an interruption of chronological time by means of something outside of it. An event strikes, it explodes onto the scene, intervening in the field of truth to create a new reality. Such a truth-event makes possible a new understanding and changes the subjects who exist and subsist and act in that field. Christ's resurrection is an event par excellence, but for Badiou, so were 1968 in Paris and the Cultural Revolution in China.[86] For Badiou, each event is a marker on the ongoing path of revolution: as an opportunity for people to build that path, the experience of the truth of a previous event gives rise to the construction of the way forward. This way is both gradual, in the sense of cumulative, but also radical, in the sense that each truth-event changes the field. But what, in this construction, constitutes a ripe moment for intervention? How would we know it? How would we create it in concert with others? Paul is compelling when he calls because he *is* called. His good news is compelling because it is a promise, not a possibility. But who calls and what is promised in Badiou's kairotic construction?

Žižek, citing Rosa Luxemburg, makes an even more temporally disjointed appeal: we must not even wait for the appointed or "ripe" moment. Instead, "we have to take the risk, and precipitate ourselves into revolutionary attempt, since it is only through a series of 'premature' attempts (and their failure) that the (subjective) conditions for the 'right' moment are created."[87] History does not generate a right moment by means of its inherent structure; rather, "things can take a messianic turn, time can become 'dense,' *at any point.*"[88] God cannot or will not help us; instead he relies on us to be his agents, to help him.[89] The event of Christ, the arrival of the Messiah, is something

A DEAD END?

that has already happened, and "it is up to humanity to live up to it, to decide its meaning, to make something of it."[90]

Badiou holds that we create the event in the ripe moment, and then the event creates the truth, and Žižek argues that only our own choice and our own action can redeem humanity. For Badiou and Žižek, it is agency alone that brings revolution: "There is no Event outside the engaged subjective decision which creates it."[91] It is precisely when the explosion of revolutionary zeal is exhausted, Žižek says, that the "real hard work . . . of translating this explosion into a New Order of Things [and] . . . remaining faithful to it" begins and continues.[92]

Žižek's structure makes sense as a call for local action on specific issues: it's up to you to make the most of redemption and heal the world. This would make a compelling call for progress-oriented leftist agendas that aim to align the law with justice and action with law, to root out localized domination and suffering, and to recenter systems in human well-being. But it is less compelling as an appeal for a radical or revolutionary agenda that could succeed at the *sublation of law itself* into some higher, spontaneous form of nondominating order. To bring about that sort of event, people must be brought to act in concert in ways that are enormously costly, and to see this concerted action and its costs as sensible, worthwhile, because likely to succeed. It may be disingenuous to think that this could be done without tremendous violence. Those nonviolent movements that have been successful (for example, Indian independence, the civil rights movement in the United States) have tended to depend on very specific political contexts: a situation in which the actions of the oppressors are hypocritical with respect to their own stated values.[93] Where there is no such dissonance, not much can be hoped for from nonviolence.

Faith in a cause is no substitute for the confident certainty of divine power or historical inevitability. A cause has no magical power to bring time to a close, to preserve the messianic community: a cause is an end, not a means. The power of Paul, like the power of Guzmán or Taiping's Hong Xiuquan, is the power to call on people on the basis that one is called. Each man is compelling because he is *compelled*. When we read Paul, his every word sparkles with urgency and purpose, effective because Paul believes in and speaks to others who believe in this proximate *inevitability*. Without this kairotic power, without a force of *now!* or *soon!*, what is there to press action? And without the soothing certainty of "someday," what is there to make patient submission worthwhile? Even withdrawal into monastic or collective life makes sense only in a situation of proximate expectation because such communities, too, predictably unravel. So with the compulsion of inevitability lost, and with the credibility of any source of legitimacy for human order undermined, what could be hoped for from radical politics?

Consider the parallels between post-secular messianism and the eschatology of submission to the church outlined above. In both cases, the promise of redemption is delayed into the future, its timing uncertain. And in both cases, each participant is called to comport herself appropriately, to perform her faith with patient but passionate devotion. In both cases, the timing is unknowable, is far off, but while the church claims confidently that God knows the time, the post-secularists make no such claim, and while the church claims with certainty that the day will come, inevitably and with certainty, the post-secularists, again, can make no such promise.

There can be no credible claim of imminence without inevitability. More typical is Agamben's claim that "*one day*, humanity will play with law" or Badiou's reply to an interviewer who asked, "So the time is more ripe than ever for international workers' revolution?" "I wouldn't say that. Certainly at the world level there can be more hope than hitherto. We're climbing a very big ladder."[94] Everything depends on what individuals choose to do or not do at the time of their choosing or not choosing. There is no compelling ground for promising that the end of capitalism will take the form of a messianic community, or that the revolution will come, and no compelling reason to wait patiently for the ground to shift. Without eschatology, it is incoherent to anticipate or expect a time without domination or decay. And without inevitability, eschatology itself becomes incoherent.

But these writers hold that believers in the cause must nonetheless keep their eyes fixed ahead on the eventual achievement of this pseudo-eschaton. Those who pursue progressive or institutional politics are traitors to that cause, seduced by the promise of partial justice. Virtue and obedience are found in scrupulously rejecting this politics, which takes the place of sin. Each failure of the project, for Badiou, like each disappointment when Christ does not return, is in fact further evidence that we are on our way up the ladder.[95] Yet Badiou offers no narrative structure that could make such a claim compelling. This post-secular, structureless messianic politics is dysfunctional. We might expect novel forms of leftist and radical politics to emerge in response. Whatever other economic and cultural forces have sparked new experiments in European leftist institutional politics, such as the emergence of populist parties like Spain's Podemos, perhaps their appeal is bolstered by the increasingly unappealing alternative. Any politics of a post-secular Paul can succeed only by subverting itself.

Conclusion

Žižek is surely right that God won't help the left and that people must help themselves. Indeed, it is possible to argue that it is only and precisely through the loss of eschatological inevitability that real freedom becomes possible.[96] After all, however freeing the experience of compulsion may be (to be free from the burdens of choice, from responsibility), it is still compulsion. To aid in bringing about the eschaton through submission to the inevitable is to be a mere tool in the course of affairs, not an author of those affairs. From this perspective, the loss of inevitability is merely rhetorical and more than made up for by the acquisition of a robust type of freedom. That is, without the interference of inevitability, it becomes possible for the political agent to act spontaneously, from the sheer force of his own will. Now, the revolutionary is the true author of his action, and the revolution a true expression of his and his comrades' freedom to choose the course of their own destiny, the means by which they will organize themselves, and freedom to commit to the norms and values that will animate their activities. It is only, on this view, through the active rejection of eschatology and narratives of inevitability that the revolution takes on this most fundamental form of value: that it is mutually chosen and freely made.

Were such a moment possible—the moment in which the revolution is freely achieved—it could be beautiful indeed. But this beautiful moment could neither come about nor persist if it did. That is to say, to imagine it is to imagine politics outside of time, to imagine a moment in isolation from its temporal context. There could be no comprehensible account of how this moment could be brought about. It is imagined to exist without a past, without a mass struggle that could only actually be brought about through persuasion. It is in this respect a childish wish, not a serious line of political thought, because it neglects the problem of motivation and substitutes the purity of the cause for its necessity, motivated by a harmonious idea, not by the real suffering of individuals. With no promise of redemption, no right time, without the compulsion of inevitability that the force of history or the raw power of divinity offers, there is nothing to make individual submission to the cause either rational or reasonable.[97]

But it is not just that this vision-of-a-moment is cut off from the reality of its necessary past. It can have no more than an imagined future either. For even if redemption could be achieved politically (not magically), it could be achieved only for an instant. Politics, if not magically sublated—time, if not magically made to stop—will enable the process of dissent, disenchantment, decay, and disintegration a moment later. It is naïve to think these threads, which left to themselves begin to unravel, could hold without force and deceit. That law can be displaced by spontaneous order, power by grace, is an example of what we might call the "temporal fallacy" that imagines a political or ontological moment, a T_1, in isolation from its temporal political context: from what politics preceded and what will follow.

This fantasy is not costless. Fidelity to this goal distracts from the hard work of justice that can take place—despite what Žižek says—not only after but in lieu of revolution. Badiou says, "The goal of all enemy propaganda is not to annihilate an existing force, but rather to annihilate an *unnoticed possibility of the situation.*"[98] This might be said of the rhetoric of the project of post-secularism itself, which seeks to annihilate an unnoticed possibility of our situation: that a better justice may indeed—may only—be possible through a better order, an order that, to legitimate itself, continually strives to meet our stringent expectations of justice and performed capacity.

Eschatology is precisely a means of creating the illusion that time ends, that its relentless constraint can be superseded. But if there is no inevitable end to time, no means to bring events to a halt, then the fundamental tension between order's enablement of fairness and justice and its unbearable constraint can never be resolved by radical politics. The moral value of constraint is sidelined or perhaps misunderstood. It is the constraints of order that make collective action possible in the first place. Political action demands organization, not spontaneity, self-discipline, not radical freedom.

The post-secularists have sought to illuminate a new way out of the dark woods the left created for itself without resort to a progressive frame that would relegitimate appeals to just order and capacity, and without resort to a proper eschatology, with its discredited claims to inevitability. But in trying to revive the critique of law necessary for this kind of radical politics, they have resurrected the brain without the body, and without the spirit also. No movement is possible. They have reached a dead end.

CONCLUSION

Transcending Time

Radical politics works toward an ideal. But even were the ideal achievable by purely human means, decay would begin a moment later. So the ideal must either be protected by force, a fruitless task, or else time must be magically made to stop. If there is to be no decay, there must be no "moment later." So eschatological rhetoric creates the illusion that it is possible to transcend time, to eradicate event and action, and hence to end the process of decay. Only in this way can a spontaneous, nonconstraining order characterized by true freedom be possible.

This creates a paradox. Since purposive action takes place over the course of event-filled time, time's negation is also the negation of purpose and hence of meaningful freedom. Meaning is always partly a function of constraint: constraint, by negating alternatives, transforms an *anything potential* into a *something actual.* One might say that the purpose of freedom is the production of meaningful constraint. That is, freedom matters because it enables commitment to and pursuit of goals. We are free when we choose or affirm our constraints, but the elimination of constraint is not freedom. A radical escape from constraint must be, at the same time, the negation of meaningful freedom.

Lacking any experience of eternity, those who look forward to or offer their followers a political program oriented toward an eschaton extrapolate from their experience of normal life. Eternity, they may imagine, would be as rich and directed. There would just be more of it. This observation goes some way to explaining why, in eschatological theory and narrative, focus on the struggle that precedes the return to Eden eclipses conditions within Eden itself. We can barely imagine what heaven would be like. It is perhaps for this reason that the absence of meaningful freedom in a condition beyond time escapes notice. Eschatological politics is, thus, not only violent and destructive but also at times perverse, a sort of temporal gluttony that neglects substance in favor of raw expanse.

It is worth asking: Would we miss event, action, and purpose in an expanse of eternity? After all, temporal constraint is not just a mechanism for constructing meaning, it drives the need for meaning in the first place. Death is the ultimate and most universal constraint.[1] Hence the first and most intensely personal question of time is: Why, if we ultimately cease to be, do we exist at all? This puzzle compels human beings to seek out, construct, or affirm meaning and purpose, a reason for being in this scheme of ultimate limitation. This is in part why the passage of life toward death, the most universally linear of all human experience, is, first, so deliberately marked and intensively celebrated and second, so often placed within larger cyclical structures, structures without *end*. It is also at these moments that belonging is reaffirmed and rehearsed: rituals surrounding birth, coming-of-age, marriage, and death are prominent loci of religious and cultural observance. These most poignant moments of individual life are superimposed on the collective life of a people. This is true at the level of family, of culture or religion, and also of state. In part because the political context provides one means of transcending death's constraint, politics can become a vehicle for sacrifice. Sacrifice in war may cut short an individual life. But through superimposition of that life

CONCLUSION

onto the collective life of the state—one temporality subordinated to a more extensive other—death is, or at least is experienced to be, transcended. This is no less evident in those cultures that see death as a precursor to rebirth. Even here, death's limit (as the condition of rebirth) creates the conditions for meaning in the life that precedes it, since the characteristics of that rebirth are a consequence of a mode of living up to the point of death. Life's linear character in the approach to death both demands and creates meaning, both through what we make of our lives and through the marking of our progress through life.

The constraints of shaped time drive the need for, but also create the mechanisms of, meaningful human life.[2] Constraint shapes meaning, and the constraints of time above all. By means of structured or constrained time, meaning is sought and achieved both within and beyond the political context. Temporal framing thus generates forms of meaning that connect and transcend lives. Fundamentally, this, combined with the ease with which temporality naturalizes the socially and politically constructed, is the source of a temporal frame's power. This book has made evident how broadly and in what numerous guises this power is deployed in politics.

Evidently, temporal frames are important among framing practices more generally, and an empirical research agenda that looked at the impact and uptake of broad narrative structures such as temporality would surely be rewarding. Attention to the ways temporal frames generate meaning and to the ways temporal structures work to naturalize or denaturalize what is socially and politically constructed generates a range of analytical tools useful for understanding political behavior. Certainly, the calendar reform puzzle with which the book began now makes sense, as do certain rhetorical peculiarities in constitutional preambles and political speeches. They are means of

CONCLUSION

tapping into the order-based and performative wells of legitimation. Additionally, attention to contrasting political frames may clarify what's at stake in certain kinds of political engagement. We saw, for example in the cases of China's and Hungary's constitutional preambles, how a shift in temporality framed a fundamental shift in regime orientation. And we saw how approaches to politics framed in opposing temporalities structure how a political problem is understood and what will count as a solution. A conception of the flow of time can dictate political values. The grand cyclic preference for glory-based politics or an eschatological insistence on purity, on a radically clean slate, may work at cross-purposes with the freedom or equality orientation of a progressive frame. Might direct engagement with diverse temporal frames facilitate mutual understanding? Even if such understanding is not possible, the engagement might clarify why.

Identifying patterns of temporal rhetoric may also illuminate historical patterns of political behavior, which in turn may aid political forecasting. For example, there are stark similarities between the way temporal frames were deployed in the rhetoric of China's Taiping Rebellion and those of the contemporary Islamic State movement. Could attention to patterns of eschatological rhetoric in the communications strategies of rebel movements illuminate internal dynamics and help identify points of stress? If this proved to be the case, attention to temporal framing may have some predictive capacity in social science. The study of temporal-rhetorical framing thus has the potential to generate analytical tools with wide application.

In addition to these empirical lines of inquiry, this study generates analytical tools in the history of political thought and political theory. Political thought is animated by problems framed in conceptions of time's flow, as I have shown. For Polybius and Machiavelli, it

CONCLUSION

is the grand cyclical frame that generates the central problem of their work: preserving glory and stalling inevitable decline. The loss frame of primitivism helps drives Rousseau's work on the social contract and education. And it is in no small part the urgent threat of eschatological politics that animated the political thought of Hobbes, Saint Thomas Aquinas, and others. Attention to temporal-rhetorical framing is thus of use not only in empirical social science and in politics itself but in the study of the history of political ideas.

From the perspective of normative political theory, the dynamic theory of legitimation I have recommended can deepen the infiltration of lived moral politics into the sometimes sterile realm of analytic political thought. I have argued that consent is the mark of, not the constituent element of, a judgment of legitimacy. But conversely, it matters that people themselves—not philosophers on their behalf—make this judgment. It matters normatively because of the role of judgment in the exercise of moral and political autonomy. The exercise of moral autonomy is not eliminated but displaced from the act of consent onto the activity of judgment. This captures both the intuition that there are substantive criteria for legitimacy for which moral arguments can be formulated and the idea that the activity of formulating and considering those arguments—who does this and under what conditions—matters too. If philosophers can inform public judgment with moral argument about what kind of power people hypothetically ought to accept, this activity must be understood *modestly.* Attention to symbolic communication about power and its justification provides insight into what leads people to make judgments about legitimacy in the first place, enriching the study of political ethics.

The dynamic conception of legitimation, by according proper place to performance, can also shed light on concrete ethical-political questions. For example, it helps to illuminate the interplay between a leader's own accumulated or threatened performance legitimacy and that of the regime and its institutions, including political parties. On the conception of legitimacy developed here, these three pillars of political order—individual officeholders, institutions, and regime—serve as mutual shock absorbers for performance failures. A political leader with banked performance legitimacy may displace blame for failures and crises onto democratic institutional structures to secure her own reserves. This opens the way for a move toward authoritarianism. Individual resignations may secure a political party's performance legitimacy. Conversely, the public's power to throw out a party helps to steady the regime type in the wake of a crisis. The sacrifice of any one of these three pillars may protect the stores of performance legitimacy of another. The odd resignation prevents, over time, institutions from falling into disrepute. The reputable function of institutions, over time, insulates the regime from challenge.

To see how this analytical tool can be put to use, consider how banked legitimacy and the interplay between order-based and performative legitimacy illuminate when and why some political agents make the rights-derogation decisions they do in times of crisis. Because a crisis—when not manufactured and controlled from the outset—is a spectacular failure to anticipate and plan for contingency, excessive or irrational constraints on liberty may be an attempt to compensate for the loss of performance legitimacy. Scholars have often approached emergency rights derogations as a threat to a regime's legal, order-based legitimacy. But from the dynamic legitimation perspective, rights derogations can be understood less as a challenge to legitimacy than as a critical means of *restoring* legitimacy, that is, performance legitimacy. Doubtless there are many more applications of this framework worth investigating.

CONCLUSION

Some questions, notably issues of intentionality and uptake of these rhetorical strategies, have not been addressed in depth here, but they also warrant further study. Often, in the cases discussed above, empirical evidence supports the claim that the use of temporal framing strategies was intentional. There is little doubt, for instance, that Khubilai's calendar reform was an explicit effort at legitimation. First, there is no reasonable competing explanation that could account for the extent of resources he poured into the project, particularly given his lack of personal or cultural connection to the practice. Second, there is written evidence in the form of Liu Ping-Chung's memo. There is also little doubt that the drafters of China's constitutional preambles used temporal framing intentionally because, as we saw in chapter 1, they have told us so. It seems reasonable, too, to assume that Abimael Guzmán, a scholar in a Catholic country, was conscious of the eschatological character of his speeches to Sendero Luminoso comrades. In other cases, intentionality is less patent. Where conscious intent is less evident, it is consonant with the cognitive science of other forms of symbolic communication, such as the study of metaphor. Just as people use metaphors such as "wasting time" without consciously attending to their status as metaphors or considering how metaphors work, people also frame claims without a fully present consciousness of why their speech is effective. Cognitive scientists like George Lakoff are at work on this phenomenon.[3]

Moreover, I have only marginally addressed the question of uptake in the cases described above. How can we know whether such rhetoric is effective? Evidently, Guzmán's and Orbán's rhetorical practices have been effective, but only with subsets of the relevant populations and in concert with a range of other legitimation strategies. How do we know to what extent the people of China were willing to accept Khubilai's legitimating efforts? Or whether the people of

CONCLUSION

Copan were even interested in the baktun propaganda that proliferated in their visual space? While social scientists have been at work on the question of what works and what doesn't in the field of framing, it may be a particularly fruitful area of empirical inquiry to consider what specifically determines susceptibility to diverse forms of temporal framing.[4] Are there characteristics common to people who find eschatology compelling, for example? This would seem to be a potentially rewarding line of inquiry with respect to the study of political movements.

We set out, in this book, with this question: What work does time talk do at moments of political change? Political leaders, I have argued, can construct arcs of time that give shape to experience and meaning to events. When political order is fractured, time, too, seems out of joint. To restore a sense of order a leader may aggressively establish a sense of time. Situating events of political change in novel arcs of time lends them meaning and sense. Hence, time's association with nature, order, and reason, and the ease with which it fades from conscious presence, helps political leaders legitimize innovation. The meaning of some event or innovation is shaped by its implied, and seemingly natural, place in an expected sequence. And the centrality of time to political performance, the other key well of legitimacy, provides further opportunities. Charting time aids planning, necessary for good performance, but beyond this, calendar reform itself can be a performance of capacity, demonstrating a regime's superior technical, scientific, or esoteric mastery. Structured time can be used as a means of performing capacity, mitigating risk, and managing contingency. These performative demands are necessary conditions for legitimacy too.

A political leader who desires not order and legitimacy but their disruption will find other time techniques at her disposal. Primitivism

CONCLUSION

and eschatology postulate a time before and a time beyond the current time of events and enforced human order. Escape from the time of events is freedom both from the inevitable decay and degeneration that time brings and from the inevitable domination that human order requires for its enforcement. Using these temporal-rhetorical frames—primitivism and eschatology—I have shown how a political leader can block both wells of legitimacy, undermining human order in anticipation of a spontaneous self-ordered mode of existence maintained through love, not law. Through such techniques, the practice of shaping time—whether in words or by means of technologies like clocks and calendars—becomes a tool in a dynamic politics of legitimation. What work does time talk do at moments of political change? We now have a plausible answer.

All politics of time rely on the interplay between openness and constraint, abstraction and determination, disjointedness and restoration. This interplay, in turn, both draws upon and gives expression to the most fundamental questions regarding our capacity for the production of meaning. Meaning depends both on intrinsic characteristics of an event, object, symbol, and so on and on the frames in which it is situated. The frame provides the cognitive constraints within which interpretation is possible. A political actor who frames an event, innovation, or claim in a conception of the flow of time, is sharply constraining the range of possible meanings and thereby enabling the determination of meaning, which is not possible in a context of radical openness. Freedom more generally shares this characteristic. The meaning of choice is always dependent on a range of limitations and structures that provide the frames for action, the means of interpreting the significance of action. This, ultimately, is why temporal framing works. It creates an intersection of connection between the meaning of an individual's action at a point in time and a point of time in the lifespan of something more grand and lasting. It is the congruence of a point in our time with a point in political-historical time that ultimately creates a sense of oneness with a people, a cause, or a political community. When this congruence is achieved, it is the most powerful form of legitimation.

Notes

Introduction

1. Lincoln said: "Four score and seven years ago our fathers brought forth, upon this continent, a new nation, conceived in Liberty, and dedicated to the proposition that all men are created equal. Now we are engaged in a great civil war. . . . It is . . . for us to be here dedicated to the great task remaining before us . . . that this nation shall have a new birth of freedom; and that this government of the people, by the people, for the people, shall not perish from the earth."

2. Maximilien Robespierre, "Speech to the Convention, February 5, 1794," World Future Fund, http://www.worldfuturefund.org/wffmaster/Reading/Communism/ROBESPIERRE'S%20SPEECH.htm.

3. Brigid Fowler, "Nation, State, Europe and National Revival in Hungarian Party Politics: The Case of the Millennial Commemorations," *Europe-Asia Studies* 60 (2004).

4. Jean-Jacques Rousseau, *The Government of Poland*, trans. Wilmoore Kendall (Indianapolis: Hackett, 1985), 13.

5. Benedict de Spinoza to Jarigh Jelles, June 2, 1674, in *The Chief Works of Benedict de Spinoza*, vol. 2, trans. R. H. M. Elwes (London: George Bell & Sons, 1901).

6. E. P. Thompson, "Time, Work Discipline, and Industrial Capitalism," *Past & Present* 38, no. 1 (1967).

7. Along these lines, a note about historical sources: in presenting the examples, anecdotes, and cases in this book, I have worked with primary materials where possible. But by necessity of their linguistic, geographic, and historical range, I have had often to rely on translations and secondary sources. In this I beg the indulgence of historians or area specialists. With these broad-brush strokes I do not intend to make any novel contribution to the historical study of these *cases* but rather to employ them as, in some cases, what Goffman called "typifications," and in others, what Lijphart called "plausibility probes" in the study of a political phenomenon. In the first case,

they provide illustration, and in the second, an initial test of a theory's explanatory power. Erving Goffman, *Frame Analysis* (New York: Harper & Row, 1974), 14; Arend Lijphart, "Comparative Politics and the Comparative Method," *American Political Science Review* 65, no. 3 (1971): 682–93.

8. There are many examples of attention to the temporal structures of narrative in the context of historiography. Fernand Braudel and the French Annalistes used the idea that history unfolds in three temporal layers as an analytical means of drawing attention to non-eventual history. More recently, building on the work of the Annalistes, Penelope Corfield has also emphasized the importance of conceptions of the flow of time in the construction of narrative history. For Corfield, this is a matter of historiographical importance, but it has also been cast as a matter of normative importance in the work of critical historians, like Hayden White, for whom all historical narrative is, by means of its (temporal) structure, ideologically inflected rhetoric. Fernand Braudel, *La Méditerranée et le monde méditerranéen à l'époque de Philippe II*, 3 vols. (Paris: Flammarion, 2009); Penelope Corfield, *Time and the Shape of History* (New Haven: Yale University Press, 2007); Hayden White, *The Content of the Form: Narrative Discourse and Historical Representation* (Baltimore: Johns Hopkins University Press, 1987).

9. Historians not only use temporalities in scholarly narratives, they produce narrative histories of temporality. Reinhart Koselleck, for instance, has devoted many essays to historical shifts in perceptions of temporality. Prior to the Enlightenment, he has argued, inevitability, either of the eschaton or of repeating patterns of events, meant the future was already present in any past moment. But with modernity comes a dramatic acceleration of time and the sense that the past contains not a determined future but rather "a future which has to be made." Reinhart Koselleck, *Futures Past,* trans. Keith Tribe (New York: Columbia, 2004), 40. The notion that the future is unknowable is certainly more prominent in modernity, but we shall see that it would be premature to consider modern temporalities decisively ascendant. Regardless, my interest is primarily in *how* conceptions of the flow of time are used politically, rather than when. Nonetheless, "when" matters when historians' own claims about the history of temporalities become politicized or politically inflected, as will be evident in the discussion of E. P. Thompson's work in chapter 4.

10. Ayatollah Ali Khamenei, "Leader's Remarks in Meeting with Commanders and Staff of the Islamic Republic of Iran Air Force," Office of the Supreme Leader, February 8, 2016, http://www.leader.ir/en/speech/14171/Ayatollah-Khamenei-meeting-with-Air-Force-commanders.

11. Shakespeare, *Hamlet,* act 1, scene 5, line 211.

Chapter 1. The Political Construction of Time

1. A similar claim is found in Norbert Elias, *Time: An Essay,* trans. Edmund Jephcott (Oxford: Blackwell, 1992), 10, 46.

2. Steven H. Strogatz, *The Mathematical Structure of the Human Sleep-Wake Cycle* (Berlin: Springer, 1986). See also Joshua Foer and Michel Siffre, "Caveman: An Interview with Michel Siffre," *Cabinet* 30 (2008).

3. Michael C. Frank, D. L. Everett, Evelina Fedorenko, and Edward Gibson, "Number as a Cognitive Technology: Evidence from Pirahã Language and Cognition," *Cognition* 108, no. 3 (2008): 819–24.

4. Michael C. Frank, Evelina Fedorenko, and Edward Gibson, "Language as a Cognitive Technology: English Speakers Match Like Pirahã When You Don't Let Them Count," *Proceedings of the 30th Annual Meeting of the Cognitive Science Society* (2008), 439.

5. J. M. E. McTaggart, "The Unreality of Time," *Mind* 17, no. 68 (1908): 457–74.

6. Douglas Dwyer, "How Atomic Clocks Work," How Stuff Works, April 1, 2000, http://science.howstuffworks.com/atomic-clock1.htm.

7. Foer and Siffre, "Caveman."

8. Strogatz, *Mathematical Structure,* 109.

9. For example, the water clock described by Al-Khazini in a twelfth-century treatise was built because it was essential "for a knowledge of times, and the calculation of the movements [of the heavens], and for obtaining the fractions of the degrees." See *On the Balance for the Hours and Their Degrees,* trans. Donald R. Hill, in *Arabic Water-Clocks* (Aleppo: University of Aleppo Institute for the History of Arabic Science, 1981), 48–49. See also Joseph Needham, Ling Wang, and Derek J. De Solla Price, *Heavenly Clockwork. The Great Astronomical Clocks of Medieval China* (Cambridge: Cambridge University Press, 1960); Nathan Sivin, *Granting the Seasons* (New York: Springer, 1999), 19–21.

10. The hours are described in *The Holy Rule of St. Benedict,* trans. Reverend Boniface Verheyen, OSB, 1949, Christian Classics Ethereal Library, http://www.ccel.org/ccel/benedict/rule2/files/rule2.html. Steven A. Epstein, "Business Cycles and the Sense of Time in Medieval Genoa," *Business History Review* 62, no. 2 (1988): 238–60.

11. Aristotle, *Physics,* in *Complete Works of Aristotle,* vol. 1, ed. Jonathan Barnes (Princeton: Princeton University Press, 1984), 219a–219b1, 220b.

12. Aristotle, *Physics,* 219a–219b1, 220b.

13. St. Augustine, *Confessions,* trans. Albert Outler (Louisville, KY: Westminster John Knox, 2006), book 11, chapter 14, section 17.

14. On the task- and situation-dependency of notions of accuracy, see the discussion of Galileo's pulse in Paul Glennie and Nigel Thrift, *Shaping the Day: A History of Timekeeping in England and Wales, 1300–1800* (Oxford: Oxford University Press, 2009), 4ff.

15. See Kimberly Hutchings, *Time and World Politics* (Manchester: Manchester University Press, 2008), 4–5, but Hutchings subsequently claims that Newtonian time is "a universally shared, precisely regulated experience of time" that *replaced* prior nature-based "imprecise, unevenly experience temporality" (6). Hutchings thereby underestimates the presence of forms of clock time in built cultures prior to modern Europe and overestimates the extent to which clock time replaces—rather than complements—other forms of time keeping. After all, the "highly complex systems of production, exchange and distribution" that she claims clock time enables have existed in other times and places, notably but not exclusively the Roman Empire and its system of trade with India and China. See, for instance, Emanuel Mayer, *The Ancient Middle Classes* (Cambridge, MA: Harvard University Press, 2012); Roberta Tomber, *Indo-Roman Trade* (London: Duckworth, 2008).

16. Benjamin Whorf, "An American Indian Model of the Universe," in *Language, Thought, and Reality* (Cambridge, MA: MIT Press, 1964).

17. Edward Evan Evans-Pritchard, *The Nuer: A Description of the Modes of Livelihood and Political Institutions of a Nilotic People* (Oxford: Oxford University Press, 1969), 101ff.

18. Kosta Gounis, "Temporality and the Domestication of Homelessness," in *The Politics of Time,* ed. Henry J. Rutz (Washington, DC: American Anthropological Association, 1992).

19. See, for example, Tomonaga Tairako, "Time and Temporality from the Japanese Perspective," in *Time and Temporality in Intercultural Perspective,* ed. Douwe Tiemermsma and Henk Oosterling (Amsterdam: Editions Rodopi, 1996), 94; Georges Gurvich, *Spectrum of Social Time,* trans. Myrtle Korenbaum (New York: Springer: 1964), 91.

20. Hans Schwartz, *Eschatology* (Grand Rapids, MI: William B. Eerdmans, 2000), 8.

21. Stephen Hanson, *Time and Revolution* (Chapel Hill: University of North Carolina Press, 1997), 2.

22. Danielle Allen, "A Schedule of Boundaries: An Exploration, Launched from the Water-clock, of Athenian Time," *Greece & Rome* 43, no. 2 (1996): 157–68.

23. Isaac Newton, *Principia Mathematica,* trans. Andre Motte (New York: Daniel Adee, 1846), 77.

24. Newton, *Principia Mathematica,* 79; my emphasis.

25. Our modern-day atomic clocks are our best current approximation. But since Einstein, we know that what Newton assumed was the "equable" flow of time in nature is only ever relative.

26. Since time is movement and all forms are unchanging, no Platonic Form partakes of time, nor is time itself a Form. Plato, *Timaeus,* trans. D. Zeyl (Indianapolis: Hackett, 2000), 37b. I am grateful to Professor Lloyd Gerson for his assistance with this passage.

27. Titus Maccius Plautus, *Comedies,* vol. 5, trans. William Warner (London: Becket & De Hondt, 1874), 363–64.

28. Allen, "A Schedule of Boundaries"; E. P. Thompson, "Time, Work Discipline, and Industrial Capitalism," *Past & Present* 38, no. 1 (1967): 56–97; Claude Javeau, "Comptes et mescomptes du temps," *Cahiers internationaux de sociologies,* n.s. 74 (1983): 72. See also the discussion in Jonathan Gershuny and Oriel Sullivan, "The Sociological Uses of Time-Use Diary Analysis," *European Sociological Review* 14 no. 1 (1998): 70ff.

29. Colorfully tying linear time to progress, Nathan Sivin describes the contemporary Western "overall frame of time [as] long and narrow and pointed upward, rising from the squalor of primitive savagery to the blessed state in which every family in the world will have two television sets and will replace them both every year." Nathan Sivin, "Chinese Conceptions of Time," *Earlham Review* 1 (1965): 82–92.

30. Mircea Eliade, *Myths, Dreams, and Mysteries,* trans. Philip Mairet (New York: Harper & Row, 1967), 23.

31. Tsvetan Todorov, *The Conquest of America: The Question of the Other* (Norman: University of Oklahoma Press, 1999), 84ff.

32. Gurvich, *Spectrum of Social Time,* 91. See also Edward T. Hall, *The Dance of Life* (New York: Anchor Books, 1983); David M. Engel, "Law, Time, and Community," *Law & Society Review* 21, no. 4 (1987): 605–38; Christopher R. Hallpike, *The Foundations of Primitive Thought* (New York: Oxford University Press, 1979); John Gunnell, *Political Philosophy and Time* (Middletown: Wesleyan University Press, 1968), 27ff.

33. For example: "Primitives' minds do not represent time exactly as ours do. Primitives do not see, extending indefinitely in imagination, something like a straight line, always homogenous by nature, upon which events fall into position, a line on

which foresight can arrange them in a unilinear and irreversible series, and on which they must of necessity occur one after the other. To the primitive time is not, as it is to us, a kind of intellectualized intuition, an 'order of succession.'" Lucien Lévy-Bruhl, *Les fonctions mentales dans les sociétés inférieures* (Ann Arbor: University of Michigan Library, 1910): 157–58. See also Donna Peuquet, *Representations of Space and Time* (New York: Guilford, 2002), 14; Dawn Elaine Bastian and Judy K. Mitchell, *Handbook of Native American Mythology* (Santa Barbara: ABC-CLIO, 2004), 34; Alfred Gell, *The Anthropology of Time* (Oxford: Berg, 1992).

34. Gershuny and Sullivan, "The Sociological Uses of Time-Use Diary Analysis," 70.

35. Hesiod, *Works and Days,* trans. Stanley Lombardo (Indianapolis: Hackett, 1993); Geoffrey Chaucer, *Parliament of Fowls,* around line 680.

36. John Stuart Mill, *Autobiography* (New York: Henry Holt, 1873), 163. See also Hutchings, *Time and World Politics,* 7.

37. John Stuart Mill, *On Coleridge,* in *Utilitarianism and Other Essays.* (New York: Penguin, 2004), 196.

38. Mill, *On Coleridge* 184.

39. Mill, *Autobiography,* 163ff; Mill, *On Coleridge,* e.g., at p. 191.

40. Giambattista Vico, *New Science,* trans. David Marsh (London: Penguin, 2000), axiom 241.

41. Auguste Comte to John Stuart Mill, October 21, 1844, in *The Correspondence of John Stuart Mill and Auguste Comte,* trans. Oscar A. Haac (London: Routledge, 1994), 263.

42. Eric Voegelin argues that there is a strong eschatological element to Comte's work. *New Science of Politics: An Introduction* (Chicago: University of Chicago Press, 1952), 131.

43. See, for example, Karl Marx and Friederich Engels, *The German Ideology* (Amherst: Prometheus, 1998), 33ff; G. W. F. Hegel, *Lectures on the Philosophy of World History,* trans. H. B. Nisbet (Cambridge: Cambridge University Press, 1975).

44. Inevitable decline is emphasized in Oswald Spengler, *Decline of the West* (New York: Vintage, 2006). Cyclicality is emphasized in Stephen Skowronek, *The Politics Presidents Make* (Cambridge, MA: Belknap, 1997); and random punctuation is the key element in Thomas Kuhn, *The Structure of Scientific Revolutions* (Chicago: University of Chicago Press, 2012).

45. This is argued most elegantly by Michael Young: "The disposition to cycles is evidently a common property of human beings." The idea of habit, for instance, of

"how we do things," is a cyclic idea that stands at the very heart of human culture and development. *The Metronomic Society* (Cambridge, MA: Harvard University Press, 1988), 120.

46. Polybius, *Histories,* trans. Evelyn Shuckburgh (Bloomington: Indiana University Press, 1962), book 6.

47. Chen Chi-yun has pointed out that the *Standard Histories* or *Zhengshi* record dynastic histories in a manner that shows their rise and fall. This can give the impression of cyclicality. But Chen points out "the difference between 'dynastic cycles' and 'historical cycles' or 'time cycles.' 'Dynastic cycles' configure the regimes of biological families, that is, the ruling dynastic houses, which would be analogous to each other in observing similar biological restraints and refrains . . . birth, maturity, decline, and death." Indeed, it was an important feature of history writing that dynasties and biographies were set down in the annals only after their subjects were gone. The very purpose of the histories was to maintain the memory of something that would otherwise have passed permanently out of the world. "Immanental Human Beings in Transcendent Time: Epistemological Basis of Pristine Chinese Historical Consciousness," in *Notions of Time in Chinese Historical Thinking,* ed. Huang Chun-Chieh and John Henderson (Hong Kong: Chinese University Press, 2006), 47–48.

48. On the subject of temporal incommensurability specifically, see Ekkehardt Malotki's critique of the Whorfian claim that we and the Hopi have radically incommensurate time notions. Malotki documented a range of linguistic evidence that the Hopi use something akin to tenses (future/nonfuture) and have words denoting duration, moment, occasion, and temporal propriety (whether an action is appropriate at a specific point in time). And Hopi expresses the seemingly universal basic association of temporal orientation with spatial orientation. Ekkehardt Malotki, *Hopi Time* (Tübingen: De Gruyter Mouton, 1983). See also, generally, Gell, *The Anthropology of Time.*

49. Maurice Bloch, "The Past and the Present in the Present," *Man* 12, no. 2 (1977): 285.

50. Historically, the uses we have for time have usually antedated the relevant technology. While new uses may be found for these technologies, it is the desire for precision, portability, adjustability, or efficiency that has driven innovation in the realm of technologies for time measurement and the marking of time. See Glennie and Thrift, *Shaping the Day,* 40.

51. I am of course not the first to recognize that each person's life is characterized by different "kinds" of time in different contexts. See, for instance, Jacques LeGoff,

"Merchant's Time and Church's Time," in *Time, Work, and Culture in the Middle Ages* (Chicago: University of Chicago Press, 1980); Glennie and Thrift, *Shaping the Day*, 103.

52. Erving Goffman, *Frame Analysis* (New York: Harper & Row, 1974), 10ff.

53. Goffman, *Frame Analysis*, 287; see also 247.

54. Goffman, *Frame Analysis*, 24.

55. The contemporary empirical study of intentional framing began with Daniel Kahneman and Amos Tversky's seminal article, "Prospect Theory: An Analysis of Decision under Risk," *Econometrica* 47 (1979): 263–91. Kahneman and Tversky demonstrated that "seemingly inconsequential changes in the formulation of choice problems caused significant shifts of preference." Amos Tversky and Daniel Kahneman, "The Framing of Decisions and the Psychology of Choice," *Science*, n.s., 211, no. 4481 (1981): 457. An overview of recent work on framing is found in Dennis Chong and James N. Druckman, "Framing Theory," *Annual Review of Political Science* 10 (June 2007): 103–26.

56. Todd Gitlin, *The Whole World Is Watching: Mass Media in the Making and Unmaking of the New Left* (Berkeley: University of California Press, 1980), 6.

57. Jim Kuypers, *Bush's War: Media Bias and Justifications for War in a Terrorist Age* (Lanham, MD: Rowman & Littlefield, 2006), 6.

58. George Lakoff, *The Political Mind* (New York: Penguin, 2009); George Lakoff and Mark Johnson, *Metaphors We Live By* (Chicago: University of Chicago Press, 2003).

59. Bryan Garsten, *Saving Persuasion* (Cambridge, MA: Harvard University Press, 2006), 2.

60. Robert D. Benford and David A. Snow, "Framing Processes and Social Movements: An Overview and Assessment," *Annual Review of Sociology* 26 (2000): 611–39.

61. David A. Snow et al., "Frame Alignment Processes, Micromobilization, and Movement Participation," *American Sociological Review* 51, no. 4 (1986): 467.

62. Snow et al., "Frame Alignment Processes," 469.

63. Snow et al., "Frame Alignment Processes," 472–73.

64. Garsten, *Saving Persuasion*, 2.

65. Steven Lukes, *Power: A Radical View* (London: Macmillan, 1974), 6.

66. Mayling Birney, "Beyond Performance Legitimacy: Procedural Legitimacy and Discontent in China" (London School of Economics, International Development Working Paper Series 2017, no. 17–189), 12.

67. Hugo Grotius, *Rights of War and Peace* (New York: M. Walter Dunne, 1901), book 1.3.8.

68. Allen Buchanan, *Justice, Legitimacy, and Self-Determination* (Oxford: Oxford University Press), 432.

69. Bruce Gilley, "The Meaning and Measure of State Legitimacy: Results for 72 Countries," *European Journal of Political Research* 45 (2006): 499–525.

70. Birney, "Beyond Performance Legitimacy." See Fritz Scharpf, *Governing in Europe: Effective and Democratic?* (Oxford: Oxford University Press, 1999).

71. David Beetham, *The Legitimation of Power* (London: Palgrave Macmillan, 2013), xiv.

72. Thomas Hobbes, *Leviathan* (Oxford: Oxford University Press, 1909), book 1, chapter 10.

73. Beetham, *Legitimation of Power*, 11.

74. This contrasts with, for example, the carefully delineated institutional "instruction books" Elazar claims are characteristic of European Western constitutions. Daniel Elazar, "Constitution Making: The Pre-eminently Political Act," in *Redesigning the State: The Politics of Constitutional Change in Industrial Nations*, ed. Keith G. Banting and Richard Siméon (New York: Springer, 1985), 232.

75. As Mayling Birney argued, Chinese officials choose to be bound by, or free of, ideological, legal, and institutional strictures depending on their relative usefulness to mandated policy aims in specific cases. "Decentralization and Veiled Corruption under 'China's Rule of Mandates,'" *World Development* 53 (2014): 55–67.

76. Preamble, *Constitution of China* (1978).

77. Preamble, *Constitution of China* (1978).

78. Preamble, *Constitution of China* (1978).

79. Preamble, *Constitution of China* (1978).

80. It is noteworthy that, in contrast to previous deposed leaders, Hua was not harmed or jailed but merely demoted, marking another worthy reform.

81. Michael Ng-Quinn, "Deng Xiaoping's Political Reform and Political Order," *Asian Survey* 22 (1982): 1201.

82. Article 7, *Constitution of China* (1982), https://www.constituteproject.org/constitution/China_2004?lang=en; Article 11, *Constitution of China* (1978).

83. Preamble, *Constitution of China* (1982).

84. Denis Feeney, *Caesar's Calendar: Ancient Time and the Beginnings of History* (Berkeley: University of California Press, 2008), 138.

85. *Constitution of China* (1982); my emphasis.

86. Zhang Youyu and Xianzheng Luncong, *An Essay Collection on Constitutional Governance* (Beijing: Mass, 1986), 27–28.

87. Zhang Youyu, "Further Researching and Implementing the New Constitution," *China Legal Studies* (1984), cited in translation by Zhang Qianfan and Yanhuang Chunqiu, "The Controversy on the Preamble to the Constitution and Its Effects," June 13, 2013, China Copyright and Media, https://chinacopyrightandmedia.wordpress.com/2013/06/10/the-controversy-on-the-preamble-to-the-constitution-and-its-effects.

Chapter 2. Calendars and the Politics of Order Alignment

Epigraph: Slogan of the Yellow Scarf Rebels who, led by a Taoist sect, sought to overthrow the corrupt Han Dynasty. Professor Hu Jing of Yale-NUS College kindly rendered this original verse translation.

1. J. G. A. Pocock, "Time, Institutions, and Action," in *Politics, Language, and Time* (Chicago: University of Chicago Press, 1989), 252.

2. H. Dabashi, *Theology of Discontent: The Ideological Foundation of the Islamic Revolution in Iran* (New York: New York University Press, 1993); Ayatollah Khomeini, *Islam and Revolution: Writings and Declarations of Imam Khomeini,* trans. H. Algar (Berkeley: Mizan, 1981). H. Ram, *Myth and Mobilization in Revolutionary Iran* (Washington, DC: American University Press, 1994).

3. Denis Feeney, *Caesar's Calendar: Ancient Time and the Beginnings of History* (Berkeley: University of California Press, 2008), 161, 188. See also Mary Beard, "A Complex of Times: No More Sheep on Romulus' Birthday," *Cambridge Classical Journal* 33 (1987): 1–15; Andrew Wallace-Hadrill, *Rome's Cultural Revolution* (Cambridge: Cambridge University Press, 2008).

4. See, for example, William Eskridge Jr. and John Ferejohn, *A Republic of Statutes* (New Haven: Yale University Press, 2010); Akhil Amar, "America's Constitution, Written and Unwritten" *Syracuse Law Review* 57 (2007): 267–87; Jack Balkin and Sanford Levinson, "The Processes of Constitutional Change," *Fordham Law Review* 75 (2006); Stephen M. Griffin, "Constitutional Change in the United States," *Fordham Law Review* 75 (2006); Cass Sunstein, *A Constitution of Many Minds* (Princeton: Princeton University Press, 2011).

5. The week, like the hour, has no natural correlate but universally functions as the means of delineating forms of market activity. It comes in a variety of lengths, although the seven-day version is naturalized enough that some languages, like Hungarian, use the same word for "seven" and "week" (*hét*). It is interesting to consider the reason for the sacralization of cycles of work and rest, which seems to have been a Jewish innovation. On this, see the fascinating discussion of Elisheva Carlbach in

Palaces of Time (Cambridge, MA: Belknap, 2011). By contrast, there is no specific holy weekday on which Buddhists or Hindus or Zoroastrians pray. Perhaps this is related to the sociopolitical functionality of the sacralization of a rest day. A society thereby prescribes which acceptable activities will constitute rest, proscribing other activities in the process, and it does not take much imagination to see how this could be both socially and politically useful.

6. Eviatar Zerubavel, "The French Republican Calendar: A Case Study in the Sociology of Time," *American Sociological Review* 42, no. 6 (1977): 868–77.

7. Clive Foss, "Stalin's Topsy-Turvy Work Week," *History Today* 54, no. 9 (2004): 46–47.

8. David Dearborn et al., "Intimachy: A December Solstice Observatory at Machu Picchu, Peru," *American Antiquity* 52, no. 2 (1987): 346–52.

9. Examples include the Islamic, Hebrew, and Sumerian calendars.

10. Claudian, "Of an Old Man of Verona Who Never Left His Home," in *Carmina Minora,* trans. Abraham Cowley (Cambridge, MA: Loeb Classical Library, 1921), 195–97.

11. Marcus Tullius Cicero, *Letters to Atticus,* trans. D. R. Shackleton Bailey (Cambridge, MA: Loeb Classic Library, 1999), 5.21.

12. Cicero, *Letters to Atticus,* 6.1.

13. There would be twenty-three or twenty-four days of February, then that month would be "put on hold" while the intercalary month ticked along. At the end of the intercalary month, February would resume with its last few days before March began.

14. L. Richardson Jr. has suggested that Cicero must have been joking in his request for this news, since he can't have expected a response to his letter in time to set his calendar straight before the actual beginning of the intercalary month. See his "Cicero, Att. 5.2.14. and the Romana Mysteria," *Phoenix* 55, no. 3 (2001): 411–13.

15. Cassius Dio relates this story about Bibulus, consul with Julius Caesar in 59 BCE. Aiming to block a controversial piece of legislation, "Bibulus . . . when no other excuse for delay was any longer left him, . . . proclaimed a sacred period for all the remaining days of the year alike, during which the people could not legally even meet in their assembly." Unfortunately, his ploy was unsuccessful and the story ends with Bibulus "thrust down the steps, his fasces . . . broken to pieces, and the tribunes as well as others received blows and wounds" Cassius Dio, *Roman History,* vol. 3 (Cambridge, MA: Loeb Classical Library, 1914), book 38.6.1. It is noteworthy that intercalation was also subject to political considerations in Assyria, as John M. Steele

makes clear in "Making Sense of Time: Observational and Theoretical Calendars," in *Oxford Handbook of Cuneiform Culture*," ed. Karen Radner and Eleanor Robson (Oxford: Oxford University Press, 2011), 475.

16. Andrew Wallace-Hadrill has argued that the Julian reform had to do with an overall drive for rationalization, a Greek fashion for the scientific and well ordered. If this is so, it bolsters the claim that Julius Caesar wished to associate himself with what was rightly ordered, natural, and rational, and the calendar reform was useful to this end. See "Time for Augustus," in *Homo Viator: Classical Essays for John Bramble*, ed. M. Whitby et al. (Bristol: Bristol Classical, 1987), 221–30.

17. In this account of Julius and Augustus, I follow the work of Denis Feeney in *Caesar's Calendar*.

18. Macrobius, *Saturnalia*, trans. Robert Kastner (Cambridge, MA: Loeb Classical Library, 2011), 1.14.9.

19. It was only with Augustus that the calendar year became 365 1/4 days long. This may have been the result of misunderstanding, as the Egyptians seem to have correctly understood the year to be roughly 365 1/4 days.

20. Feeney, *Caesar's Calendar*, 175.

21. Feeney, *Caesar's Calendar*, 174.

22. See, generally, Beard, "A Complex of Times."

23. Niccolò Machiavelli, *Discourses on Livy*, trans. N. Tarcov and Harvey Mansfield (Chicago: University of Chicago Press, 1996), 3.1.

24. Takeshi Inomata, "Spatial Mobility of Non-elite populations in Classical Maya Society and Its Political Implications," in *Ancient Maya Commoners*, ed. Jon Lohse and Fred Valdez Jr. (Austin: University of Texas Press, 2004), 175–96.

25. Key works on Copan include E. W. Andrews and William L. Fash, eds., *Copan* (Santa Fe: School of American Research Press, 2005); Ellen Bell, Marcello A. Canuto, and Robert J. Sharer, eds., *Understanding Early Classic Copan* (Philadelphia: University of Pennsylvania Museum of Archaeology and Anthropology, 2004).

26. Steven V. Roberts, "White House Confirms Reagans Follow Astrology, Up to a Point," *New York Times*, May 4, 1988.

27. Works on the Mayan calendar include Anthony Aveni, *Empires of Time: Calendars, Clocks and Cultures* (London: Tauris Parke, 1990), 185ff; Susan Millbrath, *Star Gods of the Maya* (Austin: University of Texas Press, 2000), 2ff; Prudence Rice, *Maya Political Science* (Austin: University of Texas Press, 2004). Might hot climates, where toes are habitually visible, more often feature a base-twenty than a base-ten or base-twelve (ten fingers, two hands) system of calculation?

28. Stuart, "The Beginning of the Copan Dynasty: A Review of the Hieroglyphic and Historical Evidence," in Bell, Canuto, and Sharer, *Understanding Early Classic Copan*, 239.

29. Stuart, "The Beginning of the Copan Dynasty," 240.

30. These include Stelae J, 15, 28, 63, and structures 10L-16 and 10L-26. William L. Fash et al., "Setting the Stage: Origins of the Hieroglyphic Stairway Plaza on the Great Period Ending," in *Understanding Early Classic Copan*, 78. See also Stuart "The Beginnings of the Copan Dynasty," 240, 246.

31. Aveni, *Empires of Time*, 216.

32. Stuart, "The Beginning of the Copan Dynasty," 240; Robert J. Sharer, "Founding Events and Teotihuacan Connections," in *The Maya and Teotihuacan*, ed. Geoffrey E. Braswell (Austin: University of Texas Press, 2004), 150ff.

33. T. Beach et al., "Ancient Maya Impacts on Soils and Soil Erosion," *Catena* 66 (2006): 166–78.

34. R. J. Sharer and Loa P. Taxer, *The Ancient Maya* (Stanford: Stanford University Press, 2006), 338.

35. Kazuo Aoyama, "Commentary on Lucero," *Current Anthropology* 44 (2003): 545.

36. Arthur Desmarest, *Ancient Maya: The Rise and Fall of a Rainforest Civilization* (Cambridge: Cambridge University Press, 2004), 96; Arthur Desmarest, "Commentary on Lucero," *Current Anthropology* 44 (2003): 546.

37. Stephen Houston and David Stuart, "Of Gods, Glyphs and Kings: Divinity and Rulership among the Classic Maya," *Antiquity* 70 (1996): 301.

38. Houston and Stuart, "Of Gods, Glyphs and Kings," 295.

39. Andràs Pap, *Democratic Decline in Hungary* (London: Routledge, 2018), 12, 51.

40. See, for example Kim Lane Scheppele, "Legal but Not Fair (Hungary)," *New York Times*, April 13, 2014. See also "'Destroying Democracy': Hungarians Protest Controversial New Constitution," *Spiegel Online*, January 3, 2012; Charles Gati, "Hungary's Backward Slide," *New York Times*, December 12, 2011.

41. See Viktor Orbán's speech of July 26, 2014, at Bálványos Free Summer University and Youth Camp. Orbán said that the "Hungarian nation is not a simple sum of individuals, but a community that needs to be organized, strengthened and developed, and in this sense, the new state that we are building is an illiberal state, a non-liberal state. It does not deny foundational values of liberalism, as freedom, etc. But it does not make this ideology a central element of state organization, but applies a specific, national, particular approach in its stead." See also Pap, *Democratic Decline*, 60ff; Andras György Lengyel and Gabriella Ilonszki, "Simulated Democracy and

Pseudo-Transformational Leadership in Hungary," *Historical Social Research* 37 (2012): 115.

42. Venice Commission, *Opinion on the New Constitution of Hungary:* Council of Europe, Opinion No. 621 8–10 (2011), http://www.venice.coe.int/webforms/documents/default.aspx?pdffile=CDL-AD(2011)016-e.

43. Preamble, *Hungarian Basic Law* (2012). I am grateful to Dr. Nora Forgacs for her help with the text before an English-language version was available. The text now reflects the official English version: http://www.kormany.hu/download/e/02/00000/The%20New%20Fundamental%20Law%20of%20Hungary.pdf.

44. Pap, *Democratic Decline*, 24.

45. Jan-Werner Mueller, "Eastern Europe Goes South," *Foreign Affairs*, March–April 2014, 16. See also Pap, *Democratic Decline*, 53, 62.

46. The preambles to the Treaties of Rome (1958) and Maastricht (1992), and of the later abandoned Constitution of Europe (2004) are all explicitly progressive. For example, the Treaty of Rome's preamble records that states party shall aim "to ensure the economic and social progress of their countries" and seek "the constant improvement of the living and working conditions of their peoples." Partly through "the progressive abolition of restrictions on international trade, . . . [they desire] to ensure the development of their prosperity, . . . and strengthen peace and liberty." The preamble to the Maastricht Treaty describes itself as "mark[ing] a new stage in the process of European integration" and highlights "the historic importance of the ending of the division of the European continent and the need to create firm bases for the construction of the future Europe." This treaty is clearly situated in a progressive narrative arc, confirming the member states' "attachment to the principles of liberty, democracy and respect for human rights and fundamental freedoms and of the rule of law" while also being "determined to promote economic and social progress for their peoples, . . . and advances in economic integration . . . [and] parallel progress in other fields." They are, finally, "resolved to . . . [reinforce] the European identity." These elements are even more pronounced in the discarded constitution for Europe that Hungary signed in 2004 while Fidesz was in opposition.

47. Borbála Göncz and György Lengyel, "Changing Attitudes of Hungarian Political Elites toward the EU, 2007–2014," *Historical Social Research* 41, no. 4 (2016): 119.

48. Pap, *Democratic Decline*, 18.

49. Cited in Katalin Sárváry, "Legitimisation Struggles in Hungarian Politics: The Contours of Competing Foreign Policies in Prime Ministers' Speeches," *Perspectives* 27 (2007): 75.

50. Orbán described the EU as a "colonial power" in 2012. Cited in Mueller, "Eastern Europe Goes South," 18. See also Pap, *Democratic Decline*, 40.

51. Cited in Mueller, "Eastern Europe Goes South," 16.

52. Brigid Fowler, "Nation, State, Europe and National Revival in Hungarian Party Politics: The Case of the Millennial Commemorations," *Europe-Asia Studies* 60 (2004).

53. Machiavelli, *Discourses*, 3.1.

54. Polybius, *Histories*, trans. Evelyn Shuckburgh (Bloomington: Indiana University Press, 1962), book 6, para. 57.

55. Polybius, *Histories*, book 1, para. 1. For Polybius, fortune is "fruitful . . . in change, and constantly . . . producing dramas in the life of men," book 1, para. 4.

56. Polybius, *Histories*, book 3, para. 2.

57. Polybius, *Histories*, book 6, para. 1.

58. Polybius, *Histories*, book 6, para. 57.

59. Machiavelli, *Discourses*, 1.1.

60. Machiavelli, *Discourses*, 3.1.

61. Jean-Jacques Rousseau, *The Government of Poland*, trans. Wilmoore Kendall (Indianapolis: Hackett, 1985), 13.

62. Machiavelli, *Discourses*, 3.1.

63. Emile Durkheim, *Elementary Forms of Religious Life*, trans. Joseph Ward Swain (London: George Allen & Unwin, 1915), 387.

64. Durkheim, *Elementary Forms of Religious Life*, 427.

65. Laszlo Kurti, "People vs. State: Political Rituals in Contemporary Hungary," *Anthropology Today* 6, no. 2 (1990): 6.

66. Uli Linke, "Folklore, Anthropology, and the Government of Social Life," *Comparative Studies in Society and History* 32 (1990): 117–48; C. Lane, *The Rites of Rulers: Ritual in Industrial Society—The Soviet Case* (Cambridge: Cambridge University Press, 1981); Elizabeth Pleck, "The Making of the Domestic Occasion: The History of Thanksgiving in the United States," *Journal of Social History* 32, no. 4 (1999): 775, 780. See also Stanley Brandes, "The Day of the Dead, Halloween and the Quest for Mexican National Identity," *Journal of American Folklore* 111 (1998): 359–80; J. Abink, "Seged Celebration in Ethiopia and Israel: Continuity and Change of a Falasha Religious Holiday," *Anthropos* 78 (1983): 789–810.

67. Feeney, *Caesar's Calendar*, 151ff.

68. See, generally, Pleck, "The Making of the Domestic Occasion," 773–89.

69. Pitirim Sorokin and Robert Merton, "Social Time: Methodological and Functional Analysis," *American Journal of Sociology* 42 (1937): 615–29.

Chapter 3. Khubilai Khan's Calendar and the Politics of Performance

1. Jonathan Amos, "L'Aquila Quake: Italy Scientists Guilty of Manslaughter, Analysis," *BBC News*, October 22, 2012, http://www.bbc.co.uk/news/world-europe-20025626.

2. Quoted in Liam Moloney and Shirley Wang, "Court Convicts 7 for Failing to Warn of Quake," *Wall Street Journal*, October 22, 2012.

3. Judge Marco Billi explained his reasoning in a 950-page "Motivazione" as required by Italian law. See Edwin Cartlidge, "Judge in L'Aquila Earthquake Trial Explains His Verdict," *Science*, January 21, 2013.

4. Donald P. Moynihan, "The Response to Hurricane Katrina," in *Risk Governance Deficits: An Analysis and Illustration of the Most Common Deficits in Risk Governance* (Geneva: International Risk Governance Council, 2009), https://www.irgc.org/IMG/pdf/IRGC_rgd_web_final.pdf.

5. Pew Research Center, "Hurricane Katrina Survey," September 8, 2005, http://www.people-press.org/2005/09/08/hurricane-katrina-survey/. See, for instance, P. Burns and M. Thomas, "The Failure of the Nonregime: How Katrina Exposed New Orleans as a Regimeless City," *Urban Affairs Review* 41, no. 4 (2006): 517–27; *A Failure of Initiative: Final Report of the Select Bipartisan Committee to Investigate the Preparation for and Response to Hurricane Katrina* (Washington, DC: U.S. Government Printing Office, 2006).

6. Seymour Lipset, "Some Social Requisites of Democracy: Economic Development and Political Legitimacy," *American Political Science Review* 53, no. 1 (1959): 86.

7. Lipset, "Some Social Requisites of Democracy," 89.

8. Lipset, "Some Social Requisites of Democracy," 91.

9. Dingxin Zhao, "The Mandate of Heaven and Performance Legitimation in Historical and Contemporary China," *American Behavioral Scientist* 53, no. 3 (2009); Mayling Birney, "Beyond Performance Legitimacy: Procedural Legitimacy and Discontent in China" (London School of Economics, International Development Working Paper Series 2017, no. 17–189); "Performance Legitimacy," *Economist*, July 16, 2015.

10. Joseph Raz, *The Morality of Freedom* (Oxford: Clarendon, 1986), 56.

11. Fritz Scharpf, *Governing in Europe: Effective and Democratic?* (Oxford: Oxford University Press, 1999).

12. William Reno, "Illicit Markets, Violence, Warlords, and Governance: West African Cases," *Crime, Law, and Social Change* 52 (2009): 313–22.

13. Morris Rossabi, *Khubilai Khan: His Life and Times* (Berkeley: University of California Press, 2009), 4.

14. Annecorinne Freter and Elliot Abrams, "Chronology, Construction, and the Abandonment Process," in *Human Adaptation in Ancient Mesoamerica*, ed. Kirk D. Gonlin and Nancy French (Boulder: University of Colorado Press, 2016), 110ff.

15. Nonetheless, Descartes, throughout *Meditations on First Philosophy,* and Locke (*Second Treatise of Government,* chapter 5, section 27) both maintain that God is the ultimate guarantor of reason's reliability on the one hand, and property through self-ownership on the other.

16. Jean-Jacques Rousseau, *Social Contract,* trans. G. D. H. Cole (London: J. M. Dent, 1913), 2.7.

17. *Book of Documents,* "Junshi" chapter, cited in Zhao, "Mandate of Heaven," 420.

18. Zhao, "Mandate of Heaven," 421.

19. In a contemporary study, Bruce Gilley finds moderate to strong positive correlations between "good governance, poverty reduction and the provision of civil liberties" and legitimacy. Bruce Gilley, "The Meaning and Measure of State Legitimacy: Results for 72 Countries," *European Journal of Political Research* 45 (2006): 518.

20. Miguel La Serna, *The Corner of the Living: Ayacucho on the Eve of the Shining Path Insurgency* (Chapel Hill: University of North Carolina Press, 2012), 16.

21. Vanessa Piao, "Grandson of China's Most Hated Landlord Challenges Communist Lore," *New York Times,* July 27, 2016.

22. Pierre-Joseph Proudhon, *Les confessions d'un révolutionnaire* (Paris: Garnier Frères, 1850), 17; my translation, my emphasis.

23. Anthony Giddens, "Risk and Responsibility," *Modern Law Review* 62, no. 1 (1999): 3.

24. Ulrich Beck, *Risk Society: Towards a New Modernity* (London: Sage, 1992), 21.

25. Giddens, "Risk and Responsibility," 3; my emphasis.

26. Beck, *Risk Society,* 41ff.

27. La Serna, *The Corner of the Living,* 16ff.

28. Clifford Geertz, *Negara* (Princeton: Princeton University Press, 1980), 122.

29. Geertz, *Negara,* 122.

30. George Orwell, "Shooting an Elephant," in *Inside the Whale and Other Essays,* 95–96, quoted in James Scott, *Domination and the Arts of Resistance* (New Haven: Yale University Press, 1990), 11.

31. There is even an anecdote about the consequences of telling anecdotes. Question: How many times can you tell a joke in Russia? Answer: Three times. Once to a friend. Once to the police. Once to your cellmate.

32. Indeed, Goffman famously uses the theater frame as a cue of complex unreality in *Frame Analysis* (Cambridge, MA: Harvard University Press, 1974), e.g., at 259, 419.

33. Niccolò Machiavelli, *The Prince*, trans. Harvey Mansfield (Chicago: University of Chicago Press, 1998), chapter 27.

34. Walter Bagehot, *The English Constitution* (Cambridge: Cambridge University Press, 2001). Or consider how Geertz speaks of the Balinese state's "semiotic capacity to make inequality enchant" but is careful to clarify that the enchantment, by virtue of its actuality, is actually reality. Geertz, *Negara*, 123.

35. The performance of capacity has uses for external constituencies too. For example, military parades or exercises in disputed waters have a semiotic function for foreign audiences, allowing for a more measured and retractable provocation than words would have.

36. Cited in Lizzie Davies, "L'Aquila Quake: Italian Judge Explains Why He Jailed Scientists over Disaster," *Guardian*, 18 January 2013.

37. Eleanor Robson, "Scholarly Conceptions and Quantifications of Time in Assyria and Babylonia, c. 750–250 BCE," in *Time and Temporality in the Ancient World*, ed. Ralph Rosen (Philadelphia: University of Pennsylvania Museum Publications, 2004), 47.

38. Ekart Frahm, "Keeping Company with Men of Learning: The King as Scholar," in *Oxford Handbook of Cuneiform Culture,* ed. Karen Radner and Eleanor Robson (Oxford: Oxford University Press, 2011), 513.

39. Daniel 1:3.

40. Frahm, "Keeping Company with Men of Learning," 524.

41. In the context of the letter, this is an ought statement containing a moral imperative of actualization. Translated by Simo Parpola, in *State Archives of Assyria*, vol. 10, *Letters from Assyrian and Babylonian Scholars* (Helsinki: Helsinki University Press, 1993), 166.

42. Parpola, *State Archives of Assyria*, x–xvi.

43. Parpola, *State Archives of Assyria*, xvi.

44. See, for instance, Francesca Rochberg, "Observing and Describing the World through Divination and Astronomy," 361, and Karen Radner, "Royal Decision-Making: Kings, Magnates, and Scholars," 618ff, both in Radner and Robson, *Oxford Handbook of Cuneiform Culture*. eds.

45. John M. Steele, "Making Sense of Time: Observational and Theoretical Calendars," in Radner and Robson, *Oxford Handbook of Cuneiform Culture*, 470–71.

46. Morris Rossabi, "The Reign of Khubilai Khan," in *The Cambridge History of China* (Cambridge: Cambridge University Press, 1994), 465.

47. Jan Yun-hua relates a similar story of the influence of Buddhist monks on Genghis's decision making in "Chinese Buddhism in Ta-tu," in *Yuan Thought*, ed. Hok-lam Chan and William Theodore de Bary (New York: Columbia, 1982), 382. See also Rossabi, "The Reign of Khubilai Khan."

48. Karakorum, with around ten thousand inhabitants, housed centers of worship for twelve religions, and in China, Khubilai made a point of attending to and pacifying the Buddhists, Taoists, Confucians, Christians, and Muslims who often clashed, sometimes violently, within his realm. The Mongols made a habit of providing tax exemptions for religious leaders and sponsoring the construction of monasteries and houses of worship.

49. See Hok-lam Chan, "Comprehensiveness (T'ung) and 'Change' (Pien) in Ma Tuan-lin's Historical Thought," in Chan and de Bary, *Yuan Thought*, 27; Naomi Standen, "Alien Regimes and Mental States," in *Journal of Economic and Social History of the Orient* 40, no. 1 (1997): 75.

50. The Mongols had developed sophisticated and effective military tactics both for the battlefield and for city siege—including germ warfare. Generally, when Genghis threatened a regime, he offered a choice: peaceful submission—in which case no one would be harmed and local rulers could continue to rule in exchange for the promise of tribute—or brutalization. The Mongols did not tolerate any form of rebellion and made known to all their subject states the inexorable fate rebels would meet.

51. Rossabi, "The Reign of Khubilai Khan," 414.

52. Throughout his life, Khubilai maintained a number of ties to Mongolian culture, particularly through hunting parties, the yurts at his summer residence at Shang-tu, the traditional (though somewhat private) observance of sacrificial and religious rites, and the practice of having his wives give birth in yurts. The status of Mongolian women was also substantially higher than that of Chinese women, and Mongolian women were often key political figures. Indeed, Khubilai's own mother, Sorkakteni Beki, had been given a territory to govern and had trained her sons in the art of politics. Khubilai maintained that high status, discouraging practices such as foot binding that had come into vogue under the Song. He also gave substantial weight to the advice of his highly intelligent second wife, Chabi.

53. David Morgan, *The Mongols* (Oxford: Blackwell, 2007), 104–5.

54. Timothy Brook, *The Troubled Empire: China in the Yuan and Ming Dynasties* (Cambridge, MA: Harvard University Press, 2010), 36.

55. Rossabi, *Khubilai Khan: His Life and Times*, 178.

56. Brook, *The Troubled Empire*, 29ff.

57. The Polo family, apparently, thought Khubilai ripe for conversion, but while he may have encouraged them to believe so, in the broader context, his interest in furthering the ecumenical collection is clear. Marco Polo, *The Travels of Marco Polo*, ed. Henry Yule and Henri Cordier (Mineola, NY: Dover, 1923), chapters 1–9.

58. Each new dynasty compiled the detailed records of the previous regime into a standard history, and this history always contained an important section on the calendar of the previous regime. See Richard Smith, "A Note on Qing Dynasty Calendars," *Late Imperial China* 9, no. 1 (1988): 123. See also Brook, *The Troubled Empire*, 27; Nathan Sivin, *Granting the Seasons: The Chinese Astronomical Reform of 1280* (New York: Springer, 2008), 228–29. It is interesting to note that even Hong Xiuquan, the leader of the Taiping Rebellion, made a point of reforming the calendar after conquering Nanjing and setting up his "government." Jonathan Spence, *God's Chinese Son: The Taiping Heavenly Kingdom of Hong Xiuquan* (New York: Norton, 1996), 142.

59. Sivin, *Granting the Seasons*, 559.

60. Quoted in Sivin, *Granting the Seasons*, 156.

61. Yuan shih, 9:138, translated in Sivin, *Granting the Seasons*, 152.

62. Sivin, *Granting the Seasons*, 169.

63. The term *water clock* may bring to mind a simple device similar to an hourglass, but medieval China and the medieval Arab world used water to power gears also, producing clocks of spectacular precision and great beauty. See Al-Khazini, "On the Balance for the Hours and Their Degrees," trans. Donald R. Hill, in *Arabic Water-Clocks* (Aleppo: University of Aleppo Institute for the History of Arabic Science, 1981).

64. Sivin, *Granting the Seasons*, 158.

65. Sivin, *Granting the Seasons*, 553.

66. Nathan Sivin, "A Multi-dimensional Approach to Research on Ancient Science," *East Asian Science, Technology, and Medicine* 23 (2005), 13. See also the introduction to the system provided by the compilers of the Yuan History, translated in Sivin, *Granting the Seasons*, 249–54.

67. Brook, *The Troubled Empire*, chapters 1–3.

68. The importance of simultaneity in identity building is argued in Benedict Anderson, *Imagined Communities* (London: Verso, 1991).

69. Sivin, *Granting the Seasons*, 19–33.

70. On this, see recent histories of the mathematics of risk, including Peter L. Bernstein, *Against the Gods* (New York: Wiley, 1996); and Ian Hacking, *The Taming of Chance* (Cambridge: Cambridge University Press, 1990).

Chapter 4. The Primitivist's Lament

1. Susan Jeffers, *Brother Eagle, Sister Sky* (New York: Puffin Books, 1991). It is also interesting to note the proximity of the book's invented title to the *Laudes creaturarum* of St. Francis of Assisi, which sings of Brother Sun, Sister Moon, etc.

2. Jeffers, *Brother Eagle*, 3, 18.

3. Editor's note, *New York Times*, May 3, 1992.

4. Ted Perry, film script for *Home* (Southern Baptist Radio and Television Commission, 1972), reprinted in Rudolf Kaiser, "Chief Seattle's Speech(es): American Origins and European Reception," in *Recovering the Word: Essays on Native American Literature*, ed. Brian Swann and Arnold Krupat (Berkeley: University of California Press, 1987), 525–30.

5. Jerry L. Clark, "Thus Spoke Chief Seattle: The Story of An Undocumented Speech," *Prologue* 18, no. 1 (1985).

6. Timothy Egan, "Chief's Speech of 1854 Given New Meaning (and Words)," *New York Times*, April 21, 1992. See also Eli Gifford, "The Many Speeches of Chief Seattle: The Manipulation of Record for Religious, Political, and Environmental Causes," *Sonoma State University Occasional Papers in Native American Studies*, no. 1 (1992).

7. Egan, "Chief's Speech."

8. Ad Council, Pollution: Keep America Beautiful—Iron Eyes Cody, http://www.adcouncil.org/Our-Work/The-Classics/Pollution-Keep-America-Beautiful-Iron-Eyes-Cody.

9. Patricia Dooley, "Review of *Brother Eagle, Sister Sky*," *School Library Journal* 37, no. 9 (1991): 228.

10. Arthur O. Lovejoy and George Boas, *Primitivism and Related Ideas in Antiquity* (Baltimore: Johns Hopkins University Press, 1935), 14ff.

11. Lovejoy and Boas, *Primitivism and Related Ideas in Antiquity*, 24; Chun-Chieh Huang and John Henderson, *Notions of Time in Chinese Historical Thinking* (Hong Kong: Chinese University Press, 2006), 99.

12. Stefan Maul, "Walking Backwards into the Future," in *Given World and Time: Temporalities in Context*, ed. Tyrus Miller (Budapest: Central European University Press, 2008), 20–21. The Assyrians had a story dating from second millennium BCE that the god of wisdom, Ea, "sent seven semi-divine sages to the antediluvian city of Eridu in order 'to disclose the design of the land,'" but this knowledge given to humankind was gradually lost. Hence, antiquity is associated with wisdom. The job of scholars was to attempt to find, preserve, and piece together the vestiges left over. Eleanor Robson, "Scholarly Conceptions and Quantifications of Time in Assyria and Babylonia, c. 750–250 BCE," in *Time and Temporality in the Ancient World*, ed. Ralph Rosen (Philadelphia: University of Pennsylvania Museum Press, 2004), 63.

13. A noteworthy example is found in the work of Jared Diamond. See "The Worst Mistake in the History of the Human Race," *Discover*, May 1987, 64–67.

14. Lovejoy and Boas, *Primitivism and Related Ideas in Antiquity*, 1.

15. Edward Evan Evans-Pritchard, *The Nuer: A Description of the Modes of Livelihood and Political Institutions of a Nilotic People* (Oxford: Oxford University Press, 1969), 108.

16. Claude Lévi-Strauss, *The Savage Mind* (Chicago: University of Chicago Press, 1966), 236.

17. Georges Gurvich, *The Spectrum of Social Time*, trans. Myrtle Korenbaum (New York: Springer, 1964), 91; Clifford Geertz, "Person Time and Conduct in Bali," in *The Interpretation of Cultures* (New York: Basic Books, 1977), 404.

18. Mircea Eliade, *Cosmos & History: The Myth of the Eternal Return*, trans. Willard R. Trask (New York: Harper, 1959). See also the discussion in Carlos Ivan Degregori, *How Difficult It Is to Be God* (Madison: University of Wisconsin Press, 2012), 43ff.

19. Evans-Pritchard, *The Nuer*, 103.

20. "He who says, that he perceives a figure, merely indicates thereby, that he conceives a determinate thing, and how it is determinate. This determination, therefore, does not appertain to the thing according to its being, but, on the contrary, is its non-being. As then figure is nothing else than determination, and determination is negation, figure, as has been said, can be nothing but negation." Benedict de Spinoza to Jarigh Jelles, June 2, 1674, in *The Chief Works of Benedict de Spinoza*, vol. 2, trans. R. H. M. Elwes (London: George Bell & Sons, 1901). Hegel makes the phrase famous in his account of Spinoza in *Lectures on the History of Philosophy*, placing it at the core of his own dialectical system and arguing that Spinoza himself failed to appreciate its significance. See also the discussion in Yitzhak Melamed, "'Omnis Determinatio Est Negatio': Determination, Negation, and Self-Negation in Spinoza, Kant, and Hegel,"

in *Spinoza and German Idealism,* ed. Yitzhak Y. Melamed and Eckart Forst (Cambridge: Cambridge University Press, 2012), 175ff.

21. Karl Marx, *The Poverty of Philosophy,* trans. Harry Quelch (New York: Cosimo, 2009), 57.

22. On Thompson's Marxism, see his instructive and entertaining exchange with Leszek Kolakowski. E. P. Thompson, "An Open Letter to Leszek Kolakowski," *Socialist Register* (1973); and Leszek Kolakowski, "My Correct Views on Everything: A Rejoinder to Edward Thompson's 'Open Letter to Leszek Kolakowski,'" *Socialist Register* (1974).

23. E. P. Thompson, "Time, Work Discipline, and Industrial Capitalism," *Past & Present* 38, no. 1 (1967): 60.

24. Thompson, "Time, Work Discipline, and Industrial Capitalism," 60.

25. Thompson, "Time, Work Discipline, and Industrial Capitalism," 72.

26. Thompson argues that workers and capitalists were more likely to accept this shift of circumstance because of the rise of Methodism, which disdained idleness. This reinforced the move to clock time and the separation of work from leisure. With the sense that time is moving by at a rapid pace, hurtling us toward death, time seems precious. As Benjamin Franklin wrote in the 1763 essay *Necessary Hints to Those That Would Be Rich,* "He that idly loses five shillings worth of time loses five shillings, and might as prudently throw five shillings into the sea." It may be interesting to note also the extent to which time consciousness and farm work were intertwined earlier on and in other places. Thomas Smith has collected an array of Tokugawa farmers' manuals from the mid-1680s onward that assert themes of the preciousness of time, the centrality of planning and efficiency, and the necessity of squeezing maximum labor from available hours. He cites one farm manual that exhorts, "If the farm family would escape poverty, it must treat time as precious. By rising early and shortening the daily rest period, two additional hours a day can be worked. That is seven hundred and twenty hours a year: the equivalent of sixty days." Thomas C. Smith, "Peasant Time and Factory Time in Japan," *Past and Present* 111 (1986): 168.

27. Thompson, "Time, Work Discipline, and Industrial Capitalism," 57.

28. Thompson, "Time, Work Discipline, and Industrial Capitalism," 91.

29. Thompson, "Time, Work Discipline, and Industrial Capitalism," 85.

30. Thompson, "Time, Work Discipline, and Industrial Capitalism," 93.

31. Paul Glennie and Nigel Thrift, *Shaping the Day: A History of Timekeeping in England and Wales, 1300–1800* (Oxford: Oxford University Press 2009), 43.

32. Thompson, "Time, Work Discipline, and Industrial Capitalism," 70, 86.

33. Thompson, "Time, Work Discipline, and Industrial Capitalism," 67.

34. Economic historians have provided an empirical critique of the evidence for Thompson's claims about an increase in worked hours and productivity. However, new methodologies, including statistical analysis of court testimony, seem to support Thompson's claims in this regard. John Rule, *The Experience of Labor in Eighteenth Century Industry* (London: St. Martin's, 1981); Eric Hopkins, "Working Hours and Conditions during the Industrial Revolution: A Reappraisal," *Economic History Review* 35, no. 1 (1982): 52–66; Douglas Reid, "The Decline of St. Monday," *Past and Present* 71 (1976): 76–100; Hans-Joachim Voth, "Time and Work in Eighteenth Century London," *Journal of Economic History* 58, no. 1 (1998): 29–58.

35. Glennie and Thrift, *Shaping the Day*, 138, 145. In *Macbeth* (written in 1606), for instance, there are several scenes in which clock time and the found time of nature are contrasted: "The moon is down; I have not heard the clock. / And she goes down at twelve" (act 2, scene 1, lines 2–3); "By th' clock 'tis day, / And yet dark night strangles the travelling lamp" (act 2, scene 4, lines 6–7).

36. Town Ordinances of Godalming, Surrey, 1620, cited in Glennie and Thrift, *Shaping the Day*, 142.

37. Lorna Weatherill, *Consumer Behaviour and Material Culture in Britain, 1660–1760* (New York: Routledge, 1988), 54. While luxury goods were ultimately better represented in London than in very rural areas, Weatherill notes that we may easily overemphasize the divide between town and country: those in the country of the middling class tended to go to town to obtain goods, leading to the rapid diffusion of helpful technological innovations and luxury goods (89).

38. Thompson, "Time, Work Discipline, and Industrial Capitalism," 67, 69.

39. Weatherill, *Consumer Behaviour*, 25ff.

40. When a person declared himself so impoverished that he must turn himself over to the care of the parish, the parish made a pauper inventory, a catalogue of the possessions. Peter King, "Pauper Inventories and the Material Lives of the Poor in the Eighteenth and Early Nineteenth Centuries," in *Chronicling Poverty: The Voices and Strategies of the English Poor, 1640–1840*, ed. Timothy Hitchcock et al. (London: Macmillan, 1997), 183. From the evidence of the descriptions in these inventories, it seems there was also a wide market for cheaply made clocks and watches. See Glennie and Thrift, *Shaping the Day*, 169.

41. Glennie and Thrift, *Shaping the Day*, 9.

42. "Typically, historical notions of clock time have been considerably more sophisticated than the ability of clock time at those times to deliver on them." Glennie and Thrift, *Shaping the Day*, 40.

43. See the discussion in Hatice Pamir and Nilüfer Sezgin, "The Sundial and Convivium Scene on the Mosaic from the Rescue Excavation in a Late Antique House of Antioch," *Adalya* 20 (2016): 251, 260.

44. Glennie and Thrift, *Shaping the Day*, 177.

45. Thompson, "Time, Work Discipline, and Industrial Capitalism," 61.

46. Thompson, "Time, Work Discipline, and Industrial Capitalism," 61.

47. Thompson, "Time, Work Discipline, and Industrial Capitalism," 61, 81.

48. Thompson, "Time, Work Discipline, and Industrial Capitalism," 83–84.

49. Thompson, "Time, Work Discipline, and Industrial Capitalism," 87.

50. An evident exception in the industrial revolution is train timetables, which require a level of precision and coordination that would be impossible without mechanical clocks.

51. Thompson, "Time, Work Discipline, and Industrial Capitalism," 59ff.

52. Thompson, "Time, Work Discipline, and Industrial Capitalism," 61.

53. Mary Collier, *The Woman's Labour: An Epistle to Mr. Stephen Duck* (London: J. Roberts, 1739).

54. Thompson, "Time, Work Discipline, and Industrial Capitalism," 79.

55. Cited in E. Royston Pike, *Human Documents of the Industrial Revolution* (Abingdon, UK: Routledge, 1966), 268. An interesting account of gender differences in clock ownership levels—among other luxury goods—is found in Maxine Berg, "Women's Consumption and the Industrial Classes of Eighteenth Century England," *Journal of Social History* 30, no. 2 (1996): 415–34.

56. Sociological research confirms this in the contemporary world, most notably, Arlie Hochschild and Anne Machung, *The Second Shift: Working Families and the Revolution at Home* (New York: Viking, 1989).

57. See, for example, Oriel Sullivan, "The Division of Domestic Labour: Twenty Years of Change?" *Sociology* 34, no. 3 (2000): 437–56; Oriel Sullivan, *Changing Gender Relations, Changing Families* (Oxford: Rowman & Littlefield, 2006).

58. Glennie and Thrift, *Shaping the Day*, 13.

59. Thompson, "Time, Work Discipline, and Industrial Capitalism," 79.

60. Leslie White, *The Science of Culture* (New York: Grove, 1949), 131. See also Keith Otterbein, "History of Research on Warfare," *American Anthropologist* 101, no.

4 (1999): 794–805. It was a dominant view throughout the twentieth century that when violence did occur, it was more like sport and generally nonlethal. See Leslie Sponsel, "The Natural History of Peace: The Positive View of Human Nature and Its Potential," in *A Natural History of Peace*, ed. Thomas Gregor (Nashville: Vanderbilt University Press, 1996), 95–125.

61. Lawrence Keeley, *War Before Civilization* (Oxford: Oxford University Press, 1997), 67, 91; Steven Pinker, *The Better Angels of Our Nature: Why Violence Has Declined* (New York: Viking, 2011). See also Raymond C. Kelly, *Warless Societies and the Origins of War* (Ann Arbor: University of Michigan Press, 2000); Otterbein, "History of Research on Warfare," 797. Keeley, Pinker, and others argue that the risk of violent death has a sharply inverse correlation with the complexity of the built environment.

62. Keeley, *War Before Civilization*, 179.

63. Jean-Jacques Rousseau, *Judge of Jean-Jacques*, trans. Judith Bush (Dartmouth: University Press of New England, 1990), 213.

64. Some arguments along these lines include Roger Masters, *The Political Philosophy of Rousseau* (Princeton: Princeton University Press, 1968), 42; Judith Shklar, *Men and Citizens* (Cambridge: Cambridge University Press, 1969), 19; and David Gauthier, *The Sentiment of Existence* (Cambridge: Cambridge University Press, 2006), chapter 3. However, some scholars, notably Dent, have argued that the purpose of the social contract is to promote healthy individual amour propre. Nicholas Dent, *Rousseau: An Introduction to His Psychological, Social, and Political Theory* (New York: Blackwell, 1989). For our purposes, the result is the same.

65. "We would need gods to give laws to men." Jean-Jacques Rousseau, *Du contrat social*, 2.7.

66. Rousseau, *On the Social Contract*, trans. G. D. H. Cole (London: Dent, 1913), 1.7.

67. Rousseau, *Social Contract*, 4.2n2.

68. Rousseau, *Social Contract*, 3.10.

69. Jean-Jacques Rousseau, *Emile; or, On Education*, trans. Christopher Kelly and Allan Bloom (Lebanon: Dartmouth College Press, 2010), e.g., 51. See also Shawn Fraistat, "Domination and Care in Rousseau's *Émile*," *American Political Science Review* 110 (2016): 896.

70. Fraistat, "Domination and Care," 899.

71. This is what Kant suggests in his 1784 essay "An Answer to the Question: What Is Enlightenment?" trans. James Schmidt, in *What Is Enlightenment?* (Berkeley: University of California Press, 1996), 58–64.

Chapter 5. A Dead End?

1. Eric Voegelin, *The New Science of Politics* (Chicago: University of Chicago Press, 1952).
2. David Landes, *Heaven on Earth* (Oxford: Oxford University Press, 2011), 45ff; Norman Cohn, *The Pursuit of the Millennium* (Oxford: Oxford University Press, 1970), 35–36.
3. Jonah Bromwich, "What Is Atomwaffen?" *New York Times,* February 12, 2018.
4. Compare this verse from Revelation: "Then the seventh angel blew his trumpet, and there were loud voices in heaven, saying, 'The kingdom of the world has become the kingdom of our Lord and of his Christ, and he shall reign forever and ever.'" With respect to the next verse, see also 2 Peter 3:12.
5. Abimael Guzmán, "Somos los iniciadores," quoted in Gustavo Gorriti, *The Shining Path: A History of Millenarian War in Peru,* trans. Robin Kirk (Chapel Hill: University of North Carolina Press, 1999), 35.
6. Gorriti, *The Shining Path,* 35.
7. Commission on Truth and Reconciliation, *Final Report—General Conclusions* (Lima, 2003), http://www.cverdad.org.pe/ingles/ifinal/conclusiones.php.
8. See, generally, Miguel La Serna, *The Corner of the Living: Ayacucho on the Eve of the Shining Path Insurgency* (Chapel Hill: University of North Carolina Press, 2012).
9. David Apter, *The Legitimization of Violence* (New York: NYU Press, 1997), 2. On the sociology of mass killing, see Abram de Swaan, *The Killing Compartments* (New Haven: Yale University Press, 2015).
10. Jonathan Spence, *God's Chinese Son* (New York: Norton, 1996), xxiii; *Vishnu Purana,* trans. Horace Wilson (Santa Cruz: Evinity, 2009), 4.24.
11. Neuroscientists are increasingly interested in how narrative physically impacts the brain. See, for instance, Paul Zak, "Why Inspiring Stories Make Us React: The Neuroscience of Narrative," *Cerebrum* (2015): 2.
12. John E. Smith, "Time, Times, and the Right Time," *Monist* 53, no. 1 (1969): 6.
13. 2 Peter 3:12. In the first volume of *Capital,* Marx writes: "Force is the midwife of every old society which is pregnant with a new one." (New York: Penguin, 1976), 916.
14. James Scott, *Domination and the Arts of Resistance* (New Haven: Yale University Press, 1990).
15. Voegelin, *The New Science of Politics,* 109.
16. Voegelin, *The New Science of Politics,* 111.
17. Voegelin, *The New Science of Politics,* 119.

18. Voegelin, *The New Science of Politics*, 133ff.
19. Voegelin, *The New Science of Politics*, 147.
20. Voegelin, *The New Science of Politics*, 119.
21. Voegelin, *The New Science of Politics*, 168–69.
22. Voegelin, *The New Science of Politics*, 130–31, 125, 113–14. Voegelin reserves a special ire for Comte. He is not alone in noting the Joachimite characteristics of Nazism. Karl Löwith and later commentators such as Cohn and Landes all underline that Nazism made use of Joachim's idea of a third age. The idea of a Third Reich comes down from Joachim through Merezhovsky and Moeller van den Bruck. Karl Löwith, *Meaning in History* (Chicago: University of Chicago Press, 1949), 159, 210ff.
23. Voegelin, *The New Science of Politics*, 166. It is interesting to consider what Voegelin might have made of the "post-secular" twenty-first-century eschatologies discussed at the end of this chapter. Perhaps this is not the explosion he anticipated, but it might be thought to reflect a properly dialectical progression from abstract to concrete salvation, and finally sublimation in a parody of salvation.
24. See the discussion in Eugene Webb, *Eric Voegelin: Philosopher of History* (Seattle: University of Washington Press, 1981), 258.
25. Löwith, *Meaning in History*, 145.
26. The reasoning was: Saint Matthew identifies forty-two generations between Abraham and Christ, and on the assumption that the first age remains the pattern for the second, the third age must be due forty-two generations after Christ, or around 1260 CE.
27. Many thinkers, including not only Voegelin but John Passmore, have asserted that it is Joachim we have to thank for Trinitarian historical patterns as diverse as Lessing's third age, Hitler's Third Reich, and Hegel's dialectic. Indeed, Voegelin argued that "in his Trinitarian eschatology Joachim created the aggregate of symbols which govern the self-interpretation of modern political society to this day." *The New Science of Politics*, 110. While this may be far-fetched, in some cases, such as Lessing's speculations on the culmination of history in the *Education of the Human Race*, it seems hard to contest. For a careful critical study of Joachim's reception, see Warwick Gould and Marjorie Reeves, *Joachim of Fiore and the Myth of the Eternal Evangel* (Oxford: Oxford University Press, 2001).
28. Cohn, *Pursuit of the Millennium*, 108–9.
29. See, for example, Frederico De Romanis and Marco Maiuro, *Across the Ocean: Nine Essays in Indo-Mediterranean Trade* (Leiden: Brill, 2015); Julian Reade, ed., *The Indian Ocean in Antiquity* (London: Routledge, 1996); Toby Wilkinson et al., eds.,

Interweaving Worlds: Systemic Interactions in Eurasia, 7th to 1st Millennia BC (Oakville, CT: Oxbow Books, 2011).

30. *Vishnu Purana,* 4.24, 484–85. Wendy O'Flaherty has called the dating of the Puranas and epics "more an art than a science" but notes a rough consensus around 450 CE as the most defensible estimate for the *Vishnu Purana. Hindu Myths: A Sourcebook Translated from the Sanskrit* (New York: Penguin, 2004), 17–18.

31. For instance, Horace, "Ode XVI: To the Roman People," in *Odes;* Hesiod, *Works and Days,* lines 109–201; Virgil, *Aeneid,* book 6, lines 1075ff. It would be easy to contrast the apparent cyclicality of time in the Yugas and in Roman thinking with the linearity of the Sibylline and Joachimite texts. But some scholars hold that cyclicality of the ages may be a late, and possibly politicized, inclusion in the Hindu epics. See Luis Gonzalez-Reimann, *The Mahabharata and the Yugas* (New York: Peter Lang, 2002), 202.

32. Cohn, *Pursuit of the Millennium,* 32–33.

33. While Taiping is often described as a millennial rebellion, for instance, by Landes in *Heaven on Earth* (189), Hong seems to have conceived of himself not as a bringer of the eschaton but as the founder of a new dynasty with heavenly sanction. So the status of Taiping as fully eschatological is contested, despite Hong's claims to be the brother of Jesus.

34. For a general discussion of the origins and prevalence of eschatological belief in American society, see Paul Boyer, *When Time Shall Be No More* (Cambridge, MA: Harvard University Press, 1992).

35. Pew Research Center/*Smithsonian Magazine,* "Public Sees a Future Full of Promise and Peril," April 21–26, 2010, http://www.people-press.org/2010/06/22/section-3-war-terrorism-and-global-trends. The market provides another source of evidence. The eschatology-themed *Left Behind* novels by evangelist Tim LeHaye and Jerry B. Jenkins, which deal specifically with the rapture, have reportedly sold some 70 million copies. And this is not a new phenomenon: a best-selling novel of the 1970s, Hal Lindsey's apocalyptic *Late, Great Planet Earth,* reflected similar themes.

36. Pew Research Center, "Many Americans Uneasy with Mix of Religion and Politics," August 24, 2006, http://www.people-press.org/2006/08/24/section-iv-religious-beliefs.

37. My emphasis. A survey of the directors of the National Association of Evangelicals, representing forty-five thousand churches, found that 49 percent prefer the New International Version exclusively, while 67 percent use the NIV alongside another version of the Bible. Jennifer Rile, "NIV Bible Tops List by Evangelical

Leaders," *Christian Post,* April 11, 2008. It is noteworthy, however, that prominent Evangelical Dispensationalists, such as Tim LeHaye and Oral Roberts, prefer the King James Version.

38. Jim Rutenberg et al., "Tax-Exempt Funds Aid Settlements in West Bank," *New York Times,* July 6, 2010. This article cites the preacher John Hagee in a speech to politicians in Jerusalem: "Israel exists because of a covenant God made with Abraham, Isaac and Jacob 3,500 years ago—and that covenant still stands. . . . World leaders do not have the authority to tell Israel and the Jewish people what they can and cannot do in the city of Jerusalem." Notably, Hagee was an invited speaker at the opening of the new American embassy in Jerusalem in May 2018.

39. Quoted in Boyer, *When Time Shall Be No More,* 141.

40. Pew Research Center, "Many Americans Uneasy with Mix of Religion and Politics."

41. This contentious movement, combining Marxism with Catholicism and led by Gustavo Gutiérrez, has met with a much kinder reception under Pope Francis, after something close to persecution by Pope Benedict. Stephanie Kierchgassner and Jonathan Watts, "Catholic Church Warms to Liberation Theology as Founder Heads to Vatican," *Guardian,* May 11, 2015.

42. Landes, *Heaven on Earth,* 45ff.

43. Romans 13:11; 1 Corinthians 7:29–31.

44. For an interesting comparative discussion, see Paul Weithman, "Augustine and Aquinas on Original Sin," *Journal of the History of Philosophy* 30, no. 3 (1992): 358ff. Weithman argues that Aquinas, unlike Augustine, sees political authority as a means of actually improving persons subject to it because it encourages civic-mindedness.

45. Augustine, *City of God,* 5.17.

46. Cohn, *Pursuit of the Millennium;* Richard Landes, "The Fear of an Apocalyptic Year 1000," *Speculum* 75, no. 1 (2000): 97–145.

47. Cohn, *Pursuit of the Millennium,* 41ff, 52.

48. Origen, *On First Principles* (Fig Digital, 2013): 2.11.2; St. Irenaeus, *Against Heresies,* trans. John Keble (London: James Parker, 1872). Cohn notes that such "determined efforts were made to suppress the millenarian chapters of his treatises . . . and to such good effect that it was only in 1575 that they were rediscovered." *Pursuit of the Millennium,* 29.

49. Eusebius, *The History of the Church from Christ to Constantine,* trans. G. A. Williamson (New York: Penguin, 1965), 3.27.

50. Augustine, *City of God*, 18:52.
51. Augustine, *City of God*, 18:53.
52. Marjorie Reeves notes that Joachim enjoyed the support and encouragement of three popes. It was only in 1215 at the Lateran Council after Joachim's death, that his views specifically on Peter of Lombard's Trinitarianism were condemned as heretical. *The Influence of Prophecy in the Later Middle Ages* (London: University of Notre Dame Press, 1993), 28, 30.
53. See Reeves, *Influence of Prophecy*, 60–61.
54. Reeves, *Influence of Prophecy*, 67–69.
55. St. Thomas Aquinas, *Summa theologica*, trans. Fathers of the English Dominican Province (New York: Christian Classics, 1948), 2.1, Q2.8.
56. Aquinas, *Summa theologica*, 2.1, Q92.1.
57. Aquinas, *Summa theologica*, 2.1, Q95.1.
58. Aquinas, *Summa theologica*, 2.2, Q42.2; 2.2, Q104.
59. Aquinas, *Summa theologica*, Supplement to the Third Part, Q88.3.
60. Niccolò Machiavelli, *Discourses on Livy*, trans. Nathan Tarcov and Harvey Mansfield (Chicago: University of Chicago Press, 1996), 1.12.
61. Hobbes, *Leviathan* (Oxford: Oxford University Press, 1909), 3.37.
62. This was central to Carl Schmitt's critique of Hobbes, who did not, in Schmitt's view, treat the terror of divine power seriously enough to bolster sovereignty. Carl Schmitt, *Der Leviathan in der Staatstheorie des Thomas Hobbes* (Cologne: Hohenheim, 1982). See my discussion in *States of Emergency in Liberal Democracies* (Cambridge: Cambridge University Press, 2009), 43ff.
63. Aquinas, *Summa theologica*, e.g., 1, 50–53.
64. Aquinas, *Summa theologica*, 1, 50.5.
65. Aquinas, *Summa theologica*, 1, 10.1–4. For a general account of time in Saint Thomas's thought, see Rory Fox, *Time and Eternity in Mid-Thirteenth Century Thought* (Oxford: Oxford University Press, 2006).
66. J. G. A. Pocock, "Time, History, and Eschatology in the Thought of Thomas Hobbes," in *Politics, Language and Time* (Chicago: University of Chicago Press, 1989), 148–201; Christopher Hill, *The World Turned Upside Down: Radical Ideas during the English Revolution* (New York: Penguin, 1975), 31ff; Bernard Capp, "The Millennium and Eschatology in England," *Past and Present* 57 (1972): 156–57.
67. *Book of Tribulations and Portents of the Last Hour*, book 54, hadith 44.
68. Badiou refers to Romans 3:20.

69. Alain Badiou, *St. Paul: The Foundation of Universalism*, trans. Ray Brassier (Stanford: Stanford University Press, 2003), 82.
70. Badiou, *St. Paul*, 79.
71. Giorgio Agamben, *The Time That Remains*, trans. Patricia Dailey (Stanford: Stanford University Press, 2005), 105.
72. Giorgio Agamben, *Means without End*, trans. Vincenzo Binetti and Cesare Casarino (Minneapolis: University of Minnesota Press, 2000), 112.
73. Citing 1 Corinthians 7:29–32.
74. Agamben, *Time That Remains*, 23.
75. Agamben, *Time That Remains*, 27.
76. Agamben, *Time That Remains*, 107. He cites Romans 4:13.
77. Agamben, *Time That Remains*, 93.
78. Agamben, *Time That Remains*, 119.
79. Giorgio Agamben, *The Highest Poverty: Monastic Rules and Forms of Life* (Stanford: Stanford University Press, 2013). As I have noted, Franciscans were among the most eager listeners to the message of Joachim. See Reeves, *Influence of Prophecy*, 175.
80. Slavoj Žižek, *The Ticklish Subject* (London: Verso, 1999), 146–63.
81. Slavoj Žižek, *Did Somebody Say Totalitarianism?* (London: Verso, 2001), 49–50.
82. Slavoj Žižek, *The Puppet and the Dwarf: The Perverse Core of Christianity* (Cambridge MA: MIT Press, 2003), 130.
83. Žižek, *Puppet and the Dwarf*, 130.
84. Dianna Dilworth, "Interview with Slavoj Zizek," *Believer*, July 2004, https://believermag.com/an-interview-with-slavoj-zizek/.
85. Badiou, *St. Paul*, 86.
86. See the extended discussion in Alain Badiou, *The Communist Hypothesis*, trans. David Macey and Steve Corcoran (London: Verso, 2010).
87. Žižek, *Puppet and the Dwarf*, 133.
88. Žižek, *Puppet and the Dwarf*, 134.
89. Žižek, *Puppet and the Dwarf*, 137.
90. Žižek, *Puppet and the Dwarf*, 136.
91. Žižek, *Puppet and the Dwarf*, 135.
92. Žižek, *Puppet and the Dwarf*, 135.
93. For a related perspective, see Yoav Tenembaum, "The Success and Failure of Non-violence," *Philosophy Now* 85 (July–August 2011): 34–35.

94. Giorgio Agamben, *State of Exception,* trans. Kevin Attell (Chicago: University of Chicago Press, 2005), 64; my emphasis; Stuart Jeffries, "Alain Badiou: A Life in Writing," *Guardian,* May 18, 2012, http://www.theguardian.com/culture/2012/may/18/alain-badiou-life-in-writing.

95. Badiou's *The Communist Hypothesis* can be understood as an extended account of precisely this process.

96. Thanks to Professor Elton Chan for this thoughtful argument.

97. Aquinas, *Summa theologica,* 3.2, Q88.3.

98. Badiou, "Seminar on Plato's *Republic,*" cited in Slavoj Žižek, *God in Pain: Inversions of Apocalypse* (New York: Seven Stories, 2012), 40. Žižek agrees that "enemy propaganda against radical emancipatory politics is by definition cynical [because] . . . its message is a resigned conviction that the world we live in, if not the best of all possible worlds, is the least bad one, so that any radical change can only make it worse" (40–41).

Conclusion

1. I thank Ian Shapiro for raising this important point.

2. Would an eschatologist be right to retort that, if we existed in some eternal present, the question of meaning and purpose would be moot? Could we not, in the absence of temporal constraint, exist in a purposeless now at perfect ease? Evidence from informal polling by the geneticist Nir Barzilai may be suggestive. He asked participants in longevity workshops (suggesting a bias *toward* immortality) if they would prefer an eighty-five-year lifespan characterized by the time markers of love, reproduction, child rearing, and so on to immortality without these. They chose the former. The work of scholars of positive psychology like Martin Seligman supports this too. Human well-being requires challenge, engagement, purpose, and achievement in addition to positive emotions, strong relationships, and health. Happiness is process-oriented and event-engaged. Of course, any such evidence is necessarily colored by current experience and potentially reflects a failure of imagination. But whatever the imaginary preferences of future potential people, actual existing people experience temporal constraint as the mother of purpose, of meaningful freedom. Barzilai, cited in Tad Friend, "Silicon Valley's Quest to Live Forever," *New Yorker,* April 3, 2017.

3. George Lakoff and Mark Johnson, *Metaphors We Live By* (Chicago: University of Chicago Press, 1980); see also George Lakoff, *Moral Politics* (Chicago: University of Chicago Press, 1996).

4. See, for instance, Julia Lechuga et al., "Impact of Framing on Intentions to Vaccinate Daughters against HPV: A Cross-Cultural Perspective," *Annual Review of Behavioral Medicine* 42 (2011): 221–26; Dennis Chong and James N. Druckman, "Counter-Framing Effects," *Journal of Politics* 75 (2013): 1–15; Dennis Chong and James N. Druckman, "Framing Public Opinion in Competitive Democracies," *American Political Science Review 101* (2007): 637–55.

Index

Page numbers in *italics* refer to illustrations.

Abraham (biblical figure), 180, 199
absolute time, 29
ab urbe condita dating, 33, 75–77
accuracy, 21–23, 24–25
Adam and Eve, 136, 137, 172
Addad-Sumu-Usur, 116
Agamben, Giorgio, 198–200, 204
Alexander the Great, 119
Al-Khazini, 221n9
Allen, Danielle, 28
Almagest (Ptolemy), 28
almanacs, 7, 8, 80–81, 113, 123–26
Altar Q (Copan), 79–80, *81*
anarchism, 108
anecdotes, 3–4, 112, 236n31
Annalistes school, 13, 220n8
Antichrist, 190, 196
apocalypticism, 168, 179, 190, 193, 247n35
Apter, David, 172
Ariq Boke, 119
Aristotle, 24, 91, 106, 138, 192
armillary sphere, *124*
Assurbanipal, king of Assyria, 115
Assyrian-Babylonian Empire, 5, 7, 79, 114–17, 118, 127, 136
astrology, 79, 80, 117, 122
astronomy, 80, 100, 117, 122, 123
Atatürk, Kemal, 2
atomic clocks, 21, 23, 31–32, 150
Atticus, Titus Pomponius, 72
Augustine of Hippo, Saint, 24, 177, 188, 190, 193
Augustus, emperor of Rome, 56, 64, 74–77, 88, 98, 182
auspicious timing. *See* temporal propriety
authoritarianism, 44, 46, 105–6, 214

Bacon, Francis, 106
Badiou, Alain, 197–98, 200, 201–5, 207
Bagehot, Walter, 113
baktun, 6, 79–82, 216
Bali, 140
Barzilai, Nir, 251n2
Beck, Ulrich, 109, 110
Beetham, David, 47, 48, 50
Benedict XVI, Pope, 248n41
Benford, Robert D., 40–41
Birney, Mayling, 227n75
Blair, Tony, 87
Bloch, Maurice, 37

INDEX

Boas, George, 136
Borgia, Cesare, 112–13
Braudel, Fernand, 13
Brother Eagle, Sister Sky (children's book), 131–32
Brutus Lucius Junius, 94
Buchanan, Allen, 45
Buddhism, 26
Bush, George W., 102, 109

Caesar, Julius, 1–2, 74, 75
calendars, 18, 43, 51, 215; Chinese, 2, 8, 35, 79, 80–81, 118, 122–24, 127; constructed vs. natural, 69–72; Egyptian, 74; failed reforms of, 66, 68–69; French revolutionary, 2; Gregorian, 2, 25, 32, 35, 71, 74; as infrastructure, 103, 125, 127–28; Janus-headed nature of, 5, 61, 62–69, 78, 99; Julian, 1–2, 5, 6, 32, 61, 72–77; legitimation linked to, 60–62, 66, 71, 78, 100, 113–14, 127, 211–12; linearity of, 6; lunar, 69–70, 72; Mayan, 5, 6, 35, 79–84; performative capacity framed by, 102–29; Persian, 96; pervasiveness of, 65, 66, 77; as rhetorical frame, 93; risk management and, 127; Rumi, 2. *See also* almanacs
Canada, 65
candle clocks, *36*, 149, 150
Cassius Dio, 229–30n15
Catholicism, 184–85, 190, 215
causality, 4
charisma, 60, 62, 106; cycles manipulated through, 95; legitimacy linked to, 7, 47–48, 96; as proxy for performative capacity, 7, 47, 104; of rhetoric, 172, 176, 182

Chaucer, Geoffrey, 33
Chen Chi-yun, 225n47
Chief Seattle (Sealth), 131–32, 135, 141, 142, 160
China, 28, 60, 105, 182; almanacs in, 80, 123–26; bureaucracy in, 119, 120; calendars in, 2, 8, 35, 79, 80–81, 118, 122–24, 127; constitutional preambles in, 17–18, 51–58, 76, 212, 215; crop failures in, 107, 109; eschatology in, 168–69, 172; legitimacy in, 47, 107–8, 117, 120; mandate tradition in, 7, 107, 108, 110, 114, 117, 125; primitivism in, 136; religious divisions in, 121; Taiping Rebellion in, 212
Chin Dynasty, 121–22
Christianity, 25, 26, 121, 178, 198, 200; Dispensationalist, 169, 184, 196; eschatology and, 168, 189, 172, 175, 176, 189, 190, 196; historical movement and, 180; Machiavelli's criticism of, 93–94. *See also* Catholicism; Jesus Christ; Methodism
Cicero, Marcus Tullius, 72, 74
circadian rhythm, 19, 22
civic religion, 50, 78, 99
Civitas Dei (Augustine), 177
Claudianus, Claudius, 71
clepsydra (water clock), 29, *115*, 123, 149, 150, 221n9
clocks, 9, 17, 18, 21, 26, 43, 58; as disciplinary tool, 143–44, 146; emotional resonance of, 160; pervasiveness of, 148, 149, 152, 160; societal need for, 33, 147, 149, 153; work and rest delimited by, 154, 157–59

INDEX

cognitive technology, 20, 22, 24
Cohn, Norman, 189
Collier, Mary, 155–57
colonization, 7, 104
communism, 51–52, 55, 168, 169–70, 196, 201
competence, 7, 8, 55, 102, 105
Comte, Auguste, 34–35
conceptions of the flow of time, 4–5, 93, 166; as cognitive technologies, 20–21; history distinguished from, 12–15; multiplicity of, 147–48; political values dictated by, 212–13; primitivism as, 19–20, 129, 131, 136; progress as, 17, 19, 21; purposes underlying, 37–38
conceptual time technologies, 18–20, 24
Confucianism, 7, 107, 120
conquest, 7, 78, 104
consent, 43, 44–47, 105, 106–7, 169, 213
Constantine I, emperor of Rome, 168, 189–90
constitutions: Chinese, 42, 52–58, 76, 212, 215; communist, 51–52; Hungarian, 5, 52, 61, 76, 84–89, 98, 99, 212; norms of, 106; Roman, 91–92; time talk in, 1, 42; U.S., 42
constitutive power, 84, 87, 89
consular year, 75
contingency, 7
Copan (Mayan city-state), 5, 61, 79–84, 94, 215–16
Corfield, Penelope, 13
cosmic harmony, 5, 48, 63, 78, 83, 114, 116
cosmology, 62–63, 175
Crying Indian campaign, 133, *134*, 141, 142

cultural relativism, 25–26
Cultural Revolution, 52–54, 56, 57, 76, 202
cyclicality, 4, 6, 15, 19, 140; agent-punctuated, 95–96; calendars linked to, 6; in Hungarian Basic Law, 86–89; linearity and, 26–27, 32–37, 59, 62, 78; Machiavelli's view of, 92–94; Mill's view of, 33–34; utopianism vs., 90
Cynics, 136

Dabiq, 196
Daniel, 115, 172, 190, 236n39
days, 19, 21, 58
De Bernardinis, Bernardo, 101–2, 109
Debucourt, Philibert-Louis, *67*
decay: actions to slow, 95; cyclicality linked to, 90–91; domination necessitated by, 186, 205; the Fall linked to, 172; fruition followed by, 54; of the ideal, 209; resistance to events vs., 140; Rousseau and, 163–65
decimalization, 64, 66
delegitimation, 104, 160, 182; eschatology and, 167, 168, 186; primitivism and, 144, 147; temporal-rhetorical framing and, 8, 15, 130, 143, 157
democracy, 33; consent and, 45–46; persuasion and, 41
Deng Xiaoping, 18, 52–53, 55, 57, 58, 76, 169
Descartes, René, 106
destiny, 48, 61, 78, 90, 99
determination as negation, 8–9, 137-138, 141, 217, 240n20

Discorsi (Machiavelli), 94
Discourse on the Origins of Inequality (Rousseau), 162
Dispensationalism, 169, 175, 180, 184, 196, 247n37
divination, 115
divine right, 106, 116
Dred Scott v. Sandford (1857), 42
Durkheim, Émile, 32, 97–98
Duwamish Nation, 131
dynasticism, 8, 121

Easter, 23
eclipses, 123
Eden, Garden of, 136, 137, 172
effectiveness, of governments, 104
effigies, 83
Egypt, 74, 79
Elazar, Daniel, 51
elections, 46, 61, 84, 85, 170
Eliade, Mircea, 32
Émile (Rousseau), 163–64
empire, 7, 91
English Civil War, 196
Enlightenment, 178, 182
equinoxes, 18, 96
Esarhaddon, king of Assyria, 114–15
eschatology, eschatologies, 19, 42, 93–94, 129, 131, 208–9, 212–13; in Chinese constitutional preamble, 54–57, 58; cyclicality and, 34; diversity of, 166–67, 172, 176; experience vs. imagination and, 209–10; failures of, 167–68, 185–86; human life analogized to, 37; immanent, 177–79, 180; inevitability as basis for, 169; legitimation vs., 168, 186–88, 216–17; in modern political thought, 196–205; obedience reframed by, 193; paradoxes of, 175, 186; performative legitimacy undermined by, 10; as political threat, 189–91; primitivist rhetoric and, 159, 164, 165; revolution and, 144, 145, 165, 171, 173, 215; scriptural rhetoric and, 182, 184–85; of submission, 187–88, 204–6; susceptibility to, 216; use-value of, 173–74; Vedic, 180–81, 182
eternity, 209–10
European Commission for Democracy through Law (Venice Commission), 85
European Union, 84, 87, 105
Eusebius of Caesarea, 190
Evangelicalism, 184, 247n37
Evans-Pritchard, Edward, 26, 140
expiation, 48

fairness. *See* justice
fasti (Roman consular lists), 33, 73, 75
fate, 48, 61, 78, 90, 99
Federal Emergency Management Administration (FEMA), 102, 109
Feeney, Denis, 75–76
fen (Chinese unit of time), 28
festivals and holidays, 6, 62, 70, 75, 77, 78, 95, 97
feudalism, 53
Fidesz Party, 84–89
Fordism, 153
forecasting, 103, 109, 127, 128, 212
Foucault, Michel, 117
found technologies, 18–19, 27, 31
Fourteenth Amendment, 42
Fraistat, Shawn, 164

frame alignment, 69, 160, 196;
 calendars linked to, 5, 128; defined,
 40–41, 78; innovation and, 17, 58,
 62, 63; legitimation linked to,
 50–51, 59, 63, 128, 142
Frame Analysis (Goffman), 38–39
Francis, Pope, 248n41
Franciscans, 180, 191, 199–200
Francis of Assisi, Saint, 180, 191, 239n1
Frank, Michael C., 20
Franklin, Benjamin, 241n26
Frederick II, Holy Roman Emperor, 190
French Revolution, 2, 64, 66

Galileo Galilei, 106
Gang of Four, 52–53
Garden of Eden, 136, 137, 172
Garsten, Bryan, 40
Gauguin, Paul, 136
Geertz, Clifford, 111–12, 140
Gell, Alfred, 33
genericism, 8–9, 134–42, 159, 161
Genghis Khan, 118, 119, 120
Gerard Borgo San Donnino, 191
Gershuny, Jonathan, 33
Gettysburg Address, 1
Giddens, Anthony, 109–10
Gilley, Bruce, 235n19
Gitlin, Todd, 40
Glennie, Paul, 151, 157
gnosticism, 166, 177–179
Goffman, Erving, 38–39, 41, 219n7
Gorriti, Gustavo, 169–70, 171
grace, 11, 165, 178, 187–88, 191–92, 198, 200, 297
Greece, ancient, 92, 136
Gregorian calendar, 2, 25, 32, 35, 71, 74

Grotius, Hugo, 45
Guo Shou-Chung, 122–23, *124*
Gurvich, Georges, 32–33, 140
Gutiérrez, Gustavo, 248n41
Guzmán, Abimael, 170–72, 176, 182, 204, 215
Gyurcsány, Ferenc, 87

Habermas, Jürgen, 44
Hagee, John, 248n38
Han Dynasty, 60
Hanson, Stephen, 26–28
harvest festivals, 70
Hegel, Georg Wilhelm Friedrich, 35, 200, 240–41n20
Hesiod, 33, 35, 182
hidden transcripts, 176
Hinduism, 26
Hobbes, Thomas, 47–48, 106, 111, 194–95, 213
holidays and festivals, 6, 62, 70, 75, 77, 78, 95, 97
homo sacer, 199
Hong Xiuquan, 182, 204, 238n58
Hopi nation, 2
Horace, 182
hourglasses, 4, 28, 149, 150
Hua Guofeng, 52–53, 55
humanism, 178
Hungarian Basic Law (2012), 5, 52, 61, 76, 84–89, 98, 99, 212
Hurricane Katrina, 102, 109
Hutchings, Kimberly, 222n15

identity politics, 197
illiberal democracy, 85
incrementalism, 159, 162, 164, 197
incumbency, 104
industrial revolution, 144

INDEX

inevitability: 6, 61, 78, 220n9; decline and, 90, 94, 99; eschatology and, 167, 169, 174-176, 179, 185-186, 196, 197, 203-206, 208; grand cycles and 82, 83

innovation: cyclicality compatible with, 90–91; frame alignment and, 17, 58, 62, 63; as restoration, 5–6, 51, 63–64, 77, 78, 105, 130, 143; rhetoric of time linked to, 1, 3, 15, 17

institutional recension, 65, 77

intentionality, 39–40

intercalation, 70–75, 123

Iranian revolution (1979), 13–14, 64, 98

Irenaeus, Saint, bishop of Lyon, 190

Iron Eyes Cody, 133

Islamic State (ISIS), 169, 196, 212

Jacobin Council, 2
Jeffers, Susan, 131–32, 134–35
Jelles, Jarigh, 141
Jenkins, Jerry B., 247n35
Jesus Christ, 180, 182, 184, 190, 201–3, 205. *See also* Christianity
Jiang Qing, 52
Joachim of Fiore, 177, 179–80, 182, 191
John Chrysostom, Saint, 199
Judaism, 26, 172
Julian calendar, 1–2, 5, 6, 32, 61, 72–77
Jurchen people, 125
justice, 48, 113, 173, 188, 199–201, 203, 205; in eschatological thought, 54, 55, 168; incremental, 157, 159, 164; legitimation linked to, 45, 64; order and, 10, 111, 130, 161, 170, 207; in primitivist thought, 154–55, 158, 159, 161; timekeeping and, 157–59

Kahneman, Daniel, 226n55
kairos, 174–76, 182, 187, 190, 204
Kali, age of, 181
Kant, Immanuel, 164
Keeley, Lawrence, 161
Keep America Beautiful campaign, 133, *134*, 142
Khomeini, Ruhollah, 13–14, 98
Khubilai Khan, 2, 5, 117–26, 215
King, Peter, 148, 149
K'inich Popul Huh, 80, 83
K'inich Yax K'uk' Mo', 5, 79–84, 89
Koselleck, Reinhart, 16, 220n9
Kuhn, Thomas, 35
Kurti, Laszlo, 98
Kuypers, Jim, 40

Lacan, Jacques, 200
Lakoff, George, 40, 215
lament, 160–64, 166, 169
Landes, Richard, 185, 189
L'Aquila earthquake (2009), 101–2, 109, 110, 114
Larin, Yuri, 68
La Serna, Miguel, 108
Late, Great Planet Earth (Lindsey), 247n35
law: as domination and subjection, 198–99; justice vs., 199–200, 203; love vs., 10, 165, 173, 180, 199, 200, 201, 217; pre-Christian, 180; sin and death linked to, 197–98, 200–201; temporal fallacy and, 207–8; virtue inculcated by, 182
leap days, 70
leap months, 70
leap seconds, 32
leap years, 32, 74, 75

legitimacy, legitimation, 3, 6, 43–51, 57, 130, 166, 187; agent-punctuated cycles linked to, 96; calendars linked to, 60–62, 66, 71, 78, 100, 113–14, 127, 211–12; of conquering regimes, 7, 78; eschatology vs., 168, 186–88, 216–17; festivals linked to, 95; "input" vs. "output," 105; obedience as substitute for, 193; order-based vs. performative, 214; performative capacity linked to, 102–4, 213–14; sources of, 5, 17, 60, 62–63, 84, 99–100; superfluity of, 10–11; temporal rhetorical framing linked to, 15, 16, 17, 50–51, 59, 89, 217–18; two-well theory of, 5, 17, 48–51, 60, 104–105, 212, 217. *See also* delegitimation
legitimation challenges, 44, 63, 66, 99, 117, 119
LeHaye, Tim, 247n35, 247–48n37
leisure, 69, 144, 146, 147, 152, 154–59
Lenin, Vladimir, 2
Lévi-Strauss, Claude, 140
Lévy-Bruhl, Lucien, 223–24n33
Liao Dynasty, 121–22
liberation theology, 184–85
Liberia, 66
Lin Bao, 53
Lincoln, Abraham, 1, 2
Lindsey, Hal, 247n35
linearity: cyclicality and, 26–27, 32–37, 59, 62, 78, 79, 137; eschatology and, 172, 174, 210; historical framing linked to, 6, 42, 99; human life and, 211; Western modernity linked to, 29–30, 140, 223n29, 223n33
Lipset, Seymour, 103–4, 117
Liu Ping-Chung, 121, 122, 215

Lochner, Stefan, *183*
Locke, John, 106, 164
Long Count, 79
Louis XVI, king of France, 2
Lovejoy, Arthur O., 136
Löwith, Karl, 179
Lukes, Steven, 43
lunar month, 69, 70, 71
lunar year, 70, 94
Luxemburg, Rosa, 202

Maastricht Treaty (1992), 232n46
Macbeth (Shakespeare), 242n35
Machiavelli, Niccolò, 107, 111, 112; cyclicality and, 90–94, 212–13; on declining regimes, 6, 61–62, 78, 93; eschatology and, 188, 194
Machu Picchu, 70
Macrobius, Ambrosius Aurelius Theodosius, 74
Mahabharata, 181
Malotki, Ekkehardt, 225n48
Mandate of Heaven (*tian ming*), 7, 107, 108, 110, 114, 117, 125
Mao Zedong, 17–18, 52–54
marine chronometer, 23
marks and measures: aim-specific, 28; in antiquity, 28, *29*, 30–31, 33, 35; cultural differences of, 25–28; cyclical vs. linear, 26–27, 32–37, 59, 62, 78; diversity of, 16, 24–25, 37; found vs. constructed vs. abstracted, 4, 16–17, 18, 27, 37–38, 58, 59, 173; misconceptions surrounding, 25–35; objectivity of, 21–22; time-itself vs., 22–23
martyrdom, 176
Marx, Karl, 35, 175, 188
Marxism, 64, 111, 144, 178, 182, 201

INDEX

Matthew, Saint, 246n26
Mayaland, 5–6, 35, 61, 79–82, 105
McTaggart, J. M. E., 21
Meaning in History (Löwith), 179
Medici, House of, 94
Merton, Robert, 99
messianism, 199–200, 202, 204–5
metaphor, 215
Methodism, 241n26
Mexico, 32
military watches, 28, 154
Mill, John Stuart, 33–34
millenarianism, 168, 190
Ming Dynasty, 120
Möngke Khan, 118
Mongols, 105, 118–20, 122
monsoons, 70
months, 18–19, 58, 69–72
Moses (biblical figure), 199
Motmot Marker, 80
Myanmar, 66

narrative, 3–4, 5, 12, 13, 42
naturalism, 31, 62
navigation, 23
Nazism, 178
Nebuchadnezzar, king of Babylonia, 115
negation, 8–9
neo-Nazism, 169
New Orleans, 102
New Science of Politics, The (Voegelin), 177–78
Newton, Isaac, 29–30
night watches, 28, 154
"noble savage," 142
nomadism, 119
nonviolence, 203

Nuer people, 26, 140
numeracy, 20, 26

obedience, 43, 47–48, 60, 113, 128, 187, 190–96, 205
O'Flaherty, Wendy, 247n30
Ögedei, khan of Mongolia, 118
Olympiads, 18, 69
On Coleridge (Mill), 34
Orbán, Viktor, 1, 84, 86–89, 215
Orco, Remirro de, 112
Origen, 189
Orwell, George, 112

Papirius Cursor, Lucius, 75
parliamentary systems, 105
Parpola, Simo, 116
Paul, Apostle, 187, 197–201, 204
pendulum clocks, 150
perfectibility, 162
perfection, 90–92, 116, 136, 186, 195
performative capacity, 6–7, 10–11, 47, 99, 102–29, 130, 168, 193, 216
persuasion, 40, 41; legitimation as, 43, 196
Peru, 169–72
Peter Lombard, bishop of Paris, 249n52
Physics (Aristotle), 24
Picasso, Pablo, 136
Pirahã language, 20
Plato, 30
Plautus, Titus Maccius, 30–31
Pocock, J. G. A., 64
Podemos Party, 205
Polo, Marco, 121
Pol Pot, 2
Polybius, 35, 61, 90–93, 212–13
postmodernism, 169, 196–97

preambles, constitutional, 1, 211;
  Chinese, 17–18, 51–58, 76, 212, 215;
  of European Union, 87; Hungarian,
  52, 61, 84–87, 89, 212; purposes of,
  3, 51–52, 57, 58
Prester John, 136
primitivism, 32, 35, 42, 93, 147; as
  abstraction, 138–39, 161;
  chronological vs. cultural, 136–37;
  clocks linked to, 144, 158–60; as
  conception of flow of time, 19–20,
  129, 131, 136; genericism and,
  134–42, 159, 161; moral purity
  linked to, 8, 135, 143, 158, 166;
  politics and order vs., 9, 10, 136,
  139, 145, 164, 166, 216–17; power
  of, 10
Prince, The (Machiavelli), 112
Principia Mathematica (Newton),
  29–30
progress: Chinese views of, 56–58, 76;
  as conception of the flow of time,
  17, 19, 21; cyclical vs. progressive,
  13–14, 15, 33–35; eschatology vs., 10;
  in European Union rhetoric, 84, 87;
  incremental, 159, 162, 164, 197; in
  leftist rhetoric, 147, 159, 203; liberty
  and equality linked to, 90;
  primitivism vs., 145; revolution as,
  64, 76; as temporal frame, 14–15, 17,
  19, 21, 42, 56–57, 93
property rights, 55–56
Proudhon, Pierre-Joseph, 108
Pseudo-Methodius, 182
Ptolemy, Claudius, 28
public goods, 7
Publilius Philo, Quintus, 75
punctuality, 150–51, 153
purification, 54, 55

Puritanism, 144, 178
purposive framing, 40

Quine, Willard van Orman, 39
Quiriga, 82

Ramadan, 23
rationality, 48
Raz, Joseph, 105
Reagan, Ronald, 79
redemption, 55, 159, 165, 174, 177, 188,
  198, 201, 203, 204, 206–7
Reeves, Marjorie, 249n52
regime change, 104, 129
Reno, William, 105
rest days, 66, 68
resurrection, 198, 201
revolution: in ancient Rome, 77; in
  China, 52–54, 56, 57, 76, 202;
  conditions for, 202–7; divine
  sanction for, 194; eschatology and,
  144, 145, 165, 171, 173, 215; in France,
  2, 64, 66; incompetence as cause of,
  105–6; in Iran, 13–14, 64, 98;
  justifications for, 8; legitimacy of,
  5–6; Marxist, 64, 175; rhetoric of,
  64, 172
Richardson, L., Jr., 229n14
risk mitigation, 7, 17, 101–3, 109–10,
  114, 116, 127–28, 216
risk society, 109–10
ritual, 23, 25, 32, 62, 64, 68, 83, 97,
  140; periodicity of, 98
Roberts, Oral, 247–48n37
Robespierre, Maximilien, 1
Rome, ancient, 1–2, 56, 71–77, 79,
  92–93, 98, 119, 136
Rousseau, Jean-Jacques, 6, 64, 96–97,
  106, 136, 162–64, 213

INDEX

rules, 48
rupture: Chinese views of, 54–58; eschatology linked to, 19, 37, 93–94, 171; love as means of, 200; Mill's view of, 34; as sign of power, 195; Thomist view of, 192; utopianism linked to, 90
rural time, 26

Sabbath, 23, 66
sacrifice, 55, 171, 176, 210–11
Saturnalia (Macrobius), 74
Savonarola, Girolamo, 194
Scharpf, Fritz, 47, 105
Schmitt, Carl, 198
Scholasticism, 106
Schwartz, Hans, 26
Scott, James, 176
seasons, 26, 28, 32, 35, 42, 70, 75, 124
Second Coming, 25
second shift, 243n56
Seligman, Martin, 251n2
Sendero Luminoso, 108, 169–71, *183*, 215
sequencing, 38, 42
Shakespeare, William, 242n35
Shang Dynasty, 107
Shang Shu (Book of Documents), 107
"Shooting an Elephant" (Orwell), 112
Siffre, Michel, 22
simultaneity. *See* synchronization, synchrony
Singapore, 105
Sivin, Nathan, 223n29
Skowronek, Stephen, 35
sleep/wake cycle. *See* circadian rhythm
Smith, Henry, 132
Smith, John, 174
Smith, Thomas C., 241n26
Snow, David A., 40–41

Social Contract, The (Rousseau), 162, 213
solar year, 69–72, 94
solstices, 18, 70, 123
Song Dynasty, 121–22
Sorkakteni Beki, 237n52
Sorokin, Pitirim, 99
Southern Song, 126
Soviet Union, 84, 98, 112
Sparta, 91
Spengler, Oswald, 35
Spinoza, Benedict de, 8, 141
Squamish Nation, 131
stability, of governments, 104
Stalin, Josef, 2, 66, 68–69
stars, 26–27
statelessness, 46
Stela J, 80
stellar year, 70
Stephen I, king of Hungary, 85, 86, 88, 89, 99
Stoics, 136
stopwatch, 150, 153
Stuart, David, 80
Sullivan, Oriel, 33, 157
Summa Theologica (Thomas Aquinas), 191–92, 195
sundials, 4, 150, *151*
sunrise and sunset, 18, 19, 21, 23, 24, 26, 58
synchronization, synchrony, 3, 13, 38, 150; of labor, 144, 149, 153; meaning affected by, 42, 83; political uses of, 78, 79, 82–83, 86, 89, 90, 94, 96, 99; through technology, 18, 21, 23–24, 143

Taiping Rebellion, 182, 204, 212
task orientation, 145–46

INDEX

taxation, 111, 119, 120
Taylorism, 153
teleology, 54, 138, 196
temporal accuracy, 21–23, 24–25
temporal fallacy, 207
temporal propriety: calendars linked to, 70, 79–82, 100, 113–14, 122; contingencies and, 103, 127; political order dependent on, 81, 99, 117, 121, 125
temporal relationism, 24
temporal relativism, 25–26
temporal-rhetorical framing, 5, 11–13, 40–43, 215; disguised, 59; efficacy of, 217–18; as legitimation, 15, 16, 17, 50–51, 59, 89, 217–18; meaning generated by, 211; narrative shaped by, 13; political change linked to, 15, 159; relevance of, 212–13; susceptibility to, 216
"ten days of dawn," 13–14
Tertullian, 130, 158
Thanksgiving, 98–99
Theogony (Hesiod), 35
Thomas Aquinas, Saint, 191–92, 193–94, 195, 213
Thompson, E. P., 9, 144–49, 152–60
Three-fifths Compromise, 42
Thrift, Nigel, 151, 157
Tikal, 80
Timaeus (Plato), 30
Time and Revolution (Hanson), 26–27
time technologies. *See* marks and measures
Time That Remains, The (Agamben), 198–200
Todorov, Tsvetan, 32

tradition, 48
transcendence, 12, 199
Treaty of Rome (1958), 232n46
Turkmenbashi, Saparmyrat, 2
Tversky, Amos, 226n55
types and tokens, 35, 37

Ukit Took', 82
urban time, 26
utopianism, 57, 90

Vedism, 136, 172, 175, 180–81, 182
Venice Commission (European Commission for Democracy through Law), 85
Venus, 81
Vico, Giambattista, 34–35
Virgil, 182
Vishnu Purana, 181
Voegelin, Eric, 166–67, 177–79, 185
vulgar time, 29

Wallace-Hadrill, Andrew, 230n16
Wang Hongwen, 52
Wang Hsun, 122
watches, 4–5, 148-151
water clocks, 18, 28, *30, 115,* 123, 149, 150
Watt, James, 184
weather, 18, 70, 103, 125
Weatherill, Lorna, 148–49
Weber, Max, 7, 47, 60, 63, 172
weeks, 29, 66, 68, 69, *73,* 228n5
Western Zhou Dynasty, 107, 110
White, Hayden, 13
Whorf, Benjamin, 26
Wittgenstein, Ludwig, 23, 39
work ethic, 144, 147, 153, 154
Works and Days (Hesiod), 35

Xie (Western) Xia, 125–26
Xinzi, 101

Yao Wenyuan, 52
Yax Pasaj Chan Yopat, 80
years, 18–19, 42, 69–72
Young, Michael, 224–25n45

Yuan Dynasty, 117, 121, 126

Zhang Chunqiao, 52
Zhang Youyu, 57–58
Zhou Enlai, 52
Žižek, Slavoj, 200–3, 205, 207